Library of Congress Cataloging-in-Publication Data

Wayne, Tiffany K., 1968–
    Women's roles in nineteenth-century America / by Tiffany K. Wayne.
        p. cm.— (Women's roles through history, 1553–5088)
    Includes bibliographical references and index.
    ISBN 0–313–33547–8 (alk. paper)
    1. Women—United States—History—19th century.
  2. Women—United States—Social conditions—19th century.
  3. Social role—United States—History—19th century.
  4. United States—Social conditions—19th century.   I. Title.
    HQ1418.W39   2007
    305.420973'09034—dc22   2006026206

British Library Cataloguing in Publication Data is available.

Library of Congress Catalog Card Number: 2006026206
ISBN: 0–313–33547–8
ISSN: 1553–5088

First published in 2007

Greenwood Press, 88 Post Road West, Westport, CT 06881
An imprint of Greenwood Publishing Group, Inc.
www.greenwood.com

Printed in the United States of America

The paper used in this book complies with the
Permanent Paper Standard issued by the National
Information Standards Organization (Z39.48–1984).

10 9 8 7 6 5 4 3 2 1

WOMEN'S ROLES IN NINETEENTH-CENTURY AMERICA

By Tiffany K. Wayne

Women's Roles through History

GREENWOOD PRESS
Westport, Connecticut • London

WOMEN'S ROLES IN NINETEENTH-CENTURY AMERICA

To my daughter, Lillian, a woman of the twenty-first century.

Contents

Series Foreword

Women's history is still being reclaimed. The geographical and chronological scope of the Women's Roles through History series contributes to our understanding of the many facets of women's lives. Indeed, with this series, a content-rich survey of women's lives through history and around the world is available for the first time for high school students to the general public.

The impetus for the series came from the success of Greenwood's 1999 reference *Women's Roles in Ancient Civilizations,* edited by Bella Vivante. Librarians noted the need for new treatments of women's history, and women's roles are an important part of the history curriculum in every era. Thus, this series intensely covers women's roles in Europe and the United States, with volumes by the century or by era, and one volume each is devoted to the major populated areas of the globe—Africa, the Middle East, Asia, and Latin America and the Caribbean.

Each volume provides essay chapters on major topics such as:

- Family life
- Marriage and childbearing
- Religion
- Public life
- Lives of ordinary women
- Women and the economy
- Political status
- Legal status
- Arts

Country and regional differences are discussed as necessary. Other elements include:

- Introduction, providing historical context
- Chronology
- Glossary
- Bibliography
- Period illustrations

The volumes, written by historians, offer sound scholarship in an accessible manner. A wealth of disparate material is conveniently synthesized in one source. As well, the insight provided into daily life, which readers find intriguing, further helps to bring knowledge of women's struggles, duties, contributions, pleasures, and more to a wide audience.

Acknowledgments

Writing this book has been a wonderful opportunity to revisit my favorite figures, stories, and authors in nineteenth-century women's history and to discover new ones. It is also a chance to give collective thanks to the scholars, advisors, colleagues, and friends who have kept me informed and energized through their conversations and their books. I am grateful to be a contributor to the exciting field of American women's history and acknowledge those whose work has inspired me along the way. As an undergraduate, Professor Stephanie McCurry first opened my eyes to the possibility and necessity of women's history. Reading Laurel Thatcher Ulrich during my first quarter of graduate school convinced me I should *be* a women's historian. Immersed in the prolific writings of Gerda Lerner I became interested in the nineteenth century, in particular, as the era that gave us a worldwide feminist consciousness and movement.

I want to thank my American women's history students of the past few years, whose questions and own research projects helped me envision this book as a resource they might want to read. My editor at Greenwood, Wendi Schnaufer, gently guided me through every step in the process while also honoring my own authorial vision and approach to the subject. I thank her immensely for her unwavering confidence in my ability to produce this book. My friend Larissa Brown Shapiro assisted in the early stages of compiling the bibliography and timeline before the demands of a new baby tore her away from my project to tend her own.

I am most grateful for the patience and support of my immediate family. My husband, David Wayne, built a beautiful new office for me with his own hands, a "room of my own," and does his best to make sure that I find at least a few hours here and there to use it. My children, Miles Leland Wayne and Lillian Kay Wayne, seem to take their mother's work for granted, and I see that as a sign of progress. Among the rewards of working at home with children underfoot is having my four-year-old-daughter, upon surveying the crowded bookshelves in my office, ask, "Mama, did you write *all* these books?" Certainly not, but I am glad she is growing up in a time when she can imagine that a woman—a mother, even—might write as many books as she likes.

Timeline

1789 The Constitution of the new United States is ratified.

1790 Judith Sargent Murray publishes essay, "On the Equality of the Sexes," arguing for women's need for and right to education.

1793 Cotton gin invented by Eli Whitney, making cotton production quicker and more profitable and thus entrenching slavery in the Southern states.

1803 Louisiana Purchase by President Thomas Jefferson doubles the geographical size of the United States and sets national course for westward expansion.

1804 Shoshone woman Sacagawea serves as guide on the Lewis and Clark expedition to find an overland route to the Pacific.

1807 New Jersey revokes the right of property-holding white women to vote that had been established in the New Jersey state constitution in 1776.

International slave trade abolished, fueling internal domestic trade in the United States.

1809 Elizabeth Ann Seton establishes the first Catholic sisterhood in the United States, the Sisters of Charity in Emmitsburg, Maryland.

Connecticut law allows married women to execute their own wills.

1814 Francis Cabot Lowell opens first American textile mill in Waltham, Massachusetts.

1817 As head of the Cherokee Women's Council, Nancy Ward urges her people not to sell or sign away any more land to the U.S. government.

American Colonization Society founded with plan to establish colonies for free blacks in Africa.

1819   Rebecca Gratz helps establish the Female Hebrew Benevolent Society, one of the earliest Jewish women's organizations in the United States.

Congress negotiates the Missouri Compromise in attempt to balance Northern and Southern interests, admitting Missouri as a slave state and Maine as a free state, and setting the boundary between slave and free at the 36°30' parallel.

1821   Emma Willard opens Troy Female Seminary in Troy, New York.

1823   Catherine Beecher founds Hartford Female Seminary in Connecticut.

1824   Publication of Lydia Maria Child's novel *Hobomok*.

1825   English radical Frances Wright establishes utopian community in Nashoba, Tennessee. Wright subsequently embarks on U.S. lecture tour, advocating women's marital and reproductive rights.

Publication of *Memoir of Catharine Brown: A Christian Indian of the Cherokee Nation*, the autobiography of a Cherokee woman converted to Presbyterianism.

1827   Publication of Catharine Maria Sedgwick's novel *Hope Leslie: or, Early Times in Massachusetts*.

1829   Lydia Maria Child publishes *The Frugal Housewife*.

1830   Indian Removal Act passed under President Andrew Jackson, intended as a plan for voluntary removal of Southeastern tribes in exchange for lands farther west.

Mormon religion founded by Joseph Smith in New York.

Charles Grandison Finney begins preaching in New York, setting off new phase of religious revivalism and moral reform efforts.

1831   The *Liberator* antislavery newspaper founded by radical abolitionist William Lloyd Garrison.

Maria Stewart's lecture, "Religion and the Pure Principles of Morality," appears in the *Liberator*, the first political essay published by a black woman.

1833   Oberlin College becomes the first coeducational collegiate institution in the United States, accepting men and women, as well as both black and white students.

White Quaker teacher Prudence Crandall opens a school for African American women in Canterbury, Connecticut. Crandall is forced to close the school the following year because of protests and intimidation by townspeople.

The first National Temperance Convention is held in Philadelphia, Pennsylvania.

1835 French writer Alexis de Tocqueville publishes first volume of *Democracy in America*, in which he examines the effect of political democracy on American culture and society.

1836 Angelina Grimké publishes *An Appeal to the Christian Women of the South.*

Congress imposes gag rule and refuses to read or acknowledge abolitionist petitions.

Georgia Female College established in Macon, Georgia, as first full-course college for women in the United States.

African Methodist Episcopal (AME) preacher Jarena Lee publishes her spiritual autobiography *The Life and Religious Experience of Jarena Lee, a Colored Lady, Giving an Account of Her Call to Preach the Gospel.*

1837 Sarah Josepha Hale becomes editor of *Godey's Lady's Book,* a position she holds for the next 40 years.

Mount Holyoke College for women founded by Mary Lyon in South Hadley, Massachusetts.

1838 Sarah Grimké publishes *Letters on the Equality of the Sexes and the Condition of Woman.*

Final removal of the Cherokee and other "Civilized Tribes" along the Trail of Tears from the southeast to reservation lands in Oklahoma.

1839 Mississippi is first state to pass law allowing married women to hold property in their own names, with their husbands' permission.

Margaret Fuller holds first "conversations" for women in Boston, Massachusetts.

1840 At the World Anti-Slavery Convention in London, reformers Lucretia Mott, Elizabeth Cady Stanton, and other women are barred from speaking.

Lowell Offering begins publication as newspaper written and produced by female textile factory workers.

Margaret Fuller helps found and serves as first editor of the *Dial,* literary journal of the Transcendentalist movement.

1841 Catharine Beecher publishes *A Treatise on Domestic Economy.*

Brook Farm utopian community is founded in Massachusetts.

Lydia Maria Child begins editing the *National Anti-Slavery Standard* newspaper.

1844 Lowell Female Labor Reform Association is founded in Lowell, Massachusetts.

1845 Margaret Fuller publishes *Woman in the Nineteenth Century,* the first feminist book published in the United States.

1846 First sewing machine is patented by Elias Howe of Massachusetts. Another model is patented by Isaac M. Singer in 1851.

1848 The first women's rights convention in the United States is held in Seneca Falls, New York, resulting in the signing of a "Declaration of Sentiments" outlining resolutions for the new movement.

New York State passes first comprehensive Married Women's Property Act.

Gold is discovered in California, prompting the movement of hundreds of thousands of white prospectors and settlers over the next decade.

Oneida utopian community is founded in New York.

1849 Elizabeth Blackwell becomes the first woman to receive a medical degree when she graduates from Geneva Medical College in New York.

The *Lily* is founded by Amelia Bloomer as a temperance newspaper but soon expands to include topics of dress reform and women's rights.

1850 Dr. Elizabeth Blackwell helps found the Female Medical College of Pennsylvania, the first medical school for women.

The first national women's rights convention is held in Worcester, Massachusetts, presided over by Paulina Wright Davis.

Congress passes the Fugitive Slave Act, ensuring federal assistance in the capture and return of runaway slaves. As part of a compromise with the North, California is admitted as a free state and the slave trade is banned in Washington, D.C.

Harriet Tubman begins assisting fugitive slaves in their escapes via the Underground Railroad.

Sojourner Truth publishes her autobiography, *Narrative of Sojourner Truth,* detailing her early life as a slave in New York.

1851 Sojourner Truth delivers address at women's rights convention in Akron, Ohio, later referred to as the "Ar'n't I a Woman?" speech.

Cherokee Female Seminary is opened in Oklahoma Territory.

1852 Harriet Beecher Stowe publishes *Uncle Tom's Cabin,* a fictionalized account of slavery later credited by Abraham Lincoln as one of the events sparking the Civil War.

1853 Paulina Wright Davis begins publishing the *Una,* the first paper dedicated exclusively to the issue of women's rights.

Mary Ann Shadd Cary becomes the first black woman editor of the antislavery paper, the *Provincial Freeman.*

Antoinette Blackwell is the first woman ordained as a Protestant minister.

1854   Massachusetts passes legislation granting property rights to women.

1855   Prominent reformers Lucy Stone and Henry Blackwell marry and make public their vows, which include a protest against women's subordination within marriage and against unfair marriage laws.

The court rules in *Missouri v. Celia, a Slave* that black women are property without the right to defend themselves against rape by white masters.

1859   Harriet Wilson publishes *Our Nig; or, Sketches from the Life of a Free Black,* considered the first novel by an African American woman.

1860   First kindergarten is established in the United States, founded by educational reformer Elizabeth Palmer Peabody.

1861   The American Civil War begins with shots fired at Fort Sumter, South Carolina.

Dorothea Dix begins work as Superintendent of Nursing for the Union.

Harriet Jacobs publishes her autobiography *Incidents in the Life of a Slave Girl.*

President Abraham Lincoln receives first message on newly completed transcontinental telegraph connection.

Former slave Elizabeth Keckly moves to White House to work as dressmaker to First Lady Mary Todd Lincoln. Her experiences are later published as *Behind the Scenes; or, Thirty Years a Slave and Four Years in the White House* (1868).

Woman's Union Missionary Society is founded.

Vassar College is founded in Poughkeepsie, New York.

Rebecca Harding Davis publishes novel, *Life in the Iron Mills.*

1862   Julia Ward Howe writes the "Battle Hymn of the Republic."

Charlotte Forten and Laura Towne begin teaching at a school for former slaves as part of the Port Royal experiment on South Carolina Sea Islands. Forten later publishes a series of essays on her experience as "Life on the Sea Islands."

The federal Morrill Act establishes land grants for western colleges, promoting women's education in the Midwest and Far West.

The federal Homestead Act opens the west to settlement by selling inexpensive land to individuals.

1863 President Abraham Lincoln issues Emancipation Proclamation, freeing slaves in the rebel states.

Elizabeth Cady Stanton and Susan B. Anthony organize the National Women's Loyal League with the goal of petitioning Congress for full abolition of slavery throughout the United States.

Louisa May Alcott publishes *Hospital-Sketches,* a fictionalized account of her own wartime service as a nurse.

Ellen Gould White helps found the Seventh-day Adventist Church.

1864 Rebecca Lee Crumpler graduates from New England Female Medical College, the first black woman to receive a medical degree.

Kate Mullaney organizes the Collar Laundry Union in New York for female commercial laundry workers.

1865 American Civil War ends with surrender of Confederacy at Appomattox, Virginia.

13th Amendment to the Constitution ends slavery in the United States.

Freedmen's Bureau is established to assist former slaves in transition to freedom, including assistance with employment, housing, and education.

1866 American Equal Rights Association is founded by former abolitionists and women's rights activists working together to promote civil and political rights.

1868 14th Amendment to the Constitution defines national citizenship to include former slaves.

Susan B. Anthony and Elizabeth Cady Stanton begin publishing women's rights newspaper, the *Revolution,* which becomes the main newspaper for the National Woman Suffrage Association.

Louisa May Alcott publishes best-selling novel *Little Women.*

1869 A split in the women's movement over giving black men the vote leads to creation of two separate suffrage organizations: the National Woman Suffrage Association (NWSA) and the American Woman Suffrage Association (AWSA).

Wyoming becomes the first territory to grant unrestricted suffrage to women.

The first transcontinental railroad in the United States is completed, linking eastern and western lines.

1870 15th Amendment to the Constitution states that the right to vote "shall not be denied or abridged by the United States or by any State on account of race, color, or previous condition of servitude," extending the vote to black men while still allowing states to deny the vote to women.

Women are granted the vote in Utah territory, only to have it revoked by Congress in 1876.

Woman's Journal is founded as main newspaper of the American Woman Suffrage Association.

Wellesley College is founded in Wellesley, Massachusetts.

Ada Kepley graduates from Union College of Law in Chicago (now Northwestern University), the first woman granted a law degree in the United States.

1871   Smith College is founded in Northampton, Massachusetts.

1872   Susan B. Anthony attempts to vote in the presidential election and is subsequently arrested and put on trial.

Victoria Woodhull runs for president with former abolitionist reformer Frederick Douglass as her vice presidential running mate.

1873   In *Bradwell v. Illinois,* the court establishes a state's right to exclude women from practicing law.

Comstock Law prohibits sending "obscene" materials through the U.S. mail, including information related to birth control information or devices. The prohibition is not repealed until 1936.

1874   The Woman's Christian Temperance Union (WCTU) is founded.

Massachusetts is first state to pass protective labor legislation, setting a 10-hour workday for women and children.

The court case *Minor v. Happersett* upholds a state's right to deny women the vote by categorizing women as a "special category" of citizens.

1875   The federal Page Law severely limits the immigration of Chinese women under the assumption that most would be prostitutes.

1876   Suffragists protest the Centennial celebration of the Declaration of Independence in Philadelphia, demanding that women be granted all rights of citizenship.

Sculptress Edmonia Lewis is one of only two black American artists to exhibit work at the Centennial celebration in Philadelphia.

1879   Frances Willard becomes president of the Woman's Christian Temperance Union.

Radcliffe College is founded as women's affiliate to Harvard.

Mary Baker Eddy organizes the First Church of Christ Scientists, also known as Christian Scientists.

Congress passes bill allowing female lawyers to argue before the Supreme Court and Belva Lockwood becomes first woman to do so.

Woman's National Indian Association is founded to support missionaries and to pressure the U.S. government to respect treaties and prevent white settlement on Native lands.

1881 Helen Hunt Jackson's *A Century of Dishonor* is published, documenting the wrongs against Native Americans in the settlement of the West.

Clara Barton founds the American Red Cross.

Atlanta Baptist Female Seminary (later renamed Spelman College) is founded for black women.

1882 The federal Chinese Exclusion Act prevents laborers from entering the United States, the first immigration legislation to target a specific group.

1883 Sarah Winnemucca publishes her autobiography *Life among the Piutes: Their Wrongs and Claims.*

Ladies' Home Journal is first published, with Louisa Knapp Curtis as its first editor.

1884 Helen Hunt Jackson publishes novel, *Ramona,* as part of her campaign to alert white Americans to the fate of Native Americans in the West.

1885 Bryn Mawr College is founded in Bryn Mawr, Pennsylvania, as first women's college to offer graduate degrees, including the doctorate.

1887 A federal woman suffrage amendment (also known as the Anthony Amendment) is defeated in the U.S. Senate.

The federal Dawes Severalty Act makes allotments of land to individual Native American families, breaking up land previously set aside on reservations.

Susanna Salter of Argonia, Kansas, becomes the first elected female mayor of an American city.

1889 Jane Addams and Ellen Gates Starr found Hull House in Chicago, inspiring a settlement house movement that spreads to other cities.

Barnard College is founded in New York City as a women's affiliate to Columbia.

Johns Hopkins Medical School in Baltimore, Maryland, begins admitting women.

Susan La Flesche Picotte graduates from Women's Medical College of Pennsylvania, the first Native American woman to receive a medical degree.

Woman's Art Club is founded.

Former millworker Lucy Larcom publishes her autobiography, *A New England Girlhood.*

1890   The two national suffrage organizations unite to form the National American Woman Suffrage Association (NAWSA)

General Federation of Women's Clubs (GFWC) is formed as national umbrella organization for women's club movement.

Jacob Riis publishes *How the Other Half Lives,* exposing the realities of immigrant life in urban tenements.

Forced removal of Lakota Sioux by U.S. government results in massacre at Wounded Knee, South Dakota.

Wyoming is admitted as a state, the first state in which women have the vote.

1892   Ellis Island opens as processing center for immigrants entering the United States and 15-year-old Annie Moore of Ireland is recorded as the first to pass through.

Ida B. Wells begins antilynching campaign with articles appearing in the Memphis *Free Speech* and publication of a pamphlet, *Southern Horrors: Lynch Law in All Its Phases.*

Frances Ellen Watkins Harper publishes novel, *Iola Leroy; or, Shadows Uplifted.*

1893   Colorado voters approve women's suffrage.

Woman's Building is one of the most popular exhibits at the World's Columbian Exposition in Chicago.

Congress of Jewish Women is formed as umbrella organization for Jewish women's clubs with Hannah Solomon as president.

Feminist reformer Matilda Joslyn Gage publishes *Woman, Church, and State,* arguing that Christianity is one of the primary sources of women's subordination and looks to non-Western alternatives, such as the American Iroquois society, as a model for female equality and empowerment.

1894   Julia Foote is first woman ordained as a deacon in the African Methodist Episcopal (AME) Church.

1895   Ida B. Wells publishes another account of lynchings in the South, *A Red Record.*

Elizabeth Cady Stanton and a committee of other feminist writers publish *The Woman's Bible,* a study of the Biblical origins of women's subordination.

1896   Women are granted the vote in Idaho.

Utah is admitted as a state with full suffrage for women and on condition of the Mormon Church officially denouncing polygamy.

The National Association of Colored Women is founded as umbrella organization for black women's club movement with Mary Church Terrell as first president.

Supreme Court decision in *Plessy v. Ferguson* establishes "separate but equal" standard, defining race relations in the post–Reconstruction era South.

1897 In Atlanta, 1,400 white female millworkers walk out in protest over the hiring of two black women who are subsequently fired.

1899 Carrie Nation begins new phase of temperance movement with more militant crusade against saloons and liquor dealers.

Kate Chopin's novel, *The Awakening*, is published.

Charlotte Perkins Gilman's short novel, *The Yellow Wallpaper*, is published.

1900 The International Ladies' Garment Worker's Union (ILGWU) is formed.

1903 The Women's Trade Union League (WTUL) is formed.

The Statue of Liberty is dedicated in New York Harbor and is engraved with an excerpt from Emma Lazarus's 1883 poem, "The New Colossus."

1909 Antilynching activist Ida B. Wells helps found the National Association for the Advancement of Colored People (NAACP).

1913 National Woman's Party (NWP) is founded by Alice Paul and Lucy Burns with focus on securing the vote. The NWP introduces new strategies for the women's movement, such as picketing the White House, and they also speak out against World War I.

1916 In New York, Margaret Sanger opens the first birth control clinic in the United States. The clinic was shut down after 10 days and Sanger was arrested.

1920 American women's right to vote is secured with passage of 19th Amendment to the Constitution, which states "The right of citizens of the United States to vote shall not be denied or abridged by the United States or by any State on account of sex."

Introduction

Women's Roles in Nineteenth-Century America is an overview of the lives of American women across race, class, and region. Each thematic chapter addresses ideas about women's proper roles as well as women's experiences of living in the nineteenth century. The dominant ideas about appropriate gender roles originated from within the white Protestant and primarily middle-class culture, and each chapter compares those ideas with the reality of different women's daily lives, integrating information on European American, African American, Native American, and immigrant women, and women of different economic, religious, social, and geographical locations.

This is a work of synthesis and relies upon the voluminous output of other scholars in the always expanding field of nineteenth-century women's history. Feminist scholars in a range of disciplines—historians, sociologists, anthropologists, political scientists, and literary scholars—have been drawn to the nineteenth century and continue to rework our understanding of marriage and family life, the boundaries between home and public life, women and work, and the intricacies of social and political reform, while also exploring exciting new directions in women's religious and literary roles, and in understanding the multicultural histories of the American West.

Reformers and writers often referred to their own nineteenth century as the "Woman's Century," and it was indeed a century of amazing change and progress for women in the United States. There were great leaps forward in women's legal status, their entrance into higher education and the professions, and their roles in public life. In addition, more than 4 million African American slaves, roughly half of them women, gained their freedom. It seemed the entire world was opened to women in ways never seen before. For the most part this was true, and these various advances can be traced in no small part to a century of women's own insistence on their rights as citizens and as human beings. Women who lived through and witnessed the century firsthand knew that it was one of momentous change and that women could no longer be defined strictly by their roles as wives and mothers. Writer Gertrude Baillie was one such woman who observed in 1894 that:

> No one who has kept apace with the latter half of this nineteenth century, will attempt to deny, that a momentous revolution is taking place in all the so-called spheres of women . . . A woman of lofty ambitions, high ideals, endowed with great talent and capacity, is sure, sooner or later, to become a small power in her way. She may be artist, novelist, physician, anything.[1]

Baillie rightly perceived that the revolution "in all the so-called spheres of women" had not been completed by century's end, but that it was in process, was still "taking place." In 1900 women must have felt for the first time that they could, indeed, "be anything." And yet the conclusion of Baillie's observation was that new roles brought new conflicts for women: "Should she marry, she would be none the less an artist, but she would be surrounded by numerous other cares, which as must eventually come to every married woman, and either her work or her family will feel the neglect."[2] What Baillie, looking back but also looking forward to a new century, perceived as a new dilemma for women with unprecedented new options has become nothing less than one of the enduring and unresolved conflicts for women of the twentieth and twenty-first centuries.

The themes traced in this book are integrated throughout the chapters and therefore some inevitable overlap occurs, as women's lives are not so neatly separated into chapters and subheadings. Education and immigration influenced women's entrances into wage work and the professions, which, in turn, influenced their roles in the family, including even the decision to marry or have children in the first place. Women's choices and roles in the family and in public life were also impacted by women reformers who advocated for changes in women's legal, political, and economic status. Although a separate chapter is devoted to women's roles in slavery and the Civil War, the Civil War serves as an important chronological and social marker throughout the other chapters as well. Besides the fact that the war brought freedom for some 2 million formerly enslaved women, the war had an immense political, economic, and social impact on American society and culture. Whether through encouraging westward expansion, redefining women's roles because of their wartime service, negotiating the new legal status but social restrictions on African American women's lives, or inspiring the themes of freedom, democracy, and race relations that engaged women writers, women's lives and roles were redefined in the latter half of the century in new and significant ways.

Overall, of course, there was no "typical" American woman of the nineteenth century nor a single female experience to speak of. Indeed, women's experiences and lives were so varied between 1800 and 1900 that one might ask how it is possible to come to a unified understanding of "women" in the nineteenth century at all. This book attempts to examine both the commonalities and the differences that defined women's experiences of the era within the broad themes that defined the United States in its first century. The nineteenth century opened with all of the promise and hope of an experiment in new forms of government and social organization and ended with the United States as a major industrial force and rising world power. In one sense, the nineteenth century might be characterized as a century of growth and progress, and of struggles to fulfill the Revolutionary promise of democracy and freedom. The vision of the United States as a land of unlimited opportunities and political freedom was overshadowed throughout the century, however, by the blatant *un*freedom of millions of African Americans, as well as by the aggressive decimation of Native American cultures and peoples. American women experienced and participated in all the complicated aspects of what it meant to live in the United States in the nineteenth century.

The American Revolution and the establishment of a new nation with the Constitution failed to address the issue of slavery in the United States and, in fact, served to protect private property, including slaves, with a series of compromises between the Northern and Southern states. Slavery's economic viability into the nineteenth century was ensured by technological advances, most notably the invention of the cotton gin in 1793, and by a vision of westward advancement made possible, in part, by the Louisiana Purchase in 1803 and subsequent government-sponsored explorations of the West. These political and economic forces ensured that slavery not only continued, but that it thrived and became entrenched even deeper into American society in the first half of the nineteenth century.

Some religious groups and reformers began to question not only the morality of slavery, but also its effect on society at large. The American Colonization Society was founded in 1817 and proposed to establish colonies in Africa for free blacks. Whites who supported the idea of colonization were primarily concerned with the effects of slavery upon whites, and sought to separate the races permanently and rid America of the inferior race. Many early abolitionists who called for the freedom of African Americans were not necessarily concerned with their political rights. This changed with William Lloyd Garrison who, in 1831, began his own abolitionist newspaper with a radical, even revolutionary, message. In the pages of the *Liberator,* Garrison rejected colonization and even gradual emancipation efforts, and instead called for the immediate emancipation of all slaves and the extension of civil and political rights to all black citizens. Garrison helped build the radical abolitionist movement of the 1830s and 1840s, but his critiques of the government and of the churches themselves as complicit in slavery caused a split in the movement between the radicals and the moderates.

Throughout the 1830s and 1840s abolitionists introduced new reform strategies. They held conventions with fiery lecturers, petitioned Congress to disrupt and abolish the domestic slave trade (prompting Congress to pass a "gag rule" in 1836 against abolitionist petitions and mail), boycotted Southern slave-produced goods, and worked to support antislavery candidates and political parties. They also launched a massive antislavery propaganda campaign in order to force the plight of slaves onto the American conscience, not only through the abolitionist newspapers, but also through the publication of narratives by former slaves, such as the *Narrative of Frederick Douglass* and Harriet Jacobs's *Incidents in the Life of a Slave Girl.*

While the abolitionists waged their public campaign against the moral wrongs of slavery, the U.S. government spent the first half of the nineteenth century attempting to contain the political pressure of slavery that threatened to undo the new nation. As the nation grew, both geographically and in population, slavery grew along with it, and the conflict between slave and nonslave states threatened the Union for decades before actual civil war broke out. In 1820 the Missouri Compromise was an attempt to maintain a balance between the numbers of free states and slave states as the Western territories were incorporated into the Union. Missouri was added as a slave state and Maine as a free state and the line separating North and South was agreed upon in the hopes of avoiding future conflict.

Although Congress was satisfied that this provided a permanent answer for any future states to be added to the Union, over the coming decades the line of compromise was challenged, fought over, or downright ignored as settlers and slaves poured into the Western territories. Another compromise was attempted in 1850, when California was added as a free state, and the Fugitive Slave Act was passed to assure Southerners that the U.S. government would support efforts to capture and return any slaves who escaped to free states. Responses to these events ultimately plunged the nation into a civil war, and it took the death of more than half a million Americans (and three Constitutional Amendments) to accomplish the goals of ending slavery in all the territories and states and extending the rights of citizenship to African Americans.

Black men were given the vote during the Reconstruction era and, temporarily at least, many African American men were voted into office at the state and federal levels. But even with slavery ended and black political rights protected by the federal government, white Southerners found ways to limit the exercise of those rights. Poll taxes, literary tests, intimidation, and violence prevented blacks from holding office, voting, or pursuing certain economic opportunities. In the decades after the Civil War, the KKK and mob violence and lynchings continued to terrorize the black community and limit the recently acquired freedoms of black men and women.

The new nation was growing in leaps and bounds. In 1800 there were already more than 5 million people living in the United States, most of those concentrated on the Eastern Seaboard, but the population was growing each year and the hunger for land was intense. The issue of westward expansion was one of the main concerns of the new government, and when Thomas Jefferson became president in 1800 he envisioned an agrarian republic, a nation of independent small family farmers. That vision was dependent upon the acquisition of more land for the United States and influenced all aspects of his policy making. At the time Jefferson acquired the Louisiana Territory from France in 1803, plans were already underway to send Lewis and Clark on an expedition to survey the interior of the continent and find an overland route to the Pacific.

The lands included in the Louisiana Purchase were inhabited not only by white American settlers, but also French and Spanish, as well as thousands of Native Americans. In the early decades of the nineteenth century, a pan-Indian movement arose around a powerful political leader, Tecumseh, and his brother, Tenskatawa, the Prophet or spiritual leader. The brothers visited Native American villages throughout the interior on a public speaking tour, urging Native peoples to resist white settlement, give up alcohol and dependence on other European goods, renounce Christianity, and stop conceding any lands through sale or treaty, all in an effort to rediscover Native American cultural traditions and ensure political and economic survival. Tecumseh was killed and the British were removed during the War of 1812, effectively opening up the West by removing British claims on the continent and British interference in Native American policy.

During the first three decades of the nineteenth century, the population of the United States nearly doubled and technological advances in communication and transportation both facilitated and inspired the spread of the population across a wider geographic area. The federal government sponsored the building of canals and roads to connect people and markets, such as the Erie Canal and the opening of a National Road across the Appalachians. The government also facilitated the settlement of the West through surveying, establishing territorial governments, and setting low prices for the purchase of land. It was therefore a combination of developments by mid-century that accounted for the rapid expansion of westward movement beginning in the 1840s.

In 1820 the "frontier" of white settlement referred to Ohio or Kentucky, but by 1850 the "West" reached all the way to the Pacific Coast. Much happened within a few short decades, including a new wave of European immigration which would change the economic as well as political culture of the United States. Irish immigrants fled economic devastation and settled in Northeastern urban centers of the United States, providing a steady flow of low-paid laborers for the spreading factory system. German and other northern European immigrants fled political turmoil but, possessed of more skills and economic resources, many of these found their way to newly available Midwestern lands and contributed to the agricultural growth of the plains and prairies. In the South, lands were opened up by the Indian Removal Act passed in 1830, but it took until 1838 for the final removal of all southeastern tribes along the Trail of Tears to the reservations in the Oklahoma Territory. The annexation of Texas pushed the cotton and slave economy farther west as well, and the discovery of gold and silver in the Far West opened the floodgates of pioneers and speculators to those regions. The 1850s also opened the age of the railroads and by 1869 the transcontinental railroad had opened.

By the 1840s, the term *Manifest Destiny* had been coined by a journalist to explain the sense of entitlement that white Americans felt over the entire continent. These developments also meant the removal or relocation of Native Americans was sped up, and after the Civil War, immigration, the railroads, and the discovery of gold and silver, not only in California but in Nevada, Wyoming, South Dakota, and other places, all pushed white settlement onto new areas and threatened the way of life and very existence of the Plains Indians. Whereas an estimated 4 million buffalo had roamed the plains in 1870, just four years later their numbers were reduced to half a million. The violent Indian Wars of the 1870s and 1880s culminated in the final showdown at Wounded Knee, South Dakota, in 1890.

Millions of immigrants, primarily from southern and eastern Europe, poured into the United States in the last two decades of the nineteenth century, and in 1892 Ellis Island was opened in New York specifically for the purpose of processing their entrance. These immigrants, including the first significant immigration of Jews, filled factory jobs and tenement housing in America's urban centers. Although certain groups were heavily regulated, restricted, or even outlawed from entering the United States, and although many immigrants faced extreme forms of discrimination once they arrived, as a culture Americans began to embrace their identity as a "melting pot" society. When the Statue of Liberty was erected in New York Harbor, it included an excerpt of a poem entitled "The New Colossus," written by Emma Lazarus, herself the descendent of Jewish immigrants. The inscription has become a motto for American openness and opportunity for the rest of the world:

Give me your tired, your poor,
Your huddled masses yearning to breathe free,
The wretched refuse of your teeming shore.

Send these, the homeless, tempest-tost, to me:
I lift my lamp beside the golden door.[3]

With the immigration of large numbers of Catholics, Jews, and various European Protestant groups, the United States in 1900 was one of the most religiously diverse nations in the world, yet throughout the century established religions were constantly changing and evolving to meet new circumstances, and new religious groups were founded. The century opened with a new era of religious revivalism, sometimes referred to as the second "Great Awakening," to distinguish it from the religious revivalism that spread through the colonies in the mid-eighteenth century. Camp meetings in frontier areas characterized this new form of religious activity, such as the Cane Ridge meeting in Kentucky in 1801, which attracted more than 10,000 people. Early nineteenth-century Protestant denominations, such as Baptists, Methodists, and Lutherans, promoted freedom of choice in church membership with numerous groups and denominations offering more democratic routes to salvation, or the idea that everyone could be saved. New religious groups emphasized not only self-improvement and freely chosen salvation, but also promoted moral reform in an effort to perfect society.

Beginning in the 1820s, moral reformers tackled issues from motherhood to widow's aid, to temperance and prostitution, to abolitionism and eventually women's rights, most of which remained issues through the end of the century. French observer Alexis de Tocqueville visited the United States in the early 1830s and subsequently published his observations on American politics, society, culture, and religion, in the multivolume *Democracy in America,* a text which remains as relevant to understanding America today as it did in the nineteenth century. A unique aspect of American democratic culture that Tocqueville observed was Americans' ability to address their political, moral, economic, religious, and social problems through "associations."

> Americans of all ages, all conditions, and all minds constantly unite together. . . . The Americans form associations in order to hold holiday celebrations, found seminaries, build hostels, erect churches, disseminate books, and send missionaries to the ends of the earth; in this manner they create hospitals, prisons, and schools. Finally, if it is a question of bringing a truth to light or developing a sentiment with the aid of a great example, they form associations.[4]

Women were, of course, central to the types of associations or reform organizations that Tocqueville observed in the early nineteenth century, and the post–Civil War era only brought new issues for religious groups and reformers to address, such as black civil rights, lynching, women's rights, Indian rights, and aid to immigrants. Westward movement and religious enthusiasm went hand in hand, as missionaries, preachers, and founders of Christian schools traveled west to attend to the needs of white settlements on the outskirts of society. They also attempted to convert Native people, some of whom responded by rediscovering traditional sources of spiritual power and modes of faith in the face of white encroachment and cultural genocide, such as the Ghost Dance among the Lakotas in the 1880s.

Not only were established religious groups energized, expanded, and changed by the era of revivalism and reform, but the nineteenth century also saw the creation of several new distinctly American religious groups. Mormonism was founded by Joseph Smith in New York in the early 1830s and by 1846 the sect was so numerous, and so controversial (primarily because of polygamy), that they looked to the safety valve of the West and established their own community in Utah. Utopian communities, both religious and secular, also sought new spiritual and economic models to deal with changes in American society and alternatives to mainstream Christianity. Others were motivated to found entirely new religions, and in this regard women were surprisingly prominent. Ellen G. White became the leader of the newly formed Seventh-day Adventist Church, and Christian Science emerged, led by Mary Baker Eddy.

As president between 1800 and 1808, Thomas Jefferson envisioned and promoted the growth of the United States as an agricultural nation. He specifically feared the path of industrialization and mechanization that he observed in Europe, the results of which were urbanization, overcrowding, and a permanent class of dependent wage laborers, all developments Jefferson hoped America could avoid. Yet technology, innovation, immigration, and the forces of capitalism could not be stopped or even slowed, and the United States grew to become one of the world's major industrial producers over the course of the nineteenth century.

The first textile mill opened in Waltham, Massachusetts, in 1814, introducing a new model of industry and labor. The new mills were water-powered, combined numerous tasks or steps in the process within one factory, and relied upon a new source of labor, young single women. The ability to mechanize the processing of cotton, both in the northern United States and in Britain, spurred demand from Southern cotton plantations and spread the slave economy westward. Whereas Northern industrialization might have developed exactly in the ways that Jefferson feared, the nineteenth-century agricultural South hardly represented a nation of independent small family farmers (and, indeed, Jefferson himself had been one of Virginia's wealthiest land and slave owners), as Southern society was a highly unequal stratified society of a few wealthy cotton planters organizing the labor of nonelite white farmers and millions of enslaved blacks.

Just as abolitionists began to critique the system of slavery, Northern reformers rallied around the degraded factory worker, and workers themselves began to organize and respond with the first national trade union organized in 1833. Mid-nineteenth-century workers protested and made some gains regarding shorter work days, fair pay, and safe working conditions.

Textile industries led the way in American factory system and innovation, but other industries and products that could be put to the "American system" of manufacturing interchangeable parts soon followed, and by the end of the century, the United States was in the midst of another industrial revolution and had become a leading producer of steel, guns, and numerous new consumer items. Inventions of the late nineteenth century included electricity, the bicycle, photographic film, and even the first electric automobile, as well as a host of consumer and food items marketed as conveniences to the American housewife, some of which are still on the market today, such as Ivory soap and Kellogg's breakfast cereal.

Both industry and worker organizations grew and consolidated after the Civil War and by the 1870s, America had entered into the age of big business, the "Gilded Age," the era of Rockefeller and Carnegie, the consolidation of the railroad and oil companies and department stores, and the growth of the stock market. Workers and reformers continued to protest conditions, especially for women and children exploited by the factory system, and in 1874 Massachusetts passed the first protective labor legislation, limiting the number of working hours per day for women and children. In 1890 Jacob Riis published *How the Other Half Lives,* exposing the desolate lives of immigrant working families living in urban tenements. His message was all the more shocking because his text included numerous detailed images made possible by the new photographic technology. During the 1880s and 1890s labor unions organized some of the largest and most significant strikes in American history, prompting the federal government to pass legislation to break business monopolies and to recognize the contribution of American workers to the economy by declaring Labor Day a national holiday in 1894.

Women's Roles in Nineteenth-Century America examines how the economic, political, and social history of the United States affected women's roles and how women themselves helped shape that history. In all cases, differences of race, region, and class are examined side-by-side within the thematic chapters. Chapter 1, "Marriage and Family Life," looks at women's roles and relationships as daughters, wives, and mothers, as well as the roles of women who remained single, either by choice or circumstance. Slave marriages and interracial marriages are also discussed, as well as reformers' attacks on and attempts to provide alternatives to traditional marriage. Chapter 2, "Work," acknowledges women's unpaid work within the household economy as well as their entrance into the paid workforce beginning in the nineteenth century. Whether in factories or as domestic servants (the two main employments of nineteenth-century women), the chapter looks at how women organized on their own behalf and attempted to improve the conditions of their employment. Chapter 3, "Religion," explores women's roles as churchgoers, reformers, missionaries, and preachers. Although women were denied official roles in most organized religions (Catholic nuns stand out as an exception), women were still active participants in the growth and spread of religious work and also had a role in establishing new religions in the nineteenth century. Chapter 4, "Education and the Professions," examines this century that began with almost no women having access to formal education—and most black women denied any education at all—and ended with women making up nearly half of all college graduates. By the end of the century women could be found in leading roles as teachers, college administrators, and even college presidents, and they had made several "first" entrances into professions requiring advanced educations, such as medicine, law, and the ministry. Chapter 5, "Politics and Reform," explains how, although most nineteenth-century women's lives were defined by their private or domestic roles, women were in fact consistently active in public life throughout the century. Women were moral and social reformers addressing society's ills, at the forefront of struggles to extend rights to African Americans and to women, and, in general, they worked throughout the century to make American society a safe, healthy, and equitable place for women, children, and families. Chapter 6, "Slavery and the Civil War," looks in-depth at the experience of enslaved women, their survival and resistance, as well as their first experiences of freedom during and after the Civil War. The chapter also explores the ways in which black and white women participated in and were affected by the Civil War, both North and South. Chapter 7, "The West," looks at the process of relentless westward movement in the nineteenth century through the perspective of women, whether the thousands of pioneer women who traveled into and settled the West, or the Native women who were confronted with and challenged by those settlements. Finally, Chapter 8, "Literature and the Arts," shows that although traditional studies of high culture have focused largely on a male canon of writers and artists, women in fact contributed to establishing an American tradition of literature and the arts. Beginning in the nineteenth century, women's literary sphere expanded from traditionally female genres such as domestic advice novels and sentimental literature to poetry and mainstream literature, magazine writing and editing, and recognition in the world of fine arts.

From the view at the end of the century, much remained to be done and many of the issues and themes traced in this book were not resolved by 1900, but continued well into the twentieth century and beyond. Women's struggle for the vote, that most basic right and tool of democratic citizenship, began in 1848 and continued through to the passage of the 19th Amendment, finally, in 1920. The broader women's rights movement begun in the 1840s to challenge women's economic, legal, and social subordination continues on today, into the twenty-first century. Women's access to reliable birth control information and devices remained rudimentary in the nineteenth century, and confined primarily to women of the upper classes; again, the issue of women's control over their bodies and their roles as mothers (or choice to avoid motherhood) remains just as relevant and contested a subject today as it was in the 1800s. Finally, as more and more women were pulled into, or chose to enter, the paid workforce and the professions, women's traditional roles as wives and mothers were often in conflict with their desire to play larger public roles. One need only to pick up any current magazine or newspaper to be made aware that women's efforts to juggle family and career is an issue not nearing resolution any time soon.

Even though the significance of slavery's end cannot be underestimated, at the end of the nineteenth century black women remained confined to the lowest levels of paid wage work, and they and their families continued to be subjected to extreme and even violent forms of racism and sexism in American culture and the law. The end of slavery did not guarantee the economic and political and social equality of black Americans. The struggle for civil rights that began with abolitionism in the first half of the nineteenth century continued with the movement for political and civil rights after the Civil War, was revived again in the 1950s and 1960s, and, unfortunately, continues on through today.

For Native American women, the nineteenth century saw the final push on their lands and their cultures, and women's traditional roles were radically redefined with the move to the reservation system. At the end of the century, immigrant women and their daughters provided a new generation of low-paid factory workers and often lived in squalid tenements in the nation's expanding urban centers. Although individual women were able to take advantage of new educational opportunities, they were the exception, as most immigrant women and women of color remained poor, quietly raising their children under difficult circumstances while working in factories, as domestic servants, doing agricultural labor, running family businesses, or doing piecework in their homes.

Despite the rapid and radical changes in women's roles and options brought by urbanization and industrialization, most women in the nineteenth century continued to live rurally, tied to agricultural work, and carrying out the same duties as their mothers and grandmothers had on small family farms and in the home. Even though, from the broadest perspective, an American woman's life in 1900 would have been hardly recognizable to a woman in 1800, women were still primarily defined by their roles in childbearing and rearing, food preparation and cooking, and housekeeping. Most women in the nineteenth century fulfilled these same roles, regardless of race or of region, whether in cities, on farms, or on the frontier. It was how they experienced and carried out those roles, and under what circumstances, that differed greatly.

NOTES

1. "Gertrude Stuart Baillie Asks, 'Should Professional Women Marry?,' 1894," in *Major Problems in American Women's History,* 3rd ed., ed. Mary Beth Norton and Ruth M. Alexander (Boston: Houghton Mifflin, 2003), p. 216.

2. "Gertrude Stuart Baillie," *Major Problems,* p. 216.

3. Emma Lazarus, "The New Colossus," Bette Roth Young, *Emma Lazarus in Her World: Life and Letters* (Philadelphia: Jewish Publication Society, 1997), p. 3.

4. Alexis de Tocqueville, *Democracy in America,* vol. 2, pt. 2, sec. 5, "The Use That the Americans Make of the Association in Civil Life" (1840; abr. and repr., Indianapolis, Ind.: Hackett, 2000), p. 211.

SUGGESTED READING

Clinton, Catherine, and Christine Lunardini, eds. *The Columbia Guide to American Women in the Nineteenth Century.* New York: Columbia University Press, 2000.

Collins, Gail. *America's Women: 400 Years of Dolls, Drudges, Helpmates, and Heroines.* New York: HarperCollins, 2003.

Cott, Nancy F., ed. *No Small Courage: A History of Women in the United States.* New York: Oxford University Press, 2000.

DuBois, Ellen Carol, and Lynn Dumenil, eds. *Through Women's Eyes: An American History with Documents.* Boston: Bedford/St. Martin's, 2005.

DuBois, Ellen Carol, and Vicki Ruiz, eds. *Unequal Sisters: A Multicultural Reader in U.S. Women's History,* 3rd ed. New York: Routledge, 1999.

Hewitt, Nancy, ed. *A Companion to American Women's History.* Malden, Mass.: Blackwell, 2002.

Hoffert, Sylvia, ed. *A History of Gender in America.* Upper Saddle River, N.J.: Prentice Hall/Pearson, 2003.

Kerber, Linda, and Jane Sherron De Hart, eds. *Women's America: Refocusing the Past,* 6th ed. New York: Oxford University Press, 2003.

Kerber, Linda, Alice Kessler-Harris, and Kathryn Kish Sklar, eds. *U.S. History as Women's History: New Feminist Essays.* Chapel Hill: University of North Carolina Press, 1995.

Mankiller, Wilma, Gloria Steinem, Gwendolyn Mink, Barbara Smith, and Marysa Navarro, eds. *The Reader's Companion to U.S. Women's History.* Boston: Houghton Mifflin, 1999.

Norton, Mary Beth, and Ruth M. Alexander, eds. *Major Problems in American Women's History,* 3rd ed. Boston: Houghton Mifflin, 2003.

Sherr, Lynn, and Jurate Kazickas. *Susan B. Anthony Slept Here: A Guide to American Women's Landmarks.* New York: Random House, 1994.

Zophy, Angela Howard, and Frances M. Kavenik, eds. *Handbook of American Women's History.* New York: Garland, 1990.

1

~~~

Marriage and Family Life

In 1860, the most popular women's magazine of the era, *Godey's Lady's Book,* declared, "The perfection of womanhood . . . is the wife and mother, the center of the family, that magnet that draws man to the domestic altar, that makes him a civilized being. . . . The wife is truly the light of the home."[1] *Godey's* magazine itself had a major role in spreading nineteenth-century ideals about women's domestic roles within the family. In the nineteenth century, the ideal of companionate marriage, or a partnership based on love and mutual respect, replaced an earlier economic model of marriage. Of course, in reality, marriage remained an economic arrangement with clearly defined roles for both men and women. Throughout the nineteenth century, most American women expected to marry and to have children, although the age of marriage and the number of children varied according to region, class, and race. Rural, frontier, and Southern women tended to marry earlier and have more children than their Northeastern counterparts, although the overall birthrate among all women declined as the century progressed, from seven children in 1800 to between four and five children per woman by 1900.[2]

Although most Americans continued to live rurally or tied in some way to agricultural production, the rapid industrialization and urbanization of the nineteenth century had an effect on both working-class and middle-class marriages, on family life, and on women's roles within the home. On farms and on the frontier the physical labor of everyone, including women and children, remained essential. But in the urban Northeast, more and more of women's traditional roles in household production were moved

"Godey's Fashions for December 1861," *Godey's Lady's Book,* edited by Sarah Josepha Hale, was the most popular fashion magazine of the century. Featured here are new bridal fashions; by the mid-nineteenth century, middle-class weddings were becoming more and more elaborate. (Library of Congress, Prints & Photographs Division, LC-USZC4-5143.)

to the factories, to be performed initially by young, single white women, by Irish or other immigrants, or eventually by black women.

The separation of skilled from unskilled labor and of shop from household production greatly impacted women's roles within the home and family. As a result of the industrialization of the late eighteenth and early nineteenth centuries, the home was no longer the center of all economic activity, and the daily experiences and work lives of men and women were increasingly separated. This created what historians have termed "separate spheres" of activity between the public world of men and the private world of women, each "sphere" with its own specific roles based on gender. Catharine Beecher, in her 1841 *A Treatise on Domestic Economy,* outlined this idea of separate spheres ideology and attempted to respond to the criticism that women were confined by their domestic roles:

> In no country has such constant care been taken, as in America, to trace two clearly distinct lines of action for the two sexes, and to make them keep pace one with the other, but in two pathways which are always different. . . . If, on the one hand, an American woman cannot escape from the quiet circle

of domestic employments, on the other hand, she is never forced to go beyond it.[3]

As less labor was needed at home, there was therefore less need or expectation for large families and the birthrate began to drop. Middle-class families began to focus more on children as individuals, and women, freed from the most time-consuming aspects of household or agricultural labor, spent more and more of their time on childrearing and on developing skills as efficient housekeepers. This is not to say that women's household work was not still demanding and necessary, but that women's moral and spiritual roles, particularly as mothers, were given greater emphasis. By the 1830s an entire literary genre had developed to instruct middle-class white women in their proper roles and duties within the home. Women were not simply responsible for the household, as indeed they always had been, but childrearing and housekeeping, domesticity, became seen as a separate "job" within the new economy. Women's roles in the household, including mothering, became rationalized and professionalized just as men's work away from home had become.

Pamphlets and books for women gave instructions on every aspect of housekeeping and childrearing, as if women were new employees on the job, managers in charge of ensuring efficiency and profitability. Books such as Lydia Maria Child's widely popular, *The Frugal Housewife, Dedicated to Those Who Are Not Ashamed of Economy*, and Mrs. William Parkes's *Domestic Duties; or, Instructions to Young Married Ladies, on the Management of Their Households, and the Regulations of Their Conduct in the Various Relations and Duties of Married Life*, both published in 1829, instructed women to be self-disciplined in their moral guidance of not only their children, but their husbands as well. For their part, married men were expected to provide financially for the household as well as treat the wife with respect and tenderness. But men were seen as vulnerable in new ways, with their emotional, spiritual, and financial well-being dependent upon a wife's proper adherence to her roles.

COURTSHIP, WEDDINGS, AND DIVORCE

With marriage approached as a spiritual partnership based more on mutual affection than on economics, more emphasis was placed on the importance of courtship before entering into such a relationship. In the Northeast, practices such as "bundling" extended back to the colonial era and allowed the courting couple to experience intimacy and test compatibility before marriage by sleeping in the same bed, although not engaging in sexual intercourse, of course. Although both parties in the nineteenth century were expected to agree to the union, and individual choice had become favored over parental choice, it was also proper that only men would propose. The woman's limited role in this arrangement was lamented by one young woman who explained, "true we have the liberty of refusing those we don't like, but not of selecting those we do." Whereas previously women may have expected some trials and hardships within the marriage relationship, now the pressure of a romantic and spiritual union could be too much, as one young woman reminded her fiancé before their wedding, "Every joy in anticipation depends on you, and from you must I derive every pleasure."[4]

There were some regional differences when it came to marriage customs and expectations. More openly than in the North, economics was still at the forefront of the selection of a marriage partner in the South, where wealth was measured in land and slaves. Southern white women tended to marry earlier than their Northern counterparts, becoming brides usually by age 20 compared to Northern women who began, in the nineteenth century, to delay marriage into their early to mid-20s. Southern courtship rituals were also somewhat different than in the North, with Southern planter families upholding stricter codes of feminine "honor" and purity. In the South, a couple's courtship took place under constant supervision, usually by her family. One observer noted "in the South it is deemed indecorous for them to be left alone, and the mother or some member of the family is always in the room; and if none of these, a female slave is seated on the rug at the door." The Southern "belle" had her honor and reputation to protect, but this by no means prevented her from flirting and attempting to attract potential suitors. One young woman defined attracting numerous suitors as the mark of a true "belle," announcing "she meant to have as many lovers as she could bring to her feet to be a reputed belle."[5]

The difference between North and South extended even to the very definition of marital respect and fidelity. Although the purity of women was praised by all, in the name of protecting their virtue, Southern white women's "sphere" of activity was even more limited, and they rarely engaged in activities outside of the home and immediate family. As an added insult, Southern white women of the slaveholding class were expected to bravely face and accept the infidelities of their husbands with slave women. White women were expected not only to raise their own children, but to oversee a household that might include several slaves as well as potentially their husband's children with other women. Some Southerners lamented this state of affairs, such as Mary Boykin Chesnut, writing in her diary on the eve of the Civil War: "God forgive us, but ours is a monstrous system, a wrong and an iniquity! Like the patriarchs of old, our men live all in one house with their wives and their concubines; and the mulattoes one sees in every family partly resemble the white children. Any lady is ready to tell you who is the father of all the mulatto children in everybody's household but her own. Those, she seems to think, drop from the clouds or pretends so to think."[6]

Beginning in the colonial era, informal marriage ceremonies were more common in the North and among immigrant and poorer or rural communities. In many instances, it was simply a family affair with no formal ceremony, and a couple's marriage was made known solely by their decision to take up house together. Increasingly among the middle classes, however, a more formal wedding was desired. Once an engagement was made, it was a relatively short wait until the actual wedding and announcements were sent mainly to local friends and family. In the Northeast weddings commonly took place on a weekday so as not to interfere with the minister's Sabbath-related duties on the weekend. Wedding ceremonies themselves were more elaborate and formal among the Southern planter class. Southern weddings were officiated by Anglican ministers and were an opportunity for displays of wealth as well as an excuse for a large social event and family gathering. Southern weddings were planned further in advance and the guests, including family members who would be expected to travel greater distances to attend, could expect entertainment as well as elaborate meals prepared with the help of slave labor.[7]

In the first half of the nineteenth century most Americans held a flexible view of "legal" marriage. It was more important that the community recognize and sanction a union than that a legal document was produced. The legitimacy of Rachel and Andrew Jackson's marriage was brought up during his 1828 presidential campaign. Not only had the couple been married without a license in Tennessee in 1791, but she had not obtained a legal divorce from her previous husband, revealing the looseness of the definition of legal marriage in frontier regions.[8] Even as more states adopted laws regulating the terms for marriage and divorce, in many instances it was still the community that played a primary role in regulating the actions of individual couples. A South Carolina couple having an adulterous affair in the 1870s was confronted by neighbors who called a public meeting and signed a resolution running the man out of town. Their actions eventually brought the couple to the attention of local courts, where the judge backed up the neighbors' assessment of the situation and jailed and fined the man, an action subsequently upheld all the way to the South Carolina Supreme Court.[9]

Although the culture had shifted to an emphasis on compatibility and romantic love, and the age of first marriage was delayed in more instances, some couples, of course, found themselves seeking divorce. By 1800 most states allowed legal divorce, with Southern states last to do so. Still, divorce before the Civil War was rare, with only 1.2 divorces out of every 1,000 marriages. By 1900 that number had nearly doubled, but still only 4 divorces for every 1,000 marriages.[10] Only extreme situations of breaking the marital contract warranted divorce and the reasons included adultery, physical abuse of the wife or children, or desertion, again, usually by the husband, thus explaining why more women than men sought divorce. The fact that women increasingly saw divorce as at least an option in these cases was owing, in part, to the rise of women's rights in general and women's increased education and economic opportunities as the century progressed. Still, there were economic disincentives for women to seek an end to their marriages, as there were no legal guarantees of alimony, child support, or, in most cases, of a woman's right to any of her own property. Even though the ideology of domesticity emphasized women's special role as nurturers and caregivers, the law continued to see fathers as heads of households responsible for the support of children.

SINGLE WOMEN

Not all women married, of course, and for the first time in American history, the nineteenth century saw more and more women forgoing marriage entirely, either by choice or circumstance. The new ideal of companionate marriage meant that women were discouraged from seeking marriage purely for economic or social status reasons, and women's increased access to formal education meant that pursuit of a vocation was increasingly an alternative path to marriage and motherhood. The number of "spinsters" in the United States rose steadily between the American Revolution and the Civil War, and peaked with nearly 11 percent of American women born in the immediate post–Civil War decade of 1865–1875 remaining single. By mid-century, a generation of unmarried women insisted that by not having families to tend, they were better able to devote themselves, both physically and emotionally, to the needs of others, including society at large. But they also saw the personal costs of marriage as too high, as Louisa May Alcott explained in 1868, "the loss of liberty, happiness, and self-respect is poorly repaid by the barren honor of being called 'Mrs.' instead of 'Miss,'" revealing the idea that the new single woman need not be pitied, as women such as Alcott were quite "happy in their choice."[11]

The nineteenth-century single woman by choice was most likely to be of the middle or upper class, white, and native-born, with some formal education. Among Anglo Americans, single women had more opportunities for wage-earning than married women, and, although the term *spinster* had been previously used to refer to unwed women tied to their spinning wheels, in the first half of the century, textile mills were in fact the major employer of single women in the United States. Whereas married women might have earlier participated in the paid labor force through the "putting out system" that brought farm families into the factory system, as the factories increasingly took over all aspects of production, the need for a low-paid unskilled factory labor force was found among New England's young unmarried females.

Young unmarried women were motivated to go to mills not only to earn wages, but because of the opportunity for independence as women. Of course, in many instances, those wages were needed to support the family and did not release the wage-earning woman from her family obligations. It was becoming more and more difficult to sustain a large family in a wage economy and marriage was increasingly delayed as women waited for young men to establish their own farms before marrying. As more and more household goods were mass-produced in factories, there was less work for daughters to do at home while they waited for marriage. Not only would the journey of a daughter to the mill reduce the family's living expenses, but she could contribute to its income by sending part of her wages back home, and still possibly save money for her own future marriage. In this way, young women's economic roles in the family were sometimes shifted from the dependence and unpaid domestic support labor of a daughter to her contribution of a crucial source of cash for the family.

Women's letters back home from the factories reveal their contributions to the family economy, their responsibility for their parents, and the struggles faced by many displaced farm families. After the death of her husband, Lois Barrett Larcom was responsible for the support of 10 children. After trying unsuccessfully to earn money running a boardinghouse for millworkers, Lois Larcom saw five of her daughters, Abigail, Lydia, Emeline, Octavia, and Lucy, all become mill workers themselves at various times. The girls sent as much money as possible to their mother. Emeline wrote in 1841 that she was "exceedingly grieved to have no more to send," and regretted the position her mother was in, sending comfort and consolation as well as cash: "Dear mother don't say you are poor or dependant. You are no more so than any other one. 'The earth is the Lord's and the fulness thereof.' To some of his dependant children he gives money, to some lands, to you he has given children." Women's letters back home from the factories often included notes of "dollars enclosed" and sometimes they spoke specifically to their desire to assist the family. Letters from the Larcom girls consistently noted the amounts they sent home to their mother: "Enclosed 5.00," "Enclosed 6 dollars," "Enclosed 5 dollars. Don't feel pinched for I'd rather not have a thing myself than to have you."[12] (See also Chapter 2, "Work.")

Not all single women joined the paid labor force nor did greater educational opportunities guarantee economic independence. Most unmarried women retained vital caretaking roles within their families of origin, either in the homes of their parents or their adult siblings. Clementina Smith of Pennsylvania responded directly to the myth that a single woman "could do just as I please." She complained to a friend "that even in a state of single *blessedness* when ladies are supposed to have their own way they are not always without restraint." As an unmarried adult daughter living with her parents, Smith had a round of domestic duties that led her to conclude that "Spinsters are no more independent than married people, if they are as much so indeed."[13]

Even though women's own vision of their lives was changing, most parents expected that a woman remain bound by her duties as a daughter until, if ever, she committed herself to a husband and house of her own. Those who did break away from their families of origin to pursue their own paths and independence often carried great guilt and justified their decision in terms not of self-actualization, but of contributing to some greater good. During the Civil War, Laura Towne, a Philadelphia schoolteacher, traveled to the South Carolina Sea Islands to teach former slaves, later recalling, "I have felt all along that nothing could excuse me for leaving home, and work undone there, but doing more and better work."[14]

Some women, of course, found themselves single because of circumstances beyond their control, whether it be widowhood, desertion, divorce, or simply lack of a suitable mate. The nineteenth century saw considerable shortages of marriageable young men because of both westward movement and the Civil War. More than 600,000 men were killed in the Civil War, leaving not only young widows, but also a generation of women with fewer marriage options, especially in the South. Some Southern women reveled in the possibility of independence outside of marriage and echoed Northern women's praise of "single blessedness." In 1862 young Sarah Morgan confidently stated, "I mean to be an old maid myself and show the world what such a life can be." Another young woman in Alabama, Jo Gillis, similarly declared that she had observed the lives of married women and was not attracted to the idea: "I don't care to marry. . . . I see married women have to do and submit to things that my uncurbed I may say *high* temper, never could brook . . . the slights I see some wives submit to would quite crush out life and hope." Gillis, in fact, did not escape from the expected roles for women as she not only married, but, sadly, died in childbirth.[15]

Such wartime declarations, however, were in contrast to the anxieties of many of their young female friends who were increasingly aware, as one young woman put it in 1864, "that after the war is closed, how vast a difference there will be in the numbers of males and females." While some feared spinsterhood, others began to acknowledge that "numerous ladies" might be "reduced to marry men whom they do not love," simply because the choices were limited. Others were more blunt in their assessments, such as teenager Esther Alden of South Carolina who admitted, "One looks at a man so differently when you think he may be killed to-morrow. Men whom up to this time I had thought dull and commonplace . . . seemed charming."[16]

Although the war created some anxiety about whether marriage would even be an option, by the turn of the century, more women were forgoing marriage and children by choice, and, in its place, establishing visible relationships with other women. The term *Boston marriage* was coined at the turn of the twentieth century to describe the phenomenon of long-term domestic arrangements between two white women of this class. These "marriages" defined emotional, financial, and possibly even sexual relationships between women. In a culture where traditionally married women nurtured acceptable emotional and physical relationships with other women, women in "Boston marriages" might be criticized for forgoing marriage and children, or for being feminist-minded reformers (which many of them were), but rarely were they criticized for engaging in immoral sexual practices.[17]

The increasing numbers of single-by-choice, primarily white, women in the late nineteenth century caused reflection among some critics assessing the costs of this choice on society at large, and among women themselves as they considered their expanding options. In 1894 journalist Gertrude Stuart Baillie wrote an article asking, directly, "Should Professional Women Marry?" She sought to examine "some of the formidable causes that are responsible for the celibacy of professional women," and concluded that women, now possessing the education necessary to make them intellectually equal to men and able to economically support themselves, as well as traditionally understood as morally superior to men, simply did not need men anymore as they did in earlier generations. Although women's roles were now expanding to include options outside of the family, it was still assumed that women must choose between those various options; that is, either marriage or career. Baillie was among those who cautioned that a woman could not do both, as "they could not conscientiously give their hand where their heart was not, for their heart was given to their work."[18] (See also Chapter 4, "Education and the Professions.")

SLAVE MARRIAGES

American law did not recognize marriage between African American slaves, although slaves and some white owners did. Slaveholders had an economic incentive not only to recognize but to encourage slave marriages. One plantation owner's manual pointed out the twofold advantages for white slaveholders who, by allowing their slaves to marry, would increase "the comfort, happiness, and health of those entering upon it, besides ensuring greater increase."[19] This attitude could work in slaves' favor as owners might also be reluctant to separate couples in a sale. Still, slave marriages were undermined by the fact that whites had control over their unions, regardless of whether they exercised that control in a negative or positive way.

Black women's roles as wives as well as mothers were also undermined in a system that determined the status of children, slave or free, "according to the condition of the mother," giving white men control not only over slave marriages but over the actual bodies of slave women. In this way, slavery not only degraded black women, but also undermined black partnerships by demoralizing black men. A former slave from Virginia recalled how black men stood by helplessly as wives were punished by masters, unable to fulfill their roles as protectors: "Husbands always went to de woods when dey know de wives was due fo' a whippin'." In one particular instance a pregnant woman was beaten while her husband stood nearby "not darin' to look at her or even say a word."[20] Although separation was not a desired alternative, such scenarios were surely one of the disadvantages of spouses residing on the same plantation.

White owners sometimes resented slaves' efforts to exercise control over decisions such as choosing a mate or having children. In Harriet Jacobs's 1861 autobiography, *Incidents in the Life of a Slave Girl*, she recalled her master's psychological control over her desire to have a relationship with a free black man. Her master told her, "I'll soon convince you whether I am your master, or the nigger fellow you honor so highly. If you must have a husband, you may take up with one of my slaves." She replied, "Don't you suppose, sir, that a slave can have some preference about marrying? Do you suppose that all men are alike to her?"[21] In this case, Jacobs's master revealed that he did not object to her being married, but only to marrying someone of her own choosing, and perhaps, specifically, to her having a sexual relationship with someone other than himself.

Although many slave couples considered themselves spouses or partners without any ceremony or legal acknowledgment from the white community, some slaves did have weddings, produced either with the assistance of whites or on their own. North Carolina slave Temple Herndon Durham recounted her marriage to Exter Durham, a slave owned by a different master: "We had a big wedding. We was married on the front porch of the big house. . . . Miss Betsy had Georgianna, the cook, to bake a big wedding cake all iced up white as snow with a bride and groom standing in the middle holding hands. . . . I had on a white dress, white shoes and long white gloves that come to my elbow, and Miss Betsy done made me a veil out of a white net window curtain." A black preacher married the Durhams, although Temple's white master and mistress helped organize the elaborate event.[22]

Other former slaves told how their masters required them to be married by white preachers, an interesting attempt to spiritually recognize vows that the law did not recognize. South Carolina slave Susan Hamlin pointed out that no minister ever included the traditional appeal that "what God has joined, let no man put asunder" as part of the wedding ceremony because "a couple would be married tonight and tomorrow one would be taken away and be sold."[23] Or, as in the case of the Durhams, they might not even live on the same plantation. The very next day after their elaborate wedding ceremony, Exter Durham was returned to his plantation, visiting Temple only "every Saturday night."[24]

Husbands who lived away were more likely than the wives to make the trips to visit their wives, and, later, their children, on another plantation. Some did so while traveling for work; others were given a pass to travel and visit on weekends; others traveled without permission if they had to, putting their own safety at risk. In most cases, relationships between slave partners or spouses, whether legally recognized or not, were a primary way that slaves emotionally resisted and survived the institution of slavery itself. Slaves who had a choice sought out marriage for the same reason as many whites: love, companionship, and the desire for family.

Although many white slaveholders considered their slaves as dependents and even part of their own families, slaves' family commitments were to other slaves, either those living on the same plantation, or bonds that survived the separation of husbands and wives living in different locations. Historians and sociologists have made much of the fact that many slave children grew up without knowing their fathers, and that the female-headed family unit became the norm for African Americans. But evidence suggests that even when living in different plantations, slave unions were strong and couples saw themselves as spouses and parents across the distance. One white mistress in South Carolina complained about her slave, Eliza, whose husband lived on another plantation: "I would be thankful if I could get rid of Eliza, she calls for Powel her husband, says she has been living with him five years, sends her children on messages to him, abuses me, won't let her children work for us, and is an abominable creature." Another owner found that he had to renegotiate a sale because a slave, Stephen, refused to leave the area while his wife resided on a nearby plantation.[25] In these instances, the allegiances between spouses interfered with the white owner's economic control over their slaves.

Despite their lack of social and legal rights to marriage and even to their own children, slave families struggled to exercise their human rights that bound them together by maintaining some control over their own family lives. The realities of slaves' daily work lives as well as the threat and reality of separation meant that few slaves operated within the nuclear family model practiced by whites. Older siblings or elderly women would care for infants while the parents were in the fields or in the white households working all day. On large plantations, this created a daycare system with several children watched in one place throughout the day. This arrangement was thus a necessity, but it also strengthened the bonds across generations and beyond blood ties. Former slave Laura Smalley recalled how mothers were separated from their infants by work in the fields, and the schedule on which they tended to them: "They come at ten o'clock everyday to all them babies. Them what nurse. Them what didn't nurse, they didn't come to them at all. The old lady fed them. When that horn blowed, they blowed a horn for the mothers, they'd just come just like cows, just a-running, coming to the children. . . . Ten o'clock in the day and three o'clock in the day. They come to that baby an' nurse it."[26] (See also Chapter 6, "Slavery and Civil War.")

As soon as the Civil War broke out, Southern blacks sought to legitimize their marriages, for personal reasons as well as reasons of economic and civil justice. Just as black men tried to exercise their new civil rights in joining the army, they also sought the right to have a family. Legal marriage was also required in order for black women to claim family

Multiple generations of a black family in South Carolina (1862). In the midst of the Civil War, many white plantation owners abandoned their farms, and many black families sought to reunite or keep their families together and establish new homes. (Library of Congress, Prints & Photographs Division, LC-B8171-152-A.)

benefits or potential widow's pensions for men serving in the military. As one historian explains it, "Army chaplains performed marriages for a multitude of African Americans who had lived as committed couples for years. Indeed, the army demanded that marriages be legalized before it would recognize them, regardless of how long a man and woman had thought of themselves as husband and wife and fulfilled the obligations of that state."[27] After the war, the newly formed Freedmen's Bureau found issuing marriage certificates among its many tasks in assisting the former slaves. Along with legalizing their marriages, finding and reuniting families and establishing their own homes were among the chief priorities of formerly enslaved peoples. As one officer of the Freedmen's Bureau noted, "Every mother's son seemed to be in search of his mother; every mother in search of her children."[28] White workers of the Freedmen's Bureau promoted domesticity among blacks, encouraging black men to "get a home," which "will promote virtue and build up strong family ties," and women to "learn to make good bread" and provide "perpetual sunshine in the home."[29]

INTERRACIAL MARRIAGES

Although most sexual relationships between black women and white men in the South were framed within the context of white men's control over black women's bodies in slavery, before the Civil War interracial relationships between black men and white women did not necessarily challenge racial slavery and racial inequality, especially if the woman was poor or lower class. It was more difficult for elite white women to carry on a consensual relationship with a black man, slave or free, because of her role in representing and reproducing the planter class. Before the Civil War it was rare to find actual legal marriage between white women and black men recorded, although in census records of the 1830s and 1840s, there are records of some free black men with white wives. Before war even broke out, fear of a racially mixed society, and, more specifically, of black men preying upon white women, led one white Southern minister to warn in 1860 of the social and sexual effects of the end of slavery: "Abolition preachers will be at hand to consummate the marriage of your daughters to black husbands." It was not until after the Civil War, when the legal right to marry was extended to African Americans, that the term *miscegenation* began to be used and that black-white sexual relations became strictly regulated by law as well as informally by the community.[30]

Although black-white sexual relations and intermarriage preoccupied the minds of a society where race-based slavery existed, these were not the only interracial relationships at stake. Nineteenth-century government Indian policy focused, in large part, on the regulation of marriage between whites and Native Americans. As missionary and educational efforts increased, more whites came into contact with and sought to change traditional Native forms of family life, including the traditional roles of Native women. Native Americans had different notions of private property, marriage, and the sexual division of labor, as noted and condemned by white Europeans from the era of first contact well into the nineteenth century and beyond. As one official reported to the Office of Indian Affairs, "some of the Indians had several wives, who sometimes live in different towns, and at considerable distance from each other, [and] they are allowed by the Indian to own property not subject to their husbands."[31]

White Americans held specific views about women's proper roles within the family, and, to the extent that Native Americans did not assume those same roles, marriage and the family were of particular concern to those seeking to incorporate Native Americans into the new nation. Encouraging Native peoples to assimilate so that "we shall all become Americans," President Thomas Jefferson suggested to tribal leaders in 1808 that Native men and women learn to adopt the Anglo American mode of farming as well as the white division of gender roles: "If the men will take the labor of the earth from the women they will learn to spin and weave and to clothe their families." The final part of Jefferson's vision was that "you will mix with us by marriage, your blood will run in our veins, and will spread with us over this great island."[32]

Some Native groups responded to aggressive U.S. land policies by assimilating into Anglo American culture, including through intermarriage. Thomas Jefferson and many Indian agents in the first half of the century regularly promoted or sanctioned intermarriage, at least between white men and Indian women, as part of an overall policy toward instilling white gender conventions among Native peoples. The goal was to promote monogamy, discourage polygyny as practiced among some Native tribes, and privilege those couples agreeing to male land ownership and engaging in small family farming. Although in several early cases Cherokee women won their individual claims to their own property, in some cases these rulings facilitated the transfer of control of Cherokee lands and other property to white men through intermarriage. Such legal maneuvering seemed to have been on the mind of at least one potential suitor, a white man named Townsend who, intending to marry a Cherokee woman who had claims to her uncle's land, house, and other improvements, inquired of the courts, "on the eve of his marriage . . . to know whether he could have these improvements valued as his own property provided he married the girl."[33]

Intermarriage served not only to facilitate economic goals, but it also served an important political function in Indian-white relations throughout the century, as Indian women, especially, could be useful as negotiators and interpreters between the two sides. In the late 1850s, a

Modoc woman named Winema went against family and tradition by refusing the mate prearranged for her and marrying instead a white man, a Kentucky miner named Frank Riddle. She was not only going against her family's wishes, but as the Modocs were in constant conflict with white settlers, many saw her marriage as a betrayal. But when full-scale war broke out in the 1860s, both Winema and Frank became valuable peacemakers, and she served first as an interpreter and was later called upon by the U.S. government to help negotiate the terms of an 1864 treaty of peace.[34]

Federal policy was used later in the century to enforce white gender roles and expectations among far western peoples on the new reservations. The

Winema and son (1873). After her marriage to a white man, the Native American woman Winema (also known as Tobey Riddle) was a translator and negotiator during the Modoc Wars of the 1860s and 1870s. She later received a pension from the U.S. government for her service. (Library of Congress, Prints & Photographs Division, LC-USZ62-114599.)

1887 Dawes Act divided up reservation lands into allotments for individual families, with property rights conferred on the "head of household," who was generally considered to be male. Under the Dawes Act only one allotment per "household" or couple meant that polygyny was not recognized, and, in some cases, was aggressively fought by Indian agents attempting to reorganize Indian society, both economically and socially. (See also Chapter 7, "The West.")

MARRIAGE AND REFORMERS

Even though marriage was now seen as a partnership, and the significance of both women's reproductive and spiritual roles were widely acknowledged, the political and legal status of married women was slow to change. Improving women's status as mothers and wives became the first frontier for the emerging women's rights movement of the mid-nineteenth century. Beginning in the late 1840s and 1850s, some women's rights activists began to avoid marriage, either out of principle or, sometimes, out of necessity of being able to continue their reform work. Susan B. Anthony never married and was dismayed at times that her closest friend in the cause, Elizabeth Cady Stanton, was kept from more public activity by her marriage and, more specifically, by the care of seven children. As long as marriage and motherhood went hand-in-hand, and as long as women were unable to completely control the number and spacing of births, marriage was seen as too confining for women who wanted to pursue other paths. In 1853 Stanton wrote to Anthony, "I feel as never before that this whole question of women's rights turns on the pivot of the marriage relation."[35]

Others, like Lucy Stone, chose to marry but sought to redefine the relationship from a feminist perspective. Many women's rights reformers and other publicly active women of the nineteenth century chose to take on their husband's name but to also retain their own family names—Elizabeth Cady Stanton or Paulina Wright Davis, for example—but Lucy Stone went one step further with the radical act of not taking her husband's name at all. Both Lucy Stone and Henry Blackwell were active in the abolitionist movement and supported women's rights. The Blackwell family indeed boasted several "firsts" among prominent women. Henry Blackwell's sisters were both graduates of medical college, with Elizabeth Blackwell holding the distinction of being the first female physician in the United States. Another sibling, Samuel, was married to Antoinette Brown Blackwell, the first woman ordained as a minister.

When Lucy Stone and Henry Blackwell married, they sought to challenge the traditional roles of both sexes. Lucy determined to keep her own name and therefore, symbolically, her own identity. Henry agreed, assuring her, "I wish, as a husband, to renounce all the privileges which the law confers upon me, which are not strictly mutual. Surely such a marriage will not degrade you, dearest."[36] At their 1855 wedding ceremony, they made public their commitment to a marriage between equals with a signed statement read by the minister and subsequently republished in reform journals of the time:

> While acknowledging our mutual affection by publicly assuming the relationship of husband and wife, yet in justice to ourselves and a great principle, we deem it a duty to declare that this act on our part implies no sanction of, nor promise of voluntary obedience to such of the present laws of marriage, as refuse to recognize the wife as an independent, rational being.[37]

Stone and Blackwell sought to provide a public example of an alternative approach to American beliefs about marriage and women's roles. Many feminist reformers also worked to change women's actual legal status within marriage, specifically around the issue of married women's right to their own property, a battle fought state by state through the end of the century. The American colonies had followed British common law of *feme-covert*, or coverture, which determined that women were legally "covered" by their husbands through marriage. The basis for British and American colonial common law was English jurist William Blackstone's 1765 *Commentaries on the Laws of England*, which defined *feme-covert* status:

> By marriage, the husband and wife are one person in law: that is, the very being or legal existence of the woman is suspended during the marriage, or at least incorporated and consolidated into that of the husband: under whose wing, protection, and *cover*, she performs every thing; and is therefore called . . . a *feme-covert*.[38]

Whereas still restrictive but somewhat different laws applied to unmarried women and widows—women under the legal status of *feme-sole*—a married woman could not engage in or bring forth lawsuits; she could not enter into business contracts, nor could she buy or sell or otherwise have control over any property, even that which she may have brought to the marriage. Upon marriage, all property, land, even personal possessions and wages earned, became the property of her husband, as did her children.

The American Revolution brought almost no change in women's legal status, but by the early 1800s some states began to change their laws to adjust to women's new economic roles. In 1809 Connecticut passed a law allowing married women to execute their own wills, and in 1839 Mississippi began to allow women some right to their own property, in particular, their own slaves. The Mississippi law was brought about because of a case involving a Chickasaw woman who wanted to retain the right to her own property after marrying a white man. Other Southern states amended property law to allow married women to retain rights to their inherited slave property, not necessarily as a commitment to the rights of individual women, but to make sure that such property remained within the family in case of divorce. When an organized women's rights movement emerged in the late 1840s, the issue of married women's property rights was one of the main ones targeted for reform. In 1848 New York State passed the landmark Married Women's Property Act, which became the model for other states throughout the remainder of the century.

In the decades leading up to the Civil War, the feminist reform and critique of marriage overlapped with the abolitionist critique of slavery in the minds of many Northern reformers. Reformer Lucy Stone, who, with husband Henry Blackwell, made a public statement of their intent to redefine the terms of marriage, declared, "Marriage is to woman a state of slavery. It takes from her the right to her own property, and makes her submissive in all things to her husband."[39] Reformer Paulina Wright Davis also used the analogy of wives as slaves and husbands as master. Davis edited the women's rights newspaper, the *Una*, in which she published an 1854 article titled, "Inequality of Women in Marriage," stating that "We believe that woman's enforced inferiority in the marriage relation, not only wrongs her out of the best uses of her existence, but also cheats her master of the richest and noblest blessings of the nuptial union."[40]

Some Southerners also used the analogy between women and slaves but to different ends. Whereas Northern reformers increasingly emphasized the benefits of intellectual, spiritual, and even economic equality in marriage, the antebellum Southern family was defined by hierarchy and by the subordination of masters over slaves, and of husbands over wives and children. One minister wrote that, in the Bible, "masters [are] exhorted in the same connection with husbands, parents, magistrates; slaves exhorted in the same connection with wives, children and subjects."[41]

Reformers pointed out that marriage meant not only the economic and legal subordination of women, but had physical consequences as well. Because few women of the nineteenth century could escape maternity, many reformers focused on either access to information about birth control or on redefining women's roles as mothers. Without knowledge about their own bodies and without access to birth control, marriage for most women meant unplanned and multiple pregnancies. Lucy Stone argued that property and even voting rights were secondary and meaningless "if I may not keep my body, and its uses, in my absolute right. Not one wife in a thousand can do that now, & so long as she suffers this bondage, all other rights will not help her to her true position." Her husband Henry Blackwell assured Stone that she would reserve the right to decide "how often you shall become a mother."[42]

Even though she rejected the idea that motherhood was women's primary role, or that women should be confined to the domestic sphere, women's rights activist Elizabeth Cady Stanton was herself the mother of seven children. Stanton embraced the idea that motherhood was a profession, for which women should be adequately trained and knowledgeable. In her own writings, Stanton explained how, upon becoming a mother, she had "commenced the study of medicine" in order to better perform her role as a mother and understand the latest developments in infant care and health. Stanton warned against the idea that women had "natural" or traditional wisdom regarding childcare and mothering, therefore highlighting that motherhood was but a social role imposed upon women.[43]

MARRIAGE ALTERNATIVES

Other reformers made both secular and religious arguments against traditional marriage, and, in some cases, offered alternatives to women's traditional roles in marriage and the family. Inspired by American utopian reformers, Englishwoman Frances Wright established a utopian community in Tennessee called Nashoba in 1825. Wright opposed traditional marriage and monogamy and promoted birth control and open sexual relationships among community members. She believed that sexual relationships should be based on love and commitment, on individual happiness, rather than based on a legal contract. Wright's views were so well publicized and controversial that other radical women reformers were sometimes referred to in the press as "Fanny Wrights."

By the time Wright died in 1852, "free love" constituted a separate distinct reform movement. Drawing members and ideas from among radical reformers associated with utopian communities, women's rights, health reform, and abolitionism, free love at its core was not about unrestrained sexuality, as critics charged, but instead simply promoted free *choice* in matters of love, sexuality, and maternity. Health reformers such as Mary Gove Nichols and Paulina Wright Davis, among others, emphasized the connections between women's health, women's rights, and happy marriages. Such feminist reformers argued that women could not fulfill their duties, nor find happiness, as wives and mothers without knowledge about their own bodies and the right to "voluntary motherhood." For some, voluntary motherhood meant simply that women should have some control over the frequency and timing of sexual intercourse within marriage. For other more radical reformers, it meant that women needed complete reproductive control, including accurate information about controversial topics such as methods of contraception and abortion.

Some religious reformers also rejected monogamy or even marriage outright. Shakers and Mormons were two successful nineteenth-century religious communities that practiced unorthodox family and sexual roles for women. The Shakers were founded by "Mother" Ann Lee, who emigrated to the United States from England in the 1770s and helped spread the communitarian movement that practiced strict celibacy, or refraining from marriage and sexual activity, and created new forms of family life by adopting orphans, widows, and members attracted to this idea. Ann Lee herself had been the victim of physical and sexual abuse in her own marriage and preached that the institution of marriage kept women subordinate. By the 1830s there were 19 Shaker communities in the United States with approximately 6,000 members.

Whereas the Shakers promoted celibacy, the Mormons practiced "plural marriage," or polygyny, as part of their early belief system. Unlike Shakers or feminist reformers, equality between the sexes was not the Mormons' primary goal for challenging traditional marriage. Although some Mormon women had multiple husbands, it was more common for male members to have multiple wives. In many practical ways, plural marriages protected widows with children by providing an extended network of family support. Also, in the interest of family stability and of ideal marriage, Mormons allowed divorce more often. The extensive domestic duties of Mormon women in raising larger families was exacerbated by the particular hardships of frontier living as Mormons migrated farther west in the face of outside criticism and harassment. Under these conditions, the practice of having nearby "sister-wives" may have indeed been a great help to some individual women. Accounts by nineteenth-century Mormon women often emphasized the camaraderie and tangible benefits of this particular type of sisterhood, especially when it came to their roles as mothers: "We acted as nurses for each other during confinement, we were too poor to hire nurses. One suit or outfit for new babies and confinement did for us all. . . . For many years we lived thus, working together."[44] In an era when reliable information about birth control was virtually nonexistent, plural marriage may have also relieved some women from the sexual expectations usually shouldered by the sole wife.

Of course, given little choice in the matter, not all Mormon women were happy with or accepted polygyny. Founder Joseph Smith's own wife, Emma Hale Smith, questioned the practice of polygyny and never fully accepted her husband's relationships with other women. Eventually, Emma Smith and her sons led a "Reorganized" movement within the Mormon church that opposed plural marriage. Women's rights leader Elizabeth Cady Stanton approached the issue of Mormon plural marriages from the practical standpoint of women's status and level of happiness compared to their roles and status within traditional marriage and found polygyny no better or worse: "The Mormon women, like all others, stoutly defend their religion, yet they are no more satisfied than any other sect."[45] For Stanton, it was organized

Mormon man posing with his six wives (1885). Early members of the Mormon Church (founded in 1831) practiced polygamy, but the church officially outlawed the practice after 1890 in an effort to have Utah admitted as a state. (Library of Congress, Prints & Photographs Division, LC-USZ62-83877.)

religion in general, just as much as the institution of marriage, that kept women subordinate. The practice of polygyny quickly came under increased scrutiny by the American public as well as the federal government as the sect grew in numbers and spread into the western territories. The church officially rejected the practice in the 1890s as a condition of Utah's admission as a state. (See also Chapter 3, "Religion.")

NOTES

1. *Godey's Lady's Book*, quoted in *Through Women's Eyes: An American History*, 3rd ed., ed. Ellen Carol DuBois and Lynn Dumenil (Boston: Bedford/St. Martin's, 2005), p. 138.

2. Statistics cited in *Through Women's Eyes*, p. 295.

3. Beecher quoted in Jeanne Boydston, *The Limits of Sisterhood: The Beecher Sisters on Women's Rights and Woman's Sphere* (Chapel Hill: University of North Carolina Press, 1988), p. 132.

4. Michael Goldberg, "Breaking New Ground, 1800–1848," in *No Small Courage: A History of Women in the United States*, ed. Nancy F. Cott (New York: Oxford University Press, 2000), p. 181.

5. Goldberg, "Breaking New Ground," p. 186.

6. Chesnut excerpted in DuBois and Dumenil, *Through Women's Eyes*, p. 165.

7. On Southern weddings, see Goldberg, "Breaking New Ground," pp. 186–87.

8. See Nancy F. Cott, *Public Vows: A History of Marriage and the Nation* (Cambridge, Mass.: Harvard University Press, 2000), p. 36.

9. Cott, *Public Vows*, p. 29.

10. S. J. Kleinberg, *Women in the United States, 1830–1945* (New Brunswick, N.J.: Rutgers University Press, 1999), p.141.

11. See Lee Chambers-Schiller, *Liberty, a Better Husband: Single Women in America, the Generations of 1780–1840* (New Haven, Conn.: Yale University Press, 1984), p. 3; Louisa May Alcott quoted on p. 10. The national figures obscure regional differences in education, as the number of single women in Massachusetts in 1870, for example, was more than double the national rate.

12. Thomas Dublin, ed., *Farm to Factory: Women's Letters, 1830–1860* (New York: Columbia University Press, 1993); see chap. 3, "The Larcom Letters," pp. 97–119.

13. Smith qtd. in *Liberty, a Better Husband*, pp. 157–58.

14. Towne qtd. in *Liberty, a Better Husband*, pp. 111–12.

15. Drew Gilpin Faust, *Mothers of Invention: Women of the Slaveholding South in the American Civil War* (Chapel Hill: University of North Carolina Press, 1996), chap. 6, "To Be an Old Maid: Single Women, Courtship, and Desire," quote on p. 141.

16. Faust, *Mothers of Invention*, p. 139 and p. 148.

17. Historian Carroll Smith-Rosenberg helped identify and assess the importance of relationships between women in her essay, "The Female World of Love and Ritual: Relations between Women in Nineteenth Century America," in *Disorderly Conduct: Visions of Gender in Victorian America* (New York: Knopf, 1985), pp. 53–76; on "Boston marriages," see Sarah Deutsch, *Women and the City: Gender, Space, and Power in Boston, 1870–1940* (New York: Oxford University Press, 2000), p. 109.

18. "Gertrude Stuart Baillie Asks, 'Should Professional Women Marry?,' 1894," in *Major Problems in American Women's History*, 3rd ed., ed. Mary Beth Norton and Ruth M. Alexander (Boston: Houghton Mifflin, 2003), pp. 216–17.

19. Goldberg, "Breaking New Ground," p. 184.

20. Ira Berlin, Marc Favreau, and Steven F. Miller, eds., *Remembering Slavery: African Americans Talk about Their Personal Experiences of Slavery and Emancipation* (New York: New Press, 1998), p. 140.

21. Harriet Jacobs, *Incidents in the Life of a Slave Girl, Written by Herself*, ed. Jean Fagan Yellin (Cambridge, Mass.: Harvard University Press, 2000), p. 39.

22. Durham quoted in Gail Collins, *America's Women: 400 Years of Dolls, Drudges, Helpmates, and Heroines* (New York: HarperCollins, 2003), p. 149.

23. Hamlin quoted in Emily West, *Chains of Love: Slave Couples in Antebellum South Carolina* (Urbana: University of Illinois Press, 2004), p. 31.

24. Collins, *America's Women*, p. 149.

25. West, *Chains of Love*, p. 51.

26. Smalley qtd. in *Remembering Slavery*, p. 136.

27. Darlene Clark Hine and Kathleen Thompson, *A Shining Thread of Hope: The History of Black Women in America* (New York: Broadway Books, 1998), p. 140.

28. Hine and Thompson, *Shining Thread of Hope*, p. 150.

29. Rebecca Edwards, *Angels in the Machinery: Gender in American Party Politics from the Civil War to the Progressive Era* (New York: Oxford University Press, 1997), p. 37.

30. Martha Hodes, *White Women, Black Men: Illicit Sex in the 19th-Century South* (New Haven, Conn.: Yale University Press, 1997), quotes on p. 49 and p. 144; see also Joshua Rothman, *Notorious in the Neighborhood: Sex and Families across the Color Line in Virginia, 1787–1861* (Chapel Hill: University of North Carolina Press, 2003).

31. Official qtd. in *Public Vows,* pp. 25–26.

32. "President Thomas Jefferson to Captain Hendrick, the Delawares, Mohicans, and Munries, December 21, 1808," excerpted in *Discovering the American Past: A Look at the Evidence, Vol. 1 to 1877,* 5th ed., ed. William Bruce Wheeler and Susan D. Becker (Boston: Houghton Mifflin, 2002), pp. 129–31.

33. Theda Perdue, *Cherokee Women: Gender and Culture Change, 1700–1835* (Lincoln: University of Nebraska Press, 1998), p. 154.

34. Liz Sonneborn, "Winema (aka Tobey Riddle), (1836–1932)," in *A to Z of Native American Women* (New York: Facts on File, 1998), pp. 194–97.

35. Stanton qtd. in *Public Vows,* p. 67.

36. Alice Stone Blackwell, *Lucy Stone: Pioneer of Woman's Rights* (1930; repr., Charlottesville: University of Virginia Press, 2001), p. 161.

37. Chris Dixon, *Perfecting the Family: Antislavery Marriages in Nineteenth-Century America* (Amherst: University of Massachusetts Press, 1997), p. 8.

38. Blackstone cited in Pauline E. Schloesser, *The Fair Sex: White Women and Racial Patriarchy in the Early American Republic* (New York: New York University Press, 2002), p. 30.

39. Stone qtd. in *Public Vows,* p. 64.

40. Davis qtd. in *Through Women's Eyes,* p. 249.

41. Cott, *Public Vows,* p. 59; on the effect of slavery on roles within the white non-slaveholding family, see Stephanie McCurry, *Masters of Small Worlds: Yeoman Households, Gender Relations, and the Political Culture of the Antebellum South Carolina Low Country* (New York: Oxford University Press, 1995).

42. Cott, *Public Vows,* p. 66.

43. Stanton qtd. in *Perfecting the Family,* pp. 89–90.

44. Catherine Clinton and Christine Lunardini, eds., *The Columbia Guide to American Women in the Nineteenth Century* (New York: Columbia University Press, 2000), p. 61.

45. Elizabeth Cady Stanton, *Eighty Years and More: Reminiscences, 1815–1897* (1898; repr., Boston: Northeastern University Press, 1993), p. 284.

SUGGESTED READING

Bleser, Carol, ed. *In Joy and in Sorrow: Women, Family, and Marriage in the Victorian South, 1830–1900.* New York: Oxford University Press, 1992.

Brodie, Janet Farrell. *Contraception and Abortion in 19th-Century America.* Ithaca, N.Y.: Cornell University Press, 1994.

Carter, Christine Jacobson. *Southern Single Blessedness: Unmarried Women in the Urban South, 1800–1865.* Urbana: University of Illinois Press, 2006.

Chambers-Schiller, Lee. *Liberty, a Better Husband: Single Women in America, the Generations of 1780–1840.* New Haven, Conn.: Yale University Press, 1984.

Clinton, Catherine, ed. *Southern Families at War: Loyalty and Conflict in the Civil War South.* New York: Oxford University Press, 2000.

Cott, Nancy F. *Public Vows: A History of Marriage and the Nation.* Cambridge, Mass.: Harvard University Press, 2000.

Daynes, Kathryn M. *More Wives Than One: Transformation of the Mormon Marriage System, 1840–1910.* Urbana: University of Illinois Press, 2001.

Dixon, Chris. *Perfecting the Family: Antislavery Marriages in Nineteenth-Century America.* Amherst: University of Massachusetts Press, 1997.

Faust, Drew Gilpin. *Mothers of Invention: Women of the Slaveholding South in the American Civil War.* Chapel Hill: University of North Carolina Press, 1996.

Frankel, Noralee. *Freedom's Women: Black Women and Families in Civil War Era Mississippi.* Bloomington: Indiana University Press, 1999.

Gordon, Linda. *Heroes of Their Own Lives: The Politics and History of Family Violence, Boston, 1880–1960.* Urbana: University of Illinois Press, 2002.

Herbert, T. Walter. *Dearest Beloved: The Hawthornes and the Making of the Middle-Class Family.* Berkeley: University of California Press, 1993.

Hodes, Martha. *White Women, Black Men: Illicit Sex in the 19th-Century South.* New Haven, Conn.: Yale University Press, 1997.

Luchetti, Cathy. *"I Do!": Courtship, Love and Marriage on the American Frontier.* New York: Crown, 1996.

May, Elaine Tyler. *Great Expectations: Marriage and Divorce in Post-Victorian America.* Chicago: University of Chicago Press, 1983.

McCurry, Stephanie. *Masters of Small Worlds: Yeoman Households, Gender Relations, and the Political Culture of the Antebellum South Carolina Low Country.* New York: Oxford University Press, 1995.

McMillen, Sally. *Motherhood in the Old South: Pregnancy, Childbirth, and Infant-Rearing.* Baton Rouge: Louisiana State University, 1990.

Rosenzweig, Linda W. *The Anchor of My Life: Middle-Class American Mothers and Daughters, 1880–1920.* New York: New York University Press, 1993.

Rothman, Joshua. *Notorious in the Neighborhood: Sex and Families across the Color Line in Virginia, 1787–1861.* Chapel Hill: University of North Carolina Press, 2003.

Stanley, Amy Dru. *From Bondage to Contract: Wage Labor, Marriage, and the Market in the Age of Slave Emancipation.* New York: Cambridge University Press, 1998.

Wertz, Richard W., and Dorothy C. Wertz. *Lying-In: A History of Childbirth in America.* New York: Free Press, 1977.

West, Emily. *Chains of Love: Slave Couples in Antebellum South Carolina.* Urbana: University of Illinois Press, 2004.

2

---∞∞∞---

Work

The economic success and stability of the United States in the nineteenth century depended on the work of women both inside and outside the home. The industrial as well as the commercial agricultural economies of the nation depended upon women's productive work in the household and as wage-earners and their reproductive work in childbearing and rearing. In her enormously popular 1841 *A Treatise on Domestic Economy*, author and reformer Catharine Beecher praised women's work, declaring that "No American woman, then, has any occasion for feeling that hers is an humble or insignificant lot. The value of what an individual accomplishes, is to be estimated by the importance of the enterprise achieved, and not by the particular position of the laborer." Beecher's primary objective was to encourage women in their domestic roles, but in her *Treatise* she acknowledged the many forms of women's work that supported the goals of that work.

> The woman who is rearing a family of children; the woman who labors in the schoolroom; the woman who, in her retired chamber, earns, with her needle, the mite to contribute to the intellectual and moral elevation of her country; even the humble domestic, whose example and influence may be moulding and forming young minds, while her faithful services sustain a prosperous domestic state;—each and all may be cheered by the consciousness, that they are agents in accomplishing the greatest work that ever was committed to human responsibility.[1]

Catharine Beecher (1848). Beecher was an author and reformer dedicated to promoting women's domestic roles as wives and mothers as well as women's education. Her *Treatise on Domestic Economy* (1841) was one of the most influential domestic advice guides of the century. (Schlesinger Library, Radcliffe Institute, Harvard University.)

Even as urbanization, immigration, and industrialization emerged as forces defining new American workplaces, most Americans in the nineteenth century continued to live in rural locations, in the Northeast, the South, or the new Midwest and Western frontiers. In the Southern states women's work throughout the century was tied to agriculture, whether as slaves and mistresses on the plantation or as sharecroppers and farmers after the Civil War. Throughout the United States, women were central to maintaining family farms, performing daily tasks such as gardening, tending animals, soapmaking, spinning, and sewing, in addition to working the land themselves as farm wives, slaves, homesteaders, or sharecroppers.

But regardless of whether they lived in towns, cities, or on farms, and regardless of whether they worked for wages or not, women's primary roles throughout the century revolved around childrearing and the care of the home.

The development of a middle class in the North led to changes in women's roles at home as well as in their public activities. The economic and cultural changes that helped create a new middle class gave rise to a new emphasis on domesticity intended to define and restrict the roles of white women. At the same time, the forces of urbanization, immigration, and industrialization meant that other women entered into paid wage work for the first time in factories, as schoolteachers, and, by the end of the century, made an entrance into fields such as nursing, social work, and even medicine and the law. (See also Chapter 4, "Education and the Professions.")

WOMEN'S ROLES IN THE HOUSEHOLD ECONOMY

In the first decades of the nineteenth century, most finished goods such as clothing and furniture were still produced primarily within the household and therefore involved all family members. A master craftsman's workshop would be adjacent to or within the home where he might also be responsible for one or two skilled journeymen and several young male apprentices who had been sent out by their own families to learn a trade. In addition to this system of organizing male labor, a master craftsman's trade might overflow into the regular routine of his household, with wives and young children helping out as needed in both the business and the additional tasks that came with supporting an extended household that might include apprentices and other unrelated workers. Young male apprentices usually lived within the master's house while learning the trade, receiving room and board in exchange for knowledge and training, and coming under the care of the master's wife who handled the cooking and cleaning for the entire household. In this way, social relations were controlled and maintained within the household setting and workers of different skill levels, ages, and sexes lived and worked within the same arena.

The rise of factories transformed household work and gender roles even before women began to leave the home for paid work. The skills of the master craftsman and journeyman were replaced by machines, custom goods were replaced by mass-produced products, and the family-centered household workshop was replaced by the factory. Some artisan craftsmen began doing piecework for local industries, but increasingly they and their sons either became wage workers or moved into the new business or professional class of entrepreneurs, merchants, or factory managers. By the middle of the nineteenth century, whether as skilled craftsmen or as businessmen, this new middle class of men had become physically and therefore socially removed from their own households, redefining women's economic roles within the household as well.

Regardless of the occupation of the male head of household, and regardless of whether she herself engaged in paid labor, most white women of both the working and middle classes were responsible for housework and completed a variety of tasks that contributed to the overall household economy. Martha Ballard was a woman whose life illuminates the intersection of women's paid and unpaid economic roles at the turn of the nineteenth century. Martha Ballard's husband ran a sawmill and worked as a land surveyor in frontier Maine. Martha was responsible for traditional chores related to the children and the household, but also supplied the family with income through her work as a midwife to families throughout the surrounding area. For her services as midwife, Martha accepted either cash or bartered for items her family needed, such as eggs or other services. As Martha Ballard's rural midwifery practice regularly took her significant distances from home, sometimes for days at a time and at the unpredictable and inconvenient hours that babies decide to be born, Martha relied upon others to keep the household running. Her own daughters, daughters-in-law, and occasionally a daughter of a friend or neighbor hired or apprenticed to the Ballard household, performed a variety of tasks under Martha's direction and during her absences.[2]

In households such as the Ballards', mothers, daughters, and female relatives and apprentices divided the work of tending vegetable gardens, caring for animals, collecting milk and eggs, preparing meals, washing and mending clothing and bed linens, spinning yarn, and sewing clothing. The shift toward factory-produced textiles, in particular, greatly impacted not only the work of individual women, but, as in a household organized such as the Ballards', women's roles throughout an extended family and local economy that depended on women's contributions. In Martha's case she also worked as a midwife, a traditionally female role impacted by the shift toward physicians taking over birthing practices in the early nineteenth century.

New technologies of the post–Civil War era influenced other aspects of women's household production and labor. Mechanical clothes washers and wringers lightened the workload on laundry day and pre-prepared and processed foods developed for Civil War armies began to be used by regular households during and after the war. More affluent households might even have electricity and running water by the end of the century, amenities that reduced the amount of time women needed to spend on housework. By the time of the Civil War, housekeeping, cleaning, and laundry, for example, were all tasks that middle-class households could have done inexpensively by others, in the process, of course, creating a new category of wage work for other women in domestic service.[3]

In the Southern states, white women remained tied to household management and agricultural labor throughout the century. In the antebellum era, plantation and even nonslaveholding white households operated similarly to Northern rural households. Women's roles were primarily as household managers in charge of domestic tasks such as cooking, cleaning, gardening, and childcare, whether they performed that work themselves or supervised slave labor. In many households, domestic technology and the wider availability of finished goods did not necessarily mean less work for the average white farm wife herself, as much as it might mean less need for the labor of extra females, such as daughters. With fewer hands needed, families began to have fewer children. Without any specific advance in or availability of scientific knowledge on birth control, the overall birthrate in the United States began rapidly declining, from about seven in 1800 to four by the end of the century.[4] (See also Chapter 1, "Marriage and Family Life.") As even rural households were drawn more deeply into the greater cash economy, however, daughters might still be needed as income producers, and white Northern rural households were an ideal site for recruiters looking for an unskilled labor force for the new textile factories.

THE WORK OF DOMESTICITY

The separation of skilled from unskilled, of shop from household, and of farm from factory labor all greatly impacted the home and family. As men's work moved away from the household, into small businesses or professional offices, the home was privatized. As the daily experiences and work lives of men and women of the middle classes were separated, the idea that the public world belonged to men and the private world to women came to define the middle class as much as occupation or economic status. Domesticity itself was seen as women's primary work and was increasingly exalted as having value beyond the realm of economics. As Lucy Larcom explained in her 1889 autobiography, *A New England Girlhood*, woman "is here to make this great house of humanity a habitable and a beautiful place, without and within, a true home for every one of [God's] children."[5]

Less reliance on women's labor in household production, coupled with women's increasing isolation within the home and responsibility for the entire domestic sphere, led to more concern and focus on what exactly women were supposed to do within the home. By the 1830s an entire literary genre developed to instruct middle-class white women in their proper roles and duties within the home and emphasized the moral necessity of women operating outside the realm of market forces. Domesticity and women's roles within the home, including mothering, became rationalized and professionalized just as men's work away from home had become. With less of women's, and also children's, time needed for family labor, women were expected to devote more energy to mothering and spend more time and care on raising fewer children. (See also Chapter 1, "Marriage and Family Life.")

The new economy demanded of women the same efficiency and management skills demanded of men in the workplace. Domestic guidebooks carefully detailed the rules and advice for efficient housekeeping. Promoters of domesticity emphasized the importance of women's economic as well as moral and spiritual roles in a nation now turning toward industrialization, technology, and capitalism. In 1841, Catharine Beecher, in her *Treatise on Domestic Economy,* outlined the importance of separate spheres of activity for men and women, particularly in an industrial society:

> The Americans have applied to the sexes the great principle of political economy, which governs the manufactories of our age, by carefully dividing the duties of man from those of woman. . . . In no country has such constant care been taken, as in America, to trace two clearly distinct lines of action for the two sexes, and to make them keep pace one with the other, but in two pathways which are always different.[6]

Beecher's text, and many others to follow, instructed women in everything from home design to childcare to cooking. The proper performance of women's domestic work, work that women had been doing for centuries, was now seen as nothing less than an expression of love for her family. As Shirley Murphy, author of the 1883 text *Our Homes and How to Make Them Healthy,* explained, "A clean, fresh, and well-ordered house exercises over its inmates a moral, no less than physical influence, and has a direct tendency to make members of the family sober, peaceable, and considerate of the feelings and happiness of each other."[7]

Although writers of domestic guidebooks often romanticized the larger societal and spiritual importance of women's roles within the home, the reality of domestic work could be overwhelming and monotonous. Cooking and laundry alone were tasks that consumed entire days, and even as family size was decreasing, the size of middle-class homes was increasing, making housecleaning a greater part of a woman's domestic duties. As one woman reported at the end of the century, she was glad to have a housekeeper and a new cook, "so my domestic labors are diminishing, though the responsibility is on the increase."[8] Northern women of means sought help from household servants when possible, while Southern white women in the antebellum era depended largely upon the assistance of slaves. When white women were encouraged during wartime to resume the home-based production of cloth and sewing clothing and linens, it represented a new domestic role for many formerly dependent upon slave labor. Sarah Wadley wrote in 1865, "I have commenced to learn to card and spin, and I never tried anything so difficult to me, or so tiring." Other Southern white women found themselves cooking or doing laundry for the first time without servants or slaves. Martha Horne of Missouri recalled that she "had never cooked a meal when the negro women left, and had a hard time learning."[9] (See also Chapter 6, "Slavery and the Civil War.")

Although industrialization meant that women in general may have been moving away from traditionally female tasks in spinning and weaving, sewing clothes and linens remained a significant part of the average woman's household work. It is for this reason that the invention of the mechanical sewing machine has been labeled "probably the most significant domestic labor-saving device in the late nineteenth century." Its appearance on the market at mid-century was a great success and it became immediately popular, even though it was one of the most expensive items a household could purchase. Some families even pooled their resources to "share" a machine. Women themselves found the machine of immediate practical use in their own families, but promoters of domesticity typically looked to the moral significance of this aid to women's work. *Godey's Lady's Book,* for example, imagined in 1860 that the time-saving aspect of the new machine would allow women more time for charity in "clothing the indigent and feeble," and would, "after a time, effectually banish ragged and unclad humanity from every class."[10]

Although all women were responsible for housekeeping, a commitment to "domesticity" was an ideal that did not necessarily correspond to the actual lives of many women at this time. Blacks were less likely to lead a lifestyle of separate spheres because of the economic realities of racism; that is, black men were more likely to have trouble finding regular and adequately paid employment and black women were therefore forced to work for wages more often than white women. Most women, black or white, were responsible for housekeeping and to tasks related to family farming or plantation agriculture. By mid-century many others, especially among urban and immigrant populations, began to work for wages outside the home.

WOMEN'S INDUSTRIAL WORK
IN THE PRE–CIVIL WAR ERA

Overall, relatively small numbers of women, only about 10 percent of the female population, worked outside the home in wage-earning jobs before the Civil War, and these were concentrated in a few limited occupations, such as teaching, domestic service, and jobs related to textile production.[11] The spread of common schools into rural areas before the Civil War, and the fact that educating children was seen primarily as women's work, meant that, in some areas, as many as one-quarter of all native-born white women taught school at one time in their adult lives.[12]

Woman at a sewing machine (1853). The sewing machine made its first appearance on the consumer market in the 1850s, changing forever women's textile work within the home and factory. (Library of Congress, Prints & Photographs Division, LC-USZC4-3598.)

Whether as teachers or factory workers, most women in the paid workforce in the antebellum period were young and single, expecting to be employed only temporarily until marrying and starting their own families and households.

In perhaps no area did women's roles change more quickly and drastically than in the case of textile production. At the beginning of the century, a woman would do all of the spinning and weaving in her own home, but within a few short decades those tasks were done more cost effectively in the factories. It is hard to overestimate the role of *cotton* in the lives of women workers in the nineteenth century. The invention of the cotton gin in 1793 resulted in short staple cotton replacing tobacco as the foundation of the Southern agricultural economy. The success of cotton entrenched the slave system in the South and fueled industrialization and consumer desires in the North. In the first decades of the nineteenth century, the northern United States moved from a merchant economy based on exporting American raw materials in exchange for European finished goods to a manufacturing economy focused on processing the raw materials grown and harvested in the Southern states. Both the slave-based agricultural production of cotton and the processing of cotton in the textile industries relied upon the work of women.

Slave women planted and harvested cotton in the field, tasks that involved everyone, regardless of sex or age. Throughout the antebellum period, as the North began producing its cotton in the factories, many Southern slave women continued to process cotton by hand. Marie Askin, a former slave from Missouri, remembered the work on the plantation that she, her mother, and her sisters performed in producing textiles:

> There were no sewing machines. All the women learned to sew by hand. . . . We had our own wool. Raised our own sheep, carded and spun, wove and knit. The yarn was dyed all sorts of pretty colors. . . . The indigo was bought at the drugstore. . . . For brown dye, we used walnut hulls. If we wanted black dye, we used the ripe black hulls and for all shades of brown we used young green hulls. . . . Elder and Poke berries made red dyes. We would gather them ripe and squeeze the juice.[13]

Rachel Cruze described similarly detailed work at the Tennessee plantation she had lived at, where "the material for the cotton clothes worn on the farm in summer was woven right in our own kitchen."[14]

The rise of King Cotton in the South after 1800 was accompanied by technological revolutions and the rise of the water-powered factory system in the North to process that cotton in mills. Francis Cabot Lowell established the first textile mill in Waltham, Massachusetts, in 1813. Machines began to take over the work of housewives in carding wool, spinning yarn, and, ultimately, weaving cloth. New technologies in transportation and communication, such as the telegraph, canals, and railroad, and the advent of coal-power, as well as the rapid population growth fueled by the large number of Irish and German immigrants in the 1840s and 1850s, all allowed markets for manufactured textiles and other products to reach farther westward.

Factories looking for a low-paid unskilled labor force increasingly turned to the availability of white women, and, later, immigrant workers. The textile industry provided a variety of jobs and skill levels that made it easier to bring women into the workforce. As pieceworkers, women performed tasks such as weaving the machine-spun yarn into cloth, cutting out patterns for clothes, or sewing pieces together. Married women working within their homes could integrate this work into their daily lives, weaving, cutting, or sewing alongside tasks related to childrearing, housekeeping, and preparing food. Often teenage daughters performed outwork, earning wages without ever leaving their rural homes. Wages from women's outwork would go to the family as a whole through the father or husband, who would often negotiate for the amount of work and wages as part of the family farm economy. In these ways, performing outwork for the burgeoning textile factories did not upset traditional family gender relations. Women also did home-based work for other industries such as braiding straw hats, shoe binding (stitching together the leather pieces that had been cut out by machine), and cigar rolling, all industries that lent themselves well to the separation of tasks in the outwork system.

The early piecework system of the textile industry peaked around 1820 and declined after that as more of the work was moved to the factory floor and done by hourly wage workers operating power looms. The experience of outwork was an early and necessary step, however, in drawing native-born white women into the wage economy and prompted some women to then follow the textile work into the factories where greater wages could be earned. Between 1820 and 1860 tens of thousands of young, white, mostly single women moved into paid employment outside of the home as "mill girls." As early as 1831, 70 percent of millworkers were women and by 1860 the preponderance of women in the textile factories meant that women now accounted for 25 percent of the total industrial labor force in the United States.[15]

Young women working for wages in the textile factories thus remained economically tied to their families, but at the same time they experienced for the first time the choice of how to spend their own earned money. They had to become involved in decisions about how much to send home, how much to spend on themselves, and how much to save. This financial responsibility and freedom was a new experience for young rural women. Millworker Delia Page's father realized this new role and new independence that his wage-earning daughter now had and wrote to her when she offered to buy a magazine subscription for the family.

> My dear Delia . . . I am glad to see by this offer that you are in a condition to do somewhat as you are amind to and it must be a very pleasant feeling. It is a thing much to be desired to be able to rely upon yourself with God's blessing for all the necessaries of life. If you have not already attained to this independence I think you soon will & that too without any great help from your father.

Page's mother, however, was more concerned with her daughter's moral well-being as a result of her newfound financial and social independence in her employment away from the family: "I do not think so much of you making great wages, as of your keeping good company, and being a good girl. Be sure to attend meting [*sic*] constantly on the Sabbath, unless prevented by sickness."[16]

The factory model of hiring young single women away from family farms to work in the textile mills became known as the "Lowell system" and was set up to address the concerns of parents such as Delia Page's. The Lowell system (named for the Francis Cabot Lowell factory but a model used by other factories as well) was a *paternalistic* system, meaning that managers and mill owners were intended to replace fathers in organizing and overseeing women's work and social lives. The fact that the young women were called "mill *girls*" reveals the subordinate role they took in relation to their male protectors. Factory owners, managers, and recruiters promised parents the safety and moral uprightness of mill life through same-sex dormitory living (with rent deducted directly from their pay), mandatory church attendance, enforced curfews, and company-sponsored cultural and social events.

Life in the textile mills was not always as harmonious or as uplifting as mill owners would have New England parents believe. Conditions in the mills could also be quite dangerous, and it took decades of labor reform before factories were regulated and employers held responsible for workplace injuries and deaths. In January 1860, 88 workers were killed and many others injured when a mill in Lawrence, Massachusetts, collapsed and caused a fire.[17] Although many young women voluntarily entered into factory work knowing either a sister or a cousin or a friend who had found the work tolerable and the pay satisfactory, some were lured to the mills under false pretenses by "slavers" or recruiters, as described in an 1846 labor newspaper:

> A singular-looking "long, low, black" wagon . . . makes regular trips to the north of the state [Massachusetts], cruising around in Vermont and New Hampshire, with a "commander" whose heart must be black as his craft, and who is paid a dollar a head for all he brings to the market, and more in proportion to the distance—if they bring them from such a distance that they cannot easily get back.
>
> This is done by "hoisting false colors," and representing to the girls that they can tend more machinery than is possible, and that the work is so very neat, and the wages such that they can dress in silks and spend half their time in reading. Now, is this true?[18]

In addition to their letters home the women at the Lowell factory started their own paper, the *Lowell Offering*, which also reveals much about the work culture and sense of community created by this model of factory work. Begun in 1840 with the support of the company, the *Lowell Offering* included poems, essays, and song lyrics, but soon became a forum as well for the women's views on political and economic issues, including comments on conditions at the factory. The *Lowell Offering* writers were censored from criticizing the company directly, but even before the Lowell workers started their paper, other women factory workers had begun to organize and protest low wages, long hours, and unsafe working conditions. As early as 1824, women millworkers in Rhode Island spoke out against low wages and in 1828 more than 300 operatives went on strike in New Hampshire to protest a reduction in their pay.[19] At Lowell, Massachusetts, in 1844 the millworkers formed the Female Labor Reform Association. Complaints at the Lowell factory included requests for improvements such as longer breaks for meals, establishing a fund for sick pay, and the creation of a library. In the 1840s the Lowell women led the Ten Hour movement, in which thousands of women signed petitions sent to the state legislature calling for shorter workdays. Their demand was rejected, but many women, in other industries as well, began to demand their voices be heard.

Although their experience as wage workers was short-lived, as most of the women expected to be employed only one to three years before marriage, their sense of community did contribute to the ability of the millworkers to organize as workers. The *Lowell Offering* was based in one factory, but, as more and more women entered the paid workforce, other newspapers reached out to working women across industries. The *Woman's Advocate* was founded in 1869 and wage-earning women also began to speak up in other forums, such as the many social reform organizations created in antebellum America. Working-class women were involved in early temperance or anti-alcohol societies, sometimes as the wives of working men, if not as wage-earners themselves, and contributed to efforts to address the problems specific to an industrializing urban society. In reflecting on the time she spent working in the textile mills, Lucy Larcom was honest about the hardships but concluded that "One great advantage which came to these many stranger girls through being brought together, away from their homes, was that it taught them to go out of themselves, and enter into the lives of others."[20] Larcom revealed how working women's lives in the nineteenth century expanded their sphere of influence and concern beyond the home into the workplace and into society at large.

Beginning in the late 1840s, French-Canadian and Irish women began to replace native-born New England women as an available factory labor force. These immigrants had no family ties to rural areas and arrived as a permanent class of unskilled workers living in cities. They were thus easier for factory owners to exploit with low wages and lost any benefits offered by the dormitory model of the Lowell system, such as guaranteed housing, food services, and company-sponsored cultural events for workers. The dormitories were converted to tenement housing for the next generation of entire families of immigrant factory workers.

WOMEN'S INDUSTRIAL WORK AFTER THE CIVIL WAR

Whereas native-born single, white women were drawn into factory work in unprecedented numbers before the Civil War, the face of women in the industrial workforce changed in the decades after the Civil War in two ways: more immigrant women and more married women. By the end of the century, native-born white women were moving into new types of jobs created by urbanization and the demands of a consumer culture, namely "pink-collar" jobs as salesgirls and office clerks. Additionally, women's expanded access to higher education meant that middle-class women entered the professions for the first time as professors, nurses, doctors, social workers, and lawyers. (See also Chapter 4, "Education and the Professions.") This move away from factory work by Anglo American women was facilitated, in part, by the fact that in the last decades of the nineteenth century millions of people from southern and eastern Europe entered the United States, providing a new working class for the second wave of the industrial revolution. Arriving with few or no resources or contacts, and concentrating in urban areas, immigrant men worked for below poverty-level wages, forcing immigrant wives and even children to find work either in or outside of the home for wages.

If possible, and probably owing in part to language barriers, women of these new immigrant groups in the late nineteenth century preferred factory work to domestic service. Women's experiences as wage workers during this period, however, varied depending on their ethnic and religious affiliations, and different groups came to dominate in specific industries. In eastern urban centers such as New York, Jewish workers tended to predominate in the garment industry, especially in the many ladies' clothing factories owned by fellow Jews. Jewish families were more likely to send their daughters to work in the factories, in part because of the expectation that sons would attend school instead of work. Young Italian girls were less likely to work for wages, but their mothers were able to bring in wages by working in industries, such as men's clothing, that still relied upon the piecework system of home-based tasks. By bringing in piecework, Italian women could not only still care for their own families, but could also further supplement their income by taking in boarders and providing cooking, cleaning, and laundry services for their renters. Other ethnic groups clustered in the textile mills of New England and the South, as well as in the newer urban centers of the Midwest where meat- and food-processing industries dominated.[21]

Rose Cohen lived in New York City with her father at the end of the nineteenth century and worked in the factories with the goal of saving money to bring her mother and siblings from Russia. Cohen realized the potential benefits of doing home-based work, compared to being under the boss' constant direction on the factory floor, when she complained to her father: "The boss is hurrying the life out of me . . . if I did piece work, father, I would not have to hurry so. And I could go home earlier when the other people go." Cohen's father scolded that she must do the work in whatever manner the boss preferred, and she consented that she was in a difficult personal position and could not risk losing her job because, "To lose half a dollar meant that it would take so much longer before mother and the children would come."[22]

By the end of the century, however, some women began organizing to expose the poor or dangerous conditions under which women and sometimes entire families, including children, worked, especially at home doing piecework. In the case of the cigar-rolling industry, piecework was an underground system set up and preferred by employers in order to lower factory expenses and avoid taxes on production of tobacco products. Some workers preferred the system because it allowed more women to earn wages and an 1874 article in the *New York Herald* explained the

Black women and children at work in a tobacco factory (1899). Although many African Americans sought to escape the field work they had performed under slavery, the Southern economy remained dependent upon agricultural production. Many black women continued to perform farm labor as sharecroppers or moved into paid work in processing plants such as this one. (Library of Congress, Prints & Photographs Division, LC-USZ62-69316.)

belief among Czech immigrants that "women could make better cigars than men, and it was therefore necessary that the wives should help their husbands in making cigars."[23]

Reformers could be found arguing on both sides of the issue, each side revealing certain ideas about women's proper roles within the household and their relation to paid work. Those who supported women doing piece-work in the home argued that it was the only way families could economically survive, because women and children could not always work in the factories. Reformers and male union leaders who opposed the piecework system promoted the alternative of a "family wage" for men and argued that "a union of all the cigar makers would fix uniform good wages for all the men, and would release the women to attend to household duties and the children to go to school." Others lamented the costs, both psychologically and in terms of health, when mothers rolled cigars while nursing babies.[24]

Because of racism and employment discrimination, as well as the ready availability of a European immigrant workforce in both the Northern and Southern states after the Civil War, black women were the least likely to work in the industrial and manufacturing trades. By 1900 less than 3 percent of black wage-earning women worked in factories, compared to 21 percent of foreign-born women and 38 percent of native-born white working women.[25] Even in urban areas of the South where textile mills proliferated after the Civil War, black women were more likely to work as domestic servants.

DOMESTIC WORKERS

Whereas eastern European immigrants dominated as industrial workers in the last half of the nineteenth century, domestic or household workers were more likely to be Irish or black. More women in the nineteenth century worked in domestic service than in any other single industry or occupation. At mid-century more than one-quarter of all Irish women in New York City worked as household servants. This number was surpassed, however, by free black women, more than half of whom in the North worked as domestic servants.[26] Of course, the number of black women engaged in household service was even higher than official figures reflect because, throughout the antebellum South, enslaved women worked as personal servants, housekeepers, seamstresses, child nurses, cooks, and laundresses, in addition to their other agricultural labor.

Former slave Ella Wilson began doing regular domestic work as a child. Her main job was as a nurse to her white owner's children, but she recalled that her duties extended beyond those related to their immediate care:

> I had to get up every morning at five when the cook got up and make the cof-
> fee and then I had to go in the dining-room and set the table. Then I served

breakfast. Then I went into the house and cleaned it up. Then I 'tended to the white children and served the other meals during the day.[27]

The predominance of Irish immigrant and free black women as domestics in the pre–Civil War North testifies to the fact that other groups of women avoided such work whenever possible; that is, the women least likely to be able to have a choice about their employment (because of poverty and racism) found themselves resigned to domestic service. Not only was the work difficult, the hours long, and the pay extremely low compared to even unskilled factory work, but domestic service highlighted racial and class inequalities by requiring one to be individually and directly under the supervision of a boss, usually a wealthier white woman. New England millworker Mary Paul reported before the Civil War that she and her friends would prefer to "live on 25 cents per week at sewing or school teaching rather than work at housework. . . . This all comes from the way servants are treated."[28] Many Northern women who employed servants expected them to work up to 16 hours a days at low wages, but to also behave as "loyal" members of the family. In fact, many black women wished to avoid domestic service entirely because of the close association of these attitudes and of the actual tasks performed with the work of female slaves.

Before the Civil War many middle-class families did not necessarily employ full-time live-in servants, but only hired help for specific tasks, such as cooking or laundry. Housewives commented regularly on the difficulty of finding permanent domestic help. Observer Fredrika Bremer noted that it was not unusual to find the New England "wife herself performing all the in-doors work," and suspected that this was "partly from economic causes, and partly from the difficulty there is in getting good servants."[29] In reality, servants in middle-class households would most likely be working alongside the mistress of the house to keep up with the increasing demands of women's new domestic roles. The experience of Caroline Clapp Briggs is probably a good example of the way many middle-class households used domestic help. As a young wife, Caroline Briggs shared the laundry chores with her servant, but as the household grew and the Briggses added another servant, the workload also increased. Rather than experiencing new leisure time, Caroline would try to catch up on sewing and mending while the servants cleaned.[30]

By the time of the Civil War, foreign-born servants were replacing young native-born women as the typical household servant. At mid-century 74 percent of domestic workers were Irish, and, like factory workers, were primarily young, single, and independent. Antagonism between middle-class women and their servants during this period was fueled by anti-Irish political and religious sentiment in the culture at large during the Civil

War era. Employers complained that Irish servants were disobedient in addition to being poor cooks and housekeepers. Through the end of the century, social reformers saw domestic service as an ideal way to introduce single foreign-born women to the values of the American middle-class household, but immigrant women themselves preferred almost any other work. In part, this was because of the lack of independence and free time involved with household service, with employers often expecting 12- to 13-hour days, six or seven days per week. Additionally, the general isolation from peers made such employment particularly unattractive to young single women.[31] In 1880 a full 40 percent of wage-earning women in New York City were in domestic service, and most of those were Irish or German immigrants, but this changed as the next generation moved away from such work. As one observer noted in 1905, "The German-American child wants a position in an office. . . . The daughter refuses to go into domestic service although her mother had formerly taken a 'position.'"[32] The daughters of immigrants instead looked to factory work or higher-status jobs such as office and retail clerks; some were even able to attend college and prepare for the professions. (See also Chapter 4, "Education and the Professions.") By the end of the century, domestic servants in the North were more likely to be black women than Irish.

For black women in the South, however, the very definition of "freedom" after the end of slavery included the freedom to commit themselves to their own families and to their own homes. Many former slaves resisted jobs in domestic service, jobs in white households under the direction of white women that placed them back in a position of inferiority and of vulnerability to the potential sexual advances of white men. Still, poverty, both North and South, meant that most black women had to work for wages in the decades after the Civil War. Not including farm labor, more black women worked for wages than any other group of women, including more married women and mothers, unlike white women who were more likely to work outside the home as young single women but to quit wage work upon marriage. Throughout the post–Civil War South as a whole, few black women worked as domestics through the end of the century. Only 4.1 percent of "Cotton Belt women" (that is, from the former slave states) worked as servants in white households in 1880 and only 9 percent in 1900.[33]

Black women who did have to work as domestics preferred day-service rather than living-in. One way that black women maintained some control over their own home and work lives was through task-specific employment, such as taking out laundry. Older women, married women, and mothers were more likely to be laundresses, a kind of outwork as farm women had done earlier in the century with textiles and other industries. Laundry was a particularly difficult task, however, especially in the hot humid climate of the South. One historian provided a detailed overview of the weeklong process of laundering:

> A woman would usually collect clothes on Monday from two or three families. She set up a large pot in her yard and instructed the children to help her collect water. The clothes had to be boiled, scrubbed on a washboard, rinsed, starched, wrung out, hung up, and ironed. She had to pay for the starch and soap out of her meager earnings. On Saturday she would deliver the clothes and, she hoped, collect her money. A customer's complaint could result in loss of pay for the entire week's load.[34]

Nevertheless, taking in laundry work had some benefits as it allowed a woman to work at home on her own schedule and where she could supplement with other income-producing tasks, if necessary. She might also take in boarders, usually relatives or other blacks migrating to urban areas in search of employment after the Civil War.

Even though slavery had ended, and regardless of what varieties of employment she might engage in over her lifetime, it has been noted that in the late nineteenth and early twentieth centuries, "virtually every black girl-child, except for the most affluent, knew that at some time or another she would be cleaning house for white folks."[35] Writer Fannie Barber Williams agreed, musing in a 1903 article titled "The Problem of Employment for Negro Women" that domestic work was "ours almost by birthright." By the turn of the century, black women were being urged to take pride in this work because, as Williams observed, "Girls of other nationalities do not seem to compete with colored women as domestics. It is probably safe to say that every colored woman who is in any way competent can find good employment." Considering their dominance in the field, Williams advised that it was "largely in the power of the young woman" herself to give household service "the dignity of a profession," rather than viewing it as a demeaning job.[36]

Black women's work as household servants allowed white women not only more leisure time but also the ability to live up to the high standards of nineteenth-century domesticity. Defining housework as women's work idealized white women's work in the home so that it was not seen as work at all, but as duty, love, and moral responsibility. At the same time, it meant that doing domestic work for pay was also women's work and limited other employment opportunities for poor and nonwhite women. In fact, many industrial jobs filled by women were seen as extensions of domestic tasks—for example, work in the textile-related industries as a variation on women's traditional household work in spinning, weaving, or sewing—even though these tasks were now performed in factories and required skills in operating machinery more than in women's traditional handwork.

LABOR REFORM

As most skilled craftsmen and tradesmen were replaced by unskilled women and immigrants at lower and lower wages, their labor organizations or unions largely prohibited women and immigrant workers from joining, drawing the battle lines between different workers, rather than between workers and employers. Although it would seem advantageous to increase membership numbers in the burgeoning trade unions, the goal of organized labor throughout the late nineteenth and well into the twentieth century was primarily in protecting male labor. Nevertheless, some women did emerge as labor leaders, such as Kate Mullaney, who organized the first women's trade union, the Collar Laundry Union, in 1864. Mullaney was an Irishwoman from Troy, New York, who gathered together 300 other female commercial laundry workers to organize against dangerous conditions and low pay. The union staged a series of strikes and walkouts throughout the 1860s and within just a few short years of its founding, the laundry workers saw an increase in wages from approximately $4 per week to an astounding $14 per week.[37]

While reformers and male union leaders discussed the role of white and immigrant women both in and out of the factories, African American women had to deal with discrimination not only from unions, but also from employers, and even from other working women. In 1897 white women millworkers protested the hiring of two black women at an Atlanta textile mill. In this case, an astounding 1,400 white workers organized a walk-out that resulted in the black women being fired. If they did manage to secure positions, black women risked losing those jobs if they attempted to change or better their conditions. That is exactly what happened in 1889 at a Virginia tobacco processing plant where black strikers were simply replaced by white workers.[38]

In some instances women did organize and make public their grievances, and, by doing so, inspired other workers to do the same. In 1881 the Washerwomen's Association of Atlanta went on strike, demanding higher wages per pound of laundry. The local newspaper soon reported, "Not only washerwomen, but the cooks, house servants and nurses are asking an increase." In this case, the issue extended beyond a disagreement between employers and employees to involve the entire white community attempting to undermine the women's demands. The campaign ended with the city council proposing that the laundresses should have to pay a $25 business license fee, forcing the strikers to back down from their original demands.[39]

Even though the workers were silenced in this instance, such organization and public activism was particularly important for individual household workers, who did not have unions to join.

Despite some of the early efforts by women to organize on their own behalf within individual factories or within a specific trade, by 1900 little more than 3 percent of female industrial workers were unionized.[40] One explanation for such low trade union membership is that even permanent wage-earning women, including married and immigrant women in lower-paying jobs, preferred to see themselves primarily as wives and mothers (or future wives and mothers), and as only temporary or occasional workers, just as with the Lowell "mill girls" earlier in the century. It was not until after 1900 that women began to organize on a larger scale, and they were subsequently involved in some of the largest, most significant labor disputes and strikes of the early twentieth century. Especially important to these later efforts were organizations that brought women together across skill levels within a specific trade, or across industries, such as the International Ladies' Garment Workers Union, founded in 1900, and the Women's Trade Union League, founded in 1903.

As women workers began to organize themselves and form their own unions, middle-class female reformers also sought to address some of the concerns of working women. However, as reformers were more likely to promote the home as the desired place for women, they often focused their efforts not on ameliorating the conditions for working women, but on getting women back in the home. Female reformers and social workers supported the family wage and protective labor legislation that treated women and children differently as workers. The first protective labor legislation was passed in Massachusetts in 1874 with a law establishing a maximum 10-hour workday for women and children. The passage of protective labor laws was a successful strategy for Progressive-era reformers well into the twentieth century, although in many ways, middle-class reformers undermined working women by ignoring issues related to improving working conditions and pay, in favor of legislation prohibiting women from working at night or establishing higher "family wages" for men.

Female reformers defined other women's roles in domestic terms, even while they sought to expand public roles for themselves. Late-nineteenth century white women reformers were more likely to be college graduates than their earlier counterparts and than black women reformers at any time. (See also Chapter 4, "Education and the Professions.") This generation of women graduated with decreased interest in marriage and motherhood, but only to find few public roles open to them in which they could put their educations to use. Jane Addams began her settlement house work when she could not find employment in government or other social agencies, creating a profession—social work—where there was none for her. Her work was also, of course, facilitated by an explosion of immigrant women into the paid workforce who became the "clients" of female social workers.

Addams founded Hull House in Chicago in 1889 as a place for white women reformers to aid poor immigrants by teaching them American values, helping them find employment and other services, and providing health and childcare services. This work took Addams and her colleagues into city politics in ways that women had never been involved. Women such as Addams now made it their business to campaign for clean water, health care, education, abolition of child labor, and other reforms and legislation. Although showing real concern over the degradation of labor, low wages, and the unsafe working conditions of urban industrial women workers, in particular, white reformers also assumed there was a problem within the immigrant community who made up this workforce, leading them to include within their reform agenda efforts to "Americanize" the religious and cultural practices of immigrant women and families.

The large numbers of white women employed as social reformers by the turn of the twentieth century drew upon the earlier nineteenth-century ideology of domesticity and female moral authority to enter into the public world. (See also Chapter 5, "Politics and Reform.") They justified their own work in terms of responsibility and duty in promoting what came to be termed a reform ethos of *social housekeeping*, or the idea that women were needed to clean up the mess of business and politics. As reformer Caroline Nichols Churchill explained in 1880:

> We are aware of the jealousies of many husbands in regard to any public work which the wife may become interested in, but women should remember that all the evils of society are caused by the bad management of men, and women are greatly to blame for folding their hands and permitting this state of things.[41]

Black middle-class reformers were more likely to acknowledge work, including women's social and reform work, as a necessity rather than a duty or even a necessary evil for women. The black women's club movement brought together reformers and organizations dedicated to "making the home better," an agenda that encompassed a large realm of issues. They investigated schools for black children and reported on changes needed in facilities and black teachers' salaries, and fought against segregated and unequal higher education. Reformers put together after-school care programs, playgrounds, and vacation schools, all issues aimed at accommodating and improving the lives of working mothers.

Women's increased labor force participation over the course of the nineteenth century, and the make-up of the workforce to include more black and European immigrant women, changed the focus of reformers' concerns. Using the rhetoric of domesticity and social housekeeping, women reformers critiqued industrialization, immigration, unequal education, and the poverty of a permanent working class as problems of the new economy and problems affecting women in their roles as workers, but also as wives and mothers. Women were thus at the forefront of the critique of an unchecked and rapid spread of industrialism and capitalism that characterized the United States economy by the end of the century. Whereas a woman's "work" in 1800 encompassed all of the tasks necessary to keeping a home and operating within the local economy of barter, apprenticeship, and the production of local goods, by the end of the century, millions of women worked for wages outside the home in low-paid, low-skilled jobs in factories, offices, and the homes of others.

NOTES

1. Beecher quoted in Jeanne Boydston, *The Limits of Sisterhood: The Beecher Sisters on Women's Rights and Woman's Sphere* (Chapel Hill: University of North Carolina Press, 1988), p. 134.

2. Laurel Thatcher Ulrich, *A Midwife's Tale: The Life of Martha Ballard, Based on Her Diary, 1785–1812* (New York: Vintage Books, 1991).

3. On household machines and appliances in the 19th century, see Alice Kessler-Harris, *Out to Work: A History of Wage-Earning Women in the United States*, rev. ed. (New York: Oxford University Press, 2003), pp. 111–12.

4. Kessler-Harris, *Out to Work.*

5. Larcom quoted in *Through Women's Eyes: An American History with Documents*, 3rd ed., ed. Ellen Carol DuBois and Lynn Dumenil (Boston: Bedford/St. Martin's, 2005), p. 144.

6. Boydston, *The Limits of Sisterhood*, p. 132.

7. Murphy quoted in Harvey Green, *The Light of the Home: An Intimate View of the Lives of Women in Victorian America* (New York: Pantheon Books, 1983), p. 59.

8. Green, *Light of the Home*, p. 86.

9. Drew Gilpin Faust, *Mothers of Invention: Women of the Slaveholding South in the American Civil War* (Chapel Hill: University of North Carolina Press, 1996), quotes on p. 47 and p. 78.

10. Green, *Light of the Home*, pp. 81–82.

11. Kessler-Harris, *Out to Work*, p. 47.

12. See Thomas Dublin, *Transforming Women's Work: New England Lives in the Industrial Revolution* (Ithaca, N.Y.: Cornell University Press, 1994), chap. 6, "New Hampshire Teachers," p. 207.

13. Ira Berlin, Marc Favreau, and Steven F. Miller, eds., *Remembering Slavery: African Americans Talk about Their Personal Experiences of Slavery and Emancipation* (New York: New Press, 1998), p. 98.

14. Berlin, Favreau, and Miller, *Remembering Slavery*, p. 168.

15. Catherine Clinton and Christine Lunardini, eds., *The Columbia Guide to American Women in the Nineteenth Century* (New York: Columbia University Press, 2000), p. 30 and pp. 33–35.

16. Delia Page letters reprinted in Thomas Dublin, ed., *Farm to Factory: Women's Letters, 1830–1860* (New York: Columbia University Press, 1993), pp. 166–67.

17. Dublin, *Farm to Factory*, p. 169.

18. "'Slaver Wagons, 1846," *Voice of Industry*, January 2, 1846, reprinted in *Discovering the American Past: A Look at the Evidence, Vol. I to 1877*, 5th ed., ed. William Bruce Wheeler and Susan D. Becker (Boston: Houghton Mifflin, 2002), p. 158.

19. Clinton and Lunardini, *Columbia Guide to American Women*, p. 33.

20. Lucy Larcom, *A New England Girlhood* (originally published 1889), excerpted in *Discovering the American Past*, pp. 168–69.

21. See Kessler-Harris, *Out to Work*, p. 127.

22. Rose Cohen, *Out of the Shadow: A Russian Jewish Girlhood on the Lower East Side* (originally published 1918), excerpted in *Major Problems in American Women's History*, 3rd ed., ed. Mary Beth Norton and Ruth M. Alexander (Boston: Houghton Mifflin, 2003), pp. 214–15.

23. Eileen Boris, "'A Man's Dwelling House Is His Castle': Tenement House Cigar-making and the Judicial Imperative," in *Work Engendered: Toward a New History of American Labor*, ed. Ava Baron (Ithaca, N.Y.: Cornell University Press, 1991), quote on p. 120.

24. Boris, "'A Man's Dwelling House,'" pp. 123–24.

25. Jacqueline Jones, *Labor of Love, Labor of Sorrow: Black Women, Work, and the Family from Slavery to the Present* (New York: Basic Books, 1985), p. 147.

26. Kessler-Harris, *Out to Work*, p. 54.

27. Berlin, Favreau, and Miller, *Remembering Slavery*, pp. 101–2.

28. Mary Paul quoted in Gail Collins, *America's Women: 400 Years of Dolls, Drudges, Helpmates, and Heroines* (New York: HarperCollins, 2003), p. 112.

29. Jeanne Boydston, *Home and Work: Housework, Wages, and the Ideology of Labor in the Early Republic* (New York: Oxford University Press, 1990), p. 79.

30. Boydston, *Home and Work*, pp. 80–81.

31. Kathy Peiss, *Cheap Amusements: Working Women and Leisure in Turn-of-the-Century New York* (Philadelphia: Temple University Press, 1986), p. 35.

32. Peiss, *Cheap Amusements*, pp. 39–40.

33. Jones, *Labor of Love*, p. 90.

34. Jones, *Labor of Love*, pp. 125–26.

35. Darlene Clark Hine and Kathleen Thompson, eds., *A Shining Thread of Hope: The History of Black Women in America* (New York: Broadway Books, 1998), p. 153.

36. Fannie Barber Williams, "The Problem of Employment for Negro Women," *Southern Workman* (1903), reprinted in Norton and Alexander, *Major Problems in American Women's History*, pp. 218–20.

37. Mullaney discussed in Carole Turbin, *Working Women of Collar City: Gender, Class, and Community in Troy, New York, 1864–1886* (Urbana: University of Illinois Press, 1994).

38. Jones, *Labor of Love*, p. 147.

39. Jones, *Labor of Love*, p. 148.

40. Kessler-Harris, *Out to Work*, p. 152.

41. Churchill quoted in Susan Armitage and Elizabeth Jameson, eds., *The Women's West* (Norman: University of Oklahoma Press, 1987), p. 268.

SUGGESTED READING

Baron, Ava, ed. *Work Engendered: Toward a New History of American Labor.* Ithaca, N.Y.: Cornell University Press, 1991.

Boydston, Jeanne. *Home and Work: Housework, Wages, and the Ideology of Labor in the Early Republic.* New York: Oxford University Press, 1990.

Cohen, Ruth Schwartz. *More Work for Mother: The Ironies of Household Technology from the Open Hearth to the Microwave.* New York: Basic Books, 1985.

Dublin, Thomas. *Transforming Women's Work: New England Lives in the Industrial Revolution.* Ithaca, N.Y.: Cornell University Press, 1994.

Dublin, Thomas, ed. *Farm to Factory: Women's Letters, 1830–1860.* New York: Columbia University Press, 1993.

Eisler, Benita, ed. *The* Lowell Offering: *Writings by New England Mill Women (1840–1845).* New York: Norton, 1997.

Gamber, Wendy. *The Female Economy: The Millinery and Dressmaking Trades, 1860–1930.* Urbana: University of Illinois Press, 1997.

Groneman, Carol, and Mary Beth Norton, eds. *To Toil the Livelong Day: America's Women at Work, 1780–1980.* Ithaca, N.Y.: Cornell University Press, 1987.

Jones, Jacqueline. *Labor of Love, Labor of Sorrow: Black Women, Work, and the Family from Slavery to the Present.* New York: Basic Books, 1985.

Kessler-Harris, Alice. *Out to Work: A History of Wage-Earning Women in the United States,* rev. ed. New York: Oxford University Press, 2003.

Lewenson, Sandra. *Taking Charge: Nursing, Suffrage, and Feminism in America, 1873–1920.* New York: National League for Nursing Press, 1996.

Moran, William. *The Belles of New England: The Women of the Textile Mills and the Families Whose Wealth They Wove.* New York: St. Martin's, 2002.

Peiss, Kathy. *Cheap Amusements: Working Women and Leisure in Turn-of-the-Century New York.* Philadelphia: Temple University Press, 1986.

Porter, Susan L., ed. *Women of the Commonwealth: Work, Family, and Social Change in Nineteenth-Century Massachusetts.* Amherst: University of Massachusetts Press, 1996.

Sklar, Kathryn Kish. *Florence Kelley and the Nation's Work: The Rise of Women's Political Culture, 1830–1900.* New Haven, Conn.: Yale University Press, 1997.

Stansell, Christine. *City of Women: Sex and Class in New York, 1789–1860.* Urbana: University of Illinois Press, 1987.

Sutherland, Daniel E. *Americans and Their Servants: Domestic Service in the United States from 1800 to 1920.* Baton Rouge: Louisiana State University Press, 1981.

3

⤙⤙⤙

Religion

In the first decades of the nineteenth century, women had new opportunities for participation in religious life, whether as church members themselves, as wives and mothers with moral authority at home, or as missionaries, moral reformers, and even preachers. Although a new emphasis was placed on women's spiritual roles within the home, religion became, in fact, one of the primary routes to women's participation in a broader public sphere. In 1810 New England preacher John Buckminster specifically addressed this new spiritual role for women:

> We look to you, ladies, to raise the standard of character in our own sex. . . .
> We look to you for the continuance of domestick purity, for the revival of
> domestick religion, for the increase of our charities, and the support of what
> remains of religion in our private habits and publick institutions.[1]

The United States in the nineteenth century was a religious nation, and predominantly a Protestant nation, but one where a diversity of religious groups and ideas flourished. The British North American colonies were founded, in part, as a place of refuge for religious dissenters and those seeking freedom from persecution, whether it was the Puritans in New England, Catholics in Maryland, or the Quakers who founded Pennsylvania. The Great Awakening period of revivalism in the mid-eighteenth century introduced new religious sects and a more democratic individual experience of religion. At the same time, the political creation of the new nation established the foundational freedom of worship as well as a clear separation between church and state. Churchgoers began to question the social authority of community and intellectual leaders, including elite ministers, and church membership rose through attracting the young, but also the poor, slaves, and more women, to groups that now preached self-worth and spiritual equality before God.

WOMEN'S ROLES IN THE CHURCHES

Across denominations women have usually made up the majority of churchgoers, and, as the nineteenth century began, their presence and participation in both established and new religious sects in the United States was of such great significance that some scholars have identified a "feminization of religion" during this era.[2] In the first decades of the nineteenth century, a new wave of religious revivals swept the nation, spreading a message of free will and human agency. Traveling preachers, such as Charles Grandison Finney, emphasized that it was up to individual men and women to choose morality and salvation, but also, in a new nineteenth-century emphasis, to convince *others* to make the right moral choices as well. In other words, not just to convert, but to evangelize and reform. Finney's message had particular appeal to America's new middle class, especially women, providing them with a new sense of control over their own lives and destiny, as well as a new moral justification for taking on a broader social role. (See also Chapter 5, "Politics and Reform.")

The early nineteenth-century ideology of domesticity coincided with women's increased role within the churches by promoting the idea that women were responsible for the morality and spiritual well-being of their husbands and children. Women were responsible for reading the Bible to their children, setting a good example by their own actions, involving the family in church-related activities and charitable giving, and getting the family to attend services on Sundays. Some husbands were not happy with women's new sense of moral authority and their mission of converting wayward husbands. One man complained in an 1832 newspaper editorial that preacher Charles Grandison Finney had "*stuffed* my wife with tracts, and alarmed her fears, and nothing short of meetings, night and day, could atone for the many fold sins my poor, simple spouse had committed, and at the same time, she made the miraculous discovery, that she had been 'unevenly yoked.' From this unhappy period, peace, quiet, and happiness have fled from my dwelling, never, I fear, to return."[3]

In their concern about the spiritual and educational welfare of children, both their own and others, women established church-based organizations such as charitable relief societies, schools for poor children, Sunday schools (one way that younger unmarried women could also fill a role as spiritual teachers of young children), and maternal associations. In maternal associations, women met together to discuss Christian childrearing ideas and older, more experienced, women mentored new mothers. Toward this same purpose, there were numerous publications by male clergy as well as women writers advising mothers in their "professions" and the maternal associations helped support women in this role. Revivalist preacher Charles Grandison Finney's wife, Lydia Finney, helped found the Oberlin Maternal Association in Ohio.[4] The Presbyterian Maternal Association of Utica, New York, explained its purpose in its 1824 charter:

> Deeply impressed with the great importance of bringing up our children in the nurture and admonition of the Lord, we the subscribers agree to associate for the purpose of devising and adopting such measures as may seem best calculated to assist us in the right performance of these duties.[5]

In 1833 the editor of *Mother's Magazine* supported this goal by emphasizing the particular spiritual role women had as mothers: "The church has had her seasons of refreshing and her turn of decay; but here in the circle of mothers, it is felt that the Holy Spirit condescends to dwell. It seems his blessed rest."[6]

Taking their role in promoting "domestick religion" beyond their own homes, women also reached out to other families. Christian women might go door-to-door on weekday mornings to talk with other women about either their own conversion, or to give advice to other Christian women on converting their husbands. Although male preachers and revivalists led hundreds or even thousands of communicants in worship, women predominated in unofficial roles as "exhorters," working one-on-one to facilitate the conversion of other individuals. In church, in their own separately organized meetings, or in the homes of their neighbors, women would sing and pray.

Just as some husbands may have resisted women's spiritual work, not all ministers welcomed women's expanded roles in the public forum of the churches. Perhaps perceiving a female threat to the spiritual and social authority of male ministers like himself, preacher Lyman Beecher supported a resolution stating "that in social meetings of men and women for religious worship, females are not to pray."[7] Ironically, given his limited view on women having a more visible role within the churches, Beecher was the father of two women reformers of the nineteenth century with prominent public careers: promoter of domesticity and of women's education, Catharine Beecher, and antislavery author Harriet Beecher Stowe.

WOMEN AS MISSIONARIES

Although their roles in the family meant that women were often socially isolated within the home, the moral authority that propelled women to act through the churches actually led to new and significant forms of female collectivity and public activism that took women further away from the home. Looking beyond their immediate families and even their neighbor-hoods and communities, middle-class wives gathered together under names like the Female Missionary Society, not to be missionaries themselves, but to raise funds to send young male missionaries into frontier areas where people might not be reached by the revivals and the pulpits of the regu-lar ministers. For example, the Whitestown, New York, Female Charitable Society first worked locally, then changed its name to the Oneida Female Missionary Society when it began sponsoring frontier missions. A few years later the once-more renamed Female Missionary Society of the Western District grew to include several secondary organizations that raised money to support dozens of missionaries. In addition to taking on new religious roles, women's activities ultimately gave them new organizational and financial skills beyond those necessary for running their own households.[8]

Still, women in these new organizations envisioned their work as a logical extension of their domestic roles as mothers and wives. When the Oneida Female Missionary Society appealed for support in 1819, they em-phasized their special role in reaching out to and assisting other mothers on the frontier: "Let us imagine a pious mother surrounded with a numer-ous family—none of them give evidence of possessing an interest in Christ. Without a public place of worship, and surrounded by vain amusements and unholy neighbors, the rural mother despairs of saving the souls of her children. When the itinerant minister is introduced into this sad picture by the Female Missionary Society, the mother's joy is too big for utterance; she manifests it by her tears. . . . Our missionaries often witness such af-fecting scenes."[9] Although the missionaries themselves would have been men, these women of the Missionary Society clearly and forcefully argued for recognition of their behind-the-scenes roles in the success of frontier missions.

Beyond their work for local and frontier missions, American women also supported foreign missions, whether organizationally, financially, as missionary wives, or, in a few instances, as independent missionaries them-selves. Ann Hasseltine Judson was probably the best-known missionary wife of the nineteenth century. She taught in Burma and her letters pub-lished in missionary journals describing women's cultural situation there, as well as an early biography, made Judson known to other women as a role model.[10] It was less common, but still possible, for single women to travel as missionaries. Many did so as "assistants" to married couples or families, but, as education was one of the major areas of women's missionary work, others helped found or taught in foreign schools for women and children. Women's support of and involvement in foreign missions exploded in the post–Civil War era with the 1861 founding of the Woman's Union Mis-sionary Society and the many separate denominational groups formed in the following decades. An 1869 article in the *Heathen Woman's Friend* clearly outlined the broad role missionary women saw for themselves (as indicated in the title of the journal as well): "Christian civilization does little for a nation until it has lifted woman from the condition of a thing to the dignity of a sister and wife. You cannot evangelize a country until you convert the women."[11]

Only the Quakers had a built-in tradition of female ministers and missionaries. The foundation of Quaker spirituality is the belief that each individual has an "inner light," a direct relationship with and reflection of God within each person. In Quaker religious meetings, anyone, including women, might be compelled to speak out if so moved by the spirit within. Since the sect's founding in the mid-seventeenth century, English Quakers had funded and supported women ministers traveling to the American colonies, and, in the nineteenth century, American Quaker women evangelized internationally as well as on the frontier. Most Quaker women missionaries were married and most had children, but domestic duties did not prevent them from answering the call to preach. Sarah Foulke Farquahar Emlen left five young children behind with her husband, James, when she went on a five-month evangelizing trip in 1825. She and James switched roles a few years later when he departed as a minister to the Ohio frontier while she stayed at home with the children. Apparently, the Emlens were not unusual in this regard among Quaker couples. When Rachel Price left on a mission, her husband, Philip, stayed behind with their 10 children and assured her that she was following the right path: "Having set thy hand to the work it will not do to look back, otherwise thou wilt lose the reward which I believe those are favoured to experience who are faithfully given up to it in true sincerity of heart."[12]

By mid-century much of that frontier missionizing was among Native Americans of the Plains and Far West. White missionaries and educators worked closely with government Indian affairs offices on the frontiers as, in most cases, the westward push of white settlement, efforts to convert Native Americans to Christianity, and setting up schools for Native American children all went hand-in-hand. Narcissa Prentiss Whitman and her husband, Marcus Whitman, were among the first of hundreds of missionaries who traveled overland between the 1830s and 1850s. The Whitman's purpose for going west in 1836 was to be in "service among the heathen." The Whitmans worked among the Cayuse Indians, he as a doctor and in assisting in the establishment of family farms, and she overseeing the mission kitchen and school. Eventually, Narcissa became discouraged from believing that the Indians could be helped out of "the thick darkness of heathenism." Whereas Narcissa saw Indians as uninterested or unable to be converted, hostility toward the mission was related to the more general threat of the large numbers of white settlers entering the area and of Indian deaths from new diseases. The Cayuse chief claimed the right to the land the mission had settled upon; in November 1847, a Cayuse attack on the mission killed Narcissa and her husband as well as 12 other whites.[13]

It was a widely held belief that, in order to convert Native Americans, one must focus on the mothers and the children. Sue McBeth was an unmarried Presbyterian who worked among the Nez Percé in the Pacific Northwest for 20 years, from 1873–1893. She also trained male Native Americans as ministers to build "Christian and civilized homes" among the Native people. In order to do this, Native people needed to be taught the proper roles for men and women (that is, white gender roles), and in this regard, McBeth wrote, "The mother is even more important than the father perhaps—because she has so much to do with training the children in the new way—or leading them on in the old."[14] A female Indian School Service Agent concurred that in her findings:

> It is a truism that in order to reach any heathen people the mothers and homes must be interested first. It is also just as much a truism . . . that the Indians as a whole are still pagan, and the women most conservatively pagan of all. . . . The mothers keep up the old superstitions and laugh down modern ideas and customs.[15]

Although missionaries focused on the "heathen" or "pagan" practices of Native women, in particular, many whites simply believed that Native Americans were completely without religion. Of course, spiritual practice was a part of daily life for all Native women, just as it was for white or African American women of the era. Across diverse nations and tribes, Native American women gave spiritual meaning to rituals surrounding birth, coming of age, sickness and healing, and death, finding inspiration in their origin myths, histories, dreams, and visions. Among many Native peoples, women held positions as religious leaders and medicine women. Many Native Americans, of course, did convert to Christianity and some Native women even worked as missionaries themselves. Earlier in the century, Cherokee Catharine Brown of Alabama sought out an education at a missionary school and became a Presbyterian. She subsequently converted others within her own family and circle of friends before her death in 1823, although her influence and her missionizing continued through her published autobiography, *Memoir of Catharine Brown: A Christian Indian of the Cherokee Nation.*[16]

WOMEN AS PREACHERS

Although they could not be ordained or officially lead congregations as regular ministers, women throughout the Protestant denominations could not be prevented from responding to the spiritual call to preach. In most denominations, women were church members, not leaders, but women did work with male leadership within the churches and within their reform organizations. The revivalism of the early nineteenth century, however, emphasized emotional expressiveness and individual inspiration from the Holy Spirit, including the inspiration to speak, and these avenues were open equally to women. Still, women who felt called by the Holy Spirit to preach faced social opposition, primarily based on the apostle Paul's instructions in I Corinthians 14:34 to "Let your women keep silence in the churches; for it is not permitted unto them to speak." But as women acted upon the moral and spiritual authority granted by new religious ideas, they and their supporters increasingly called upon woman's *duty* to share their gift and their message.

Women preachers themselves regularly emphasized that they were acting on God's authority, not their own, in reluctantly deciding to pursue a path of public speaking. Deborah Pierce, in her 1820 *A Scriptural Vindication of Female Preaching, Prophesying, or Exhortation,* emphasized that women preachers spoke from a position of spiritual authority, rather than from a position of social equality. Increasingly, however, those two aspects overlapped and as women appeared more regularly on the church podium, on the camp-meeting stage, and on the moral reform lecture circuit, they had to defend not only their duty but also their *right* to be there.

Free Will Baptist Nancy Towle received the call to preach in a dream and traveled extensively as an itinerant preacher throughout New England, the mid-Atlantic states, into South Carolina, and internationally to Canada, England, and Ireland. Towle even preached before the U.S. Congress. In addition to speaking and converting, Towle served as a role model and urged more women across denominations to pursue preaching. As with other women preachers of the early nineteenth century, Towle was supported by some male church members and invited to preach in their congregations, but others opposed her public speaking.[17]

In the 1830s women were central to a renewal or "Holiness" movement within the Methodist Church. Preacher Phoebe Palmer had followed the same path of religious and communal experience of many devout Protestant women in the first half of the nineteenth century, but emerged as one of the primary leaders of the new Methodism. A member of female missionary and charitable societies, Palmer led women's prayer meetings and a Bible group, but her role was extended in 1840 to leadership of a "Tuesday Meeting for the Promotion of Holiness" that was attended by both women and men. Palmer subsequently became an itinerant preacher in the United States and England and the author of numerous publications. In her 1869 text, *Tongues of Fire on the Daughters of the Lord,* Palmer defended women's need, duty, even right, to preach, saying "God has eminently endowed woman with gifts for the social circle. He has given her the power of persuasion, and the ability to captivate. Who may win souls to Christ, if she may not?"[18] In all of her writing, Palmer, like most other female preachers of the century, assured her critics that their public ministries were not efforts to expand or challenge women's traditional roles, but only represented God's will: "Women who speak in assemblies for worship, under the influence of the Holy Spirit, assume thereby no *personal authority* over others. They are instruments through which divine instruction is communicated to other people."[19]

Black women of this era became some of the first, often forgotten, female public speakers through their preaching activities. Jarena Lee was a free black woman who, in 1836, published an account of her conversion and preaching career as *The Life and Religious Experience of Jarena Lee, a Colored Lady, Giving an Account of Her Call to Preach the Gospel.* In this spiritual autobiography, Lee recounted hearing a voice that told her to "Go Preach the Gospel!" and explained how she approached her minister, the Reverend Richard Allen of the African Methodist Episcopalian (AME) Church, about this dilemma.

> I now told him, that the Lord had revealed it to me, that I must preach the gospel. . . . He then replied, that a Mrs. Cook, a Methodist lady, had also some time before requested the same privilege; who it was believed, had done much good in the way of exhortation, and holding prayer meetings; and who had been permitted to do so by the verbal license of the preacher in charge at the time. But as to women preaching, he said that our Discipline knew nothing at all about it—that it did not call for women preachers.[20]

By her own account, then, Lee sought to work through the existing denominational structure and was reluctant to present preaching as her own idea, but it is also interesting that the Rev. Allen indicated she was not the first woman to make such a request. He and other male ministers were carefully coming to terms with the valuable work that women might do by taking on such public roles, but without challenging male authority. Jarena Lee was eventually authorized by the church to lead prayer meetings in her own home and to travel as an itinerant speaker.

Zilpha Elaw was raised near Philadelphia and worked for a Quaker family before converting to Methodism in 1808. In 1817 she attended a camp meeting where she fell into a "trance of ecstasy" and subsequently began leading prayer meetings. Urged by other women and supported by her ministers, Elaw became a preacher in front of both black and white audiences. Elaw's main critic was her husband, but, like Jarena Lee, Zilpha Elaw felt the choice to preach was not hers to make but was God's purpose for her life. In her 1846 *Memoirs of the Religious Experience, Ministerial Travels and Labors of Mrs. Zilpha Elaw, An American Female of Colour; Together with Some Account of the Great Religious Revivals in America,* Elaw presented her husband's opposition to his wife's public speaking as a spiritual crisis borne of the fact that he was not a Christian. Elaw acknowledged: "That woman is dependant on and subject to man, is the dictate of nature; that the man is not created for the woman, but the woman for the man, is that of Scripture." She herself resisted the call to preach for some time until, like Jarena Lee, she had a mystical experience in which she heard a voice saying, "Now thou knowest the will of God concerning thee; thou must preach the gospel; and thou must travel far and wide." After she was widowed, Elaw did just that, traveling throughout England and the United States, even into the slaveholding states of the South where, as a free black woman, her own personal safety was at risk.[21] The public careers of Lee and Elaw influenced other women to organize and support each other, although the male hierarchy of the Methodist Church continued to refuse to officially recognize women as preachers.

Although the AME church was the primary denominational supporter of most black female preachers in the first half of the nineteenth century, the majority of white women preachers were members of the Society of Friends, or Quakers. If moved by the Holy Spirit, women could become preachers and missionaries. Some men among the Quakers struggled with the idea of women taking on a more public role, but still could not deny their spiritual right to do so. Upon observing the public presence of Quaker women in the United States in the 1830s, English Quaker Joseph Gurney concluded:

> I do not approve of ladies speaking in public, even in the antislavery cause, except under the immediate influences of the Holy Spirit. Then, and then only all is safe. Should my dear ladies have to speak in this way, I have no objections."[22]

Gurney's own wife, Eliza Kirkbride Gurney, however, was called upon to speak not only when moved by the spirit, but also as a translator and at public events during the couple's travels through Europe.[23]

Preacher Mary Moon Meredith was one of the best-regarded Quaker women preachers of her era, and in 1880 she spoke to the argument still made by some that the Bible mandated "women keep silence in the churches." Meredith argued: "There is one thing sure: either God makes a mistake, or Paul makes a mistake, or the people who put Paul in such an awkward position make one. As for me, I shall not place the mistake on God, neither upon that great champion of the cross, the Apostle Paul. . . . People talk about this new departure [of women speaking]! Why it is as old as the Church."[24] In the end, a belief in spiritual equality, the idea that the Holy Spirit could work through any person—male or female, black or white, rich or poor—was used by women preachers among Quakers as well as non-Quakers to justify their work. For the Quakers in particular, however, spiritual equality also provided a foundation for a commitment to social equality and explains not only the predominance of women speakers among the Quakers, but also their active leadership role in moral reform movements such as abolitionism, and, later, women's rights. (See also Chapter 5, "Politics and Reform.")

Just as with members of female moral reform and benevolent associations, women preachers also operated in unofficial roles, affiliated with but not representing the official churches, supported by but not always recognized by male preachers. Assessing women's access into religious leadership roles, Frances Willard estimated in 1889 that there were some "five hundred women who have already entered the pulpit as evangelists . . . (exclusive of the 350 Quaker preachers) who are pastors." Willard went on to report the following denominations as having "regularly ordained" women: "Methodist, Baptist, Free Baptist, Congregational, Universalist and Unitarian."[25] Indeed, women had roles as preachers and exhorters, both officially and unofficially, throughout the Protestant denominations by the end of the century. In 1880 Anna Howard Shaw became the first ordained female Methodist minister, but the church revoked the ordination four years later. In 1894 the AME church ordained Julia Foote as the first female deacon, an alternative church role for women. Other women chose to pursue formal training as ministers, and Antoinette Blackwell became the first woman to graduate from divinity school in 1850 and had the distinction of becoming the first ordained female minister in the United States in 1853.

Other women took on leadership roles in completely new religious sects. Women founded two of the most popular new religious groups of the late nineteenth century. Ellen Gould White was one of the founders and early leaders of the Seventh Day Adventist Church, organized in 1863, and Mary Baker Eddy founded Christian Science in 1879. White became one of the most prolific women writers of the nineteenth century, and her religious and philosophical texts are still read by church members around the world. Eddy may have been influenced by Mother Ann Lee, founder of the Shakers, for Eddy offered a similar belief in God as both male and female. Eddy explained that men's and women's spiritual roles combined in the idea of God, because "The ideal man corresponds to creation, to intelligence, and Truth. The ideal woman corresponds to Life and Love." Whereas other Christian religions focused on Eve's role in the downfall of man, Eddy emphasized the figure of Eve as a spiritual role model for women. Additionally, as Christian Science attracted members and grew, both men and women could be leaders of societies, missionaries for the religion, or healers, as a rejection of the male physician model of medicine was an integral part of Eddy's Christian Science message.[26]

RELIGION AND WOMEN'S RIGHTS

Nineteenth-century women soon moved from justifying their right to preach to demanding their right to speak publicly about other issues related to moral and social reform. Black women early on addressed the sin of slavery and lent their voices as preachers to the emerging antislavery movement. Nor was it coincidental that Quaker women took leadership of the most important reform movements of the nineteenth century. Their roles as female preachers and missionaries in the public sphere combined with their spiritual imperative toward social equality. (See also Chapter 5, "Politics and Reform.") Just as women's roles within the churches were expanding, taking them more into the public sphere and allowing them to exercise more spiritual authority, traditional religion was also increasingly subject to feminist critique. Female preachers were powerful role models of women speaking in public, and, by the 1820s and 1830s, women began acting on their moral duties as Christians to challenge the traditional church hierarchy and the limits of women's prescribed roles.

Daughters of a South Carolina slaveholder, sisters Angelina and Sarah Grimké moved to Philadelphia and converted to Quakerism, a spirituality that inspired in them a sense of both woman's call to speak and a humanitarian objection to slavery. The sisters participated in a range of religious activities typical of other women of the century. They led prayer meetings and Christian women's groups, contributed to charitable organizations to help the poor, and Angelina taught at a "colored Sunday school." While still in South Carolina, the women of the Grimké family had reached out to African Americans by holding prayer meetings attended by their own family slaves as well as others in the community.[27]

Still, although Quakers encouraged and supported many women preachers, the Grimkés' speaking and publishing throughout the 1830s eventually crossed over into political issues, a development that brought attention and criticism upon them as women. In her 1836 tract, *Appeal to the Christian Women of the South*, Angelina Grimké created controversy by addressing the issue of white men fathering children with slave women. The following year the sisters embarked upon a tour of Northern churches, in which they spoke out against slavery and began to link the degradation of enslaved women with the general and pervasive subordination of all women.

In the face of criticism over their ideas and opposition to their public presence, the Grimké sisters had to defend themselves not only against male ministers and critics, but also against other women reformers and writers who insisted a woman's main influence was in the home, not in public. Angelina responded directly to the issue of women's right to speak in *Letters to Catharine Beecher*. Unlike women preachers, however, the Grimkés argued that women not only might be compelled to preach by receiving a calling from the Holy Spirit, but also must take it upon themselves to act on their duty and right to speak out on moral issues.

In response to their intense public speaking tours in the mid-1830s, the Grimkés came under criticism from the General Association of

Massachusetts Churches, which published an open "Pastoral Letter" in a New England journal clearly outlining the line between appropriate and inappropriate roles women might take within the churches:

> There are social influences which females use in promoting piety and the great objects of Christian benevolence which we cannot too highly commend. We appreciate the unostentatious efforts of woman in advancing the cause of religion at home and abroad; in Sabbath schools; in leading religious inquirers to the pastors for instruction; and in all such associated efforts as becomes the modesty of her sex; and earnestly hope that she may abound more and more in these labors of piety and love.
>
> . . . But when she assumes the place and tone of man as a public reformer . . . she yields the power which God has given her for protection, and her character becomes unnatural.[28]

The Grimké sisters had crossed the line from a supporting spiritual role within the churches to a more independent public role as moral reformers. But the warning of the Massachusetts ministers did not deter them from their purpose and in fact compelled Sarah Grimké to respond with a series of "Letters on the Equality of the Sexes and the Condition of Woman" (1838), writing that provided a model and rhetoric for other women abolitionists and for the emerging women's rights movement of the following decade.

The limited role of women within the churches was addressed again a few years later at the first women's rights convention at Seneca Falls, New York, in July 1848. Reformers Elizabeth Cady Stanton, Lucretia Mott, and others cited religion as one of the foundational sources of women's oppression that they included in the "Declaration of Sentiments," a list of grievances against man's social, economic, and legal subordination of women:

> He has monopolized nearly all the profitable employments, and from those she is permitted to follow, she receives but a scanty remuneration. He closes against her all the avenues to wealth and distinction which he considers most honorable to himself. As a teacher of theology, medicine, or law, she is not known. . . .
>
> He allows her in Church, as well as State, but a subordinate position, claiming Apostolic authority for her exclusion from the ministry, and, with some exceptions, from any public participation in the affairs of the Church. . . .
>
> He has usurped the prerogative of Jehovah himself, claiming it as his right to assign for her a sphere of action, when that belongs to her conscience and to her God.[29]

The "Declaration of Sentiments" addressed the larger questions of women's access to the ministry, her influence within the church, and, like Sarah

Grimké's critique, the question of men being presumptuous enough to define what her duties should be as a Christian woman. In emphasizing that women were denied religious education and the ministry as a professional route, the women of Seneca Falls recognized that most women who wished to pursue spiritual vocations did so as lay preachers, unpaid, with or without the blessing or support of their home denominations, and that this created inequality within the churches and within society.

Elizabeth Cady Stanton and other nineteenth-century feminists eventually extended their critique beyond women's educational and vocational exclusions within the church to questioning Christian doctrine itself. At the end of the century, Stanton, in conjunction with several other writers, published the controversial *Woman's Bible*, which emphasized the basis for social inequality and women's subordination in both the Old and New Testaments. One of Stanton's co-authors, Matilda Joslyn Gage, also looked to Christianity as a primary source of inequality and published her own treatise, *Woman, Church, and State*, in 1893. The attacks on Christianity by these radical feminists were the culmination of a century of efforts by women to gain an equal spiritual and social footing both within Protestant churches and in society at large. But their radical views ultimately put them at odds with other women's rights activists, who continued to pursue their social and political rights as Christian women.

RELIGION AND UTOPIAN REFORM

Other reformers challenged women's traditional religious, economic, and social roles by creating alternative religious communities. Some utopian communities were based on religious beliefs, others on socialist blueprints for society, but they all reconsidered women's roles within society and the family. Most utopian communities rejected monogamy and many of them rejected marriage outright, believing at some level that the nuclear family and private property were at the root of many of the spiritual and economic problems of modern society. Two religious communities that flourished in the mid-nineteenth century and created alternative family and social arrangements, and, in particular, presented new roles for women as members, were the Shakers and the Mormons.

The Shakers were founded by an English woman known as Mother Ann Lee, who brought her group to the colonies on the eve of the American Revolution. Lee died in 1784 but was succeeded by a series of other female leaders throughout the nineteenth century and beyond. The Shakers were created out of Lee's own traumatic experiences as a wife and mother, and, therefore, the foundation of her religious vision was one in which women's roles within the family and church were completely redefined. Lee had suffered through difficult childbearing and all four of her children had died very young. She subsequently had a vision in which she perceived the sexual act itself as humanity's fall from grace and began to espouse a belief in celibacy, or abstaining from sexual intercourse. Celibacy could be freeing for women, considering their economic and legal subordination within traditional marriage and the lack of adequate birth control that had impacted Lee's own life. The spiritual basis of Lee's teaching was an androgynous vision of God—that is, God as both Father and Mother—that translated into a commitment to earthly equality between the sexes.[30] In Shaker communities men and women lived in separate quarters, with practical chores split between them, although women were still primarily responsible for domestic labor such as cleaning and laundry. The communities sought to be self-sustaining, and women also participated in a wide range of economic roles such as furniture making or crafts and dairy farming.

Writing at the end of the century, Shaker historian and elderess Anna White noted the influence of Shakerism on changes in women's status, in particular linking the rise of Shakerism to the emergence of a women's rights movement in the nineteenth century:

> To Ann Lee may woman look for the first touch that struck off her chains and gave her absolute right to her own person. . . . The daughters of Ann Lee, alone among women, rejoice in true freedom, not alone from the bondage of man's domination, but freedom also from the curse of that desire "to her husband" by which, through the ages, he has ruled over her.[31]

Women also had a unique spiritual and community role within Mormonism, even though they were barred from church leadership as in most other Protestant sects. The Mormon religion was founded in 1830 by Joseph Smith, and, throughout the nineteenth century, many Mormons practiced polygyny, or had multiple wives, as modeled by the patriarchs of the Old Testament. At a time when the American birthrate in general was decreasing, and when nineteenth-century women were slowly increasing their access to birth control knowledge, Mormon women were encouraged to have as many children as possible as part of their spiritual role. One nineteenth-century wife, Mrs. Whitney, explained how Mormon women viewed motherhood as a spiritual quest and noted that polygyny was accepted as a way to increase family size beyond what a single wife could accomplish:

> Our children are considered stars in a mother's crown, and the more there are, if righteous, the more glory they will add to her and their father's eternal kingdom. . . . Nothing but this, and a desire to please our Father in heaven, could tempt the majority of Mormon men or women either, to take upon themselves the burdens and responsibilities of plural marriage.[32]

Although some women committed themselves to their spiritual roles as wives and mothers, other women no doubt found the practice of plural marriage degrading despite their religious commitment. Joseph Smith's own first wife, for example, never completely accepted the practice of plural marriage. In his 1843 "Revelation on the Eternity of the Marriage Covenant, including Plurality of Wives," Joseph Smith relayed God's message to Emma Smith, in particular, instructing her to accept her husband's leadership on the issue: "And let mine handmaid, Emma Smith, receive all those that have been given unto my servant Joseph, and who are virtuous and pure before me." Although some Mormon women also had multiple husbands, or polyandry, such a practice was rare, and Joseph Smith's revelation clarified that this was not an option for Emma Smith: "And I command mine handmaid, Emma Smith, to abide and cleave unto my servant Joseph, and to none else."[33]

CATHOLIC WOMEN

Barred from becoming ordained preachers, missionary work and becoming a nun were the only recognized official religious vocations for Christian women. As one historian points out, "becoming a missionary functioned for Protestant women as the alternative of a religious vocation did for Roman Catholics."[34] Catholicism established a presence in the American colonies with the founding of Maryland, and, subsequently, of two Catholic colleges in the late 1700s: Georgetown and St. Mary's. The history of the growth and success of the Catholic Church in the United States, however, would be tied directly to the large influx of Irish Catholics in the mid-nineteenth century, which made the Roman Catholic Church the single largest religious denomination in the United States by 1850.[35] By the end of the nineteenth century, the United States was home to a large number of not only Irish but Italian and Mexican Catholics as well, in addition to smaller numbers of French and German Catholics.

Most Catholic women, like their Protestant counterparts, saw their own primary roles in relation to the family, as wives and mothers and spiritual keepers of home, tradition, and ritual. A small number of Catholic women devoted themselves to the church and to God directly in roles as members of convents, or nuns. Elizabeth Seton established the first American sisterhood, the Sisters of Charity of St. Joseph, in Maryland in 1809, with subsequent orders established in Philadelphia in 1814 and New York in 1817. Seton was a widow and a former Protestant who had been involved in charity and reform organizations before converting to Catholicism and expanding the educational and charitable work of Catholic women in the United States.[36] Women religious (nuns) established schools and provided free education for poor children as well as academies for families willing and able to pay tuition for what was perceived by even many Protestants as a superior educational alternative, especially for daughters. As one nun so confidently explained, even in the face of increased anti-Catholic sentiment by mid-century, Protestant "parents have to choose between the inferiority of the other schools and what they call the *superstition* of ours; but, as many prefer having their children well instructed, they send them to us. Our boarding school is the best in Indiana, and would be considered very good even in France."[37] By 1900, there were more than 3,800 parochial schools in the United States and 663 girls' academies, the teachers for all of which were primarily Catholic sisters.[38] The flood of Irish immigration in the pre–Civil War decades spurred the founding of numerous other convents to meet the needs of a growing American Catholic, primarily poor and working-class, population.

Besides convents and schools, American nuns also established and served in orphanages and hospitals. At a time when women were barred from the medical profession and nursing was not a regular organized profession for women, Catholic nuns ran more than 200 American hospitals, work that made them especially valuable during several mid-century cholera and yellow fever epidemics and during the Civil War.[39] It is estimated that more than 600 of the 3,200 volunteer Civil War nurses were Catholic sisters. Even non-Catholics had to praise this wartime service, as an 1861 *Chicago Tribune* article enthusiastically reported:

> The Sisters of Mercy have taken hold of the hospitals in Jefferson City as nurses for the sick there.... Pray permit me, Standing so far from these women in ecclesiastical and theological ideas, to testify to their beautiful, holy and unselfish devotions where I have found them in our hospitals.[40]

Despite their valuable social and humanitarian roles, nuns were sometimes in conflict not only with the male leadership of the Roman Catholic Church (from whom they received authorization and support), but also from the dominant American Protestant culture. The increased presence of Irish Catholics in the United States gave rise to *nativism,* a political and cultural movement of racial hatred against the Irish, and, more generally, against all things Catholic. Fears of a Catholic takeover of all American educational institutions, and rumors of Protestant girls being held captive in convents and forced to endure deprivations, or, worse, seduced by priests, led to a wave of attacks that resulted in the burning of at least 10 convents in the mid-nineteenth century.[41] Nevertheless, nuns represented a model of public female service and independence that was largely unavailable to most women, Catholic or non-Catholic. As Sister St. Francis Xavier reported, her Indiana convent received applications from many "good lad[ies]" who "would like to be Sisters, but have not yet decided to become Catholics."[42]

JEWISH WOMEN

The Jewish population in America was extremely small before the nine-teenth century, when significant numbers of German Jews began immi-grating at mid-century and even greater numbers of eastern European Jews at the very end of the century. A small community of close-knit families thrived in the colonial era, concentrated in cities such as New York; Provi-dence, Rhode Island; Richmond, Virginia; and Charleston, South Carolina; but it was not until the nineteenth century that the first rabbi came to the United States. Like their Christian counterparts, Jewish women's daily lives revolved around home, family, and religious tradition. In the nineteenth century, Jewish women took on broader public roles through charitable and reform work, often working with Christian women in the same or-ganizations. The Jewish community was especially concerned, given their small numbers, about the welfare and education of orphaned children, and organizations such as the Hebrew Orphan Society of Charleston, founded in 1801, were characteristic of Jewish women's efforts in the first half of the century.

Women immigrants at Ellis Island (ca 1900). Ellis Island opened as a national immigration processing center in 1892. Men and women would have been separated and given health examinations before admittance to the United States. (Library of Congress, Prints & Photo-graphs Division, LC-USZ62-26602.)

One of the best-known Jewish women of the early nineteenth century was Rebecca Gratz. Born in Philadelphia, Gratz never married but devoted her life to caring for her own siblings and their families. Gratz helped found several organizations committed to the causes of children, women, and the poor, including the Female Association for the Relief of Women and Children in Reduced Circumstances, founded in 1801 when Gratz was only 20 years old, the Female Hebrew Benevolent Society in 1819, and later, in the 1850s, the Jewish Foster Home and Orphanage. She also established the first Hebrew Sunday School in 1838, opening up a role for Jewish women as teachers, and inspiring the establishment of such schools across the United States through the end of the century. In 1858 Gratz explained the role that religious education had for Jewish children living as a religious minority in the United States:

> As Israelites in a Christian community, where our youth associate and compete with their fellow-citizens in all the branches of the arts and sciences, it is essential they should go provided with a knowledge of their own doctrines—that they should feel the requirements of their own peculiar faith, and by a steadfast, unobtrusive observance of them, claim the respect of others.[43]

Developments in European Judaism also affected the greater public role of Jewish women in America at mid-century. In 1846 a conference on Reformed Judaism issued recommendations for some radical changes in women's traditional status that spoke directly to their roles in religious practice and in the education of children. The reforms included, but were not limited to, mandates that women be included in services "from which they had traditionally been exempt," that women's religious vows "could not be invalidated by her husband or father," and that "the man's traditional morning prayer, thanking God that he had not been born a woman, was abolished."[44]

Eastern European Jews who migrated to the United States in the last decades of the nineteenth century were more orthodox, however, and were the least likely to accept such changes promoted by Reformed Judaism. Their large numbers meant that at least first-generation members of these later waves of immigration were able to recreate their communities within the United States and focus more on retaining traditional culture and religious beliefs than on assimilating to new American forms of Judaism. But new opportunities and ideas provided by American culture at large meant that younger Jewish women increasingly sought to expand their religious, social, and educational roles as well. (See also Chapter 4, "Education and the Professions.")

By the 1890s a new generation of Jewish women, daughters of immigrants, claimed identity as both Jews and as Americans. In 1893, as president of the Congress of Jewish Women, Hannah Solomon made it her mission to "gather together America's outstanding Jewish women," and she spoke to the generational differences that now divided the American Jewish community: "We are removed but one generation from those who in love, reverence, and fear obeyed every injunction . . . [and] To many of our generation the ceremonial and the holiday have lost their appeal." In assessing women's roles at the end of the century, Solomon, like many leaders of Christian women's groups in the 1890s, looked back upon the nineteenth century as one of steady progress and improvement for women, and one in which women's contributions, not only to their religious communities but to American society in general, were numerous and significant:

> We have established nine mission schools, reaching several thousand children who are being instructed in our religion and ethics. . . . Many women have been placed upon the school boards of Sabbath-schools through our efforts, and many Sabbath-schools have been established by our members in cities where no synagogues exist. . . . Our philanthropies take the form of industrial schools—sewing, manual training, kindergarten, crèche, summer outing and personal service. In addition several thousand dollars were raised for the army and navy. If the deed is the supreme test of religion, then does our faith, as exemplified in this branch of our work, reach the highest ideal.[45]

NOTES

1. Nancy F. Cott, *The Bonds of Womanhood: "Woman's Sphere" in New England, 1780–1835,* 2nd ed. (New Haven, Conn.: Yale University Press, 1997), p. 148.

2. See Ann Douglas, *The Feminization of American Culture* (New York: Knopf, 1977).

3. On women's roles in revivals, see Paul E. Johnson, *A Shopkeeper's Millennium: Society and Revivals in Rochester, New York, 1815–1837* (New York: Hill and Wang, 1978), chap. 5, "Pentecost"; quote on p. 108.

4. Susan Hill Lindley, *"You Have Stept Out of Your Place": A History of Women and Religion in America* (Louisville, Ky.: Westminster John Knox Press, 1996), p. 63.

5. Mary Ryan, *Cradle of the Middle Class: The Family in Oneida County, New York, 1790–1865* (New York: Cambridge University Press, 1981), p. 89.

6. Ryan, *Cradle of the Middle Class,* p. 98.

7. Catherine Clinton and Christine Lunardini, eds., *The Columbia Guide to American Women in the Nineteenth Century* (New York: Columbia University Press, 2000), p. 55.

8. Ryan, *Cradle of the Middle Class,* pp. 83–84.

9. Ryan, *Cradle of the Middle Class,* p. 86.

10. On Judson, see Lindley, *"You Have Stept Out of Your Place,"* p. 72.

11. Lindley, *"You Have Stept Out of Your Place,"* p. 79.

12. Margaret Hope Bacon, *Mothers of Feminism: The Story of Quaker Women in America* (New York: Harper, 1986), pp. 169–71.

13. Account of Narcissa Whitman from Michael Goldberg, "Breaking New Ground, 1800–1848," in *No Small Courage: A History of Women in the United States,* ed. Nancy F. Cott (New York: Oxford University Press, 2000), pp. 209–12; see also Julie Roy Jeffery, *Converting the West: A Biography of Narcissa Whitman* (Norman: University of Oklahoma Press, 1991).

14. Lindley, *"You Have Stept Out of Your Place,"* pp. 161–62.

15. S. J. Kleinberg, *Women in the United States, 1830–1945* (New Brunswick, N.J.: Rutgers University Press, 1999), pp. 135–36.

16. Theda Perdue, "Catharine Brown: Cherokee Convert to Christianity," in *Sifters: Native American Women's Lives,* ed. Theda Perdue (New York: Oxford University Press, 2001), pp. 77–91.

17. Jon Butler, *Awash in a Sea of Faith: Christianizing the American People* (Cambridge, Mass.: Harvard University Press, 1990), p. 281.

18. Palmer quoted in Marilyn Westerkamp, *Women and Religion in Early America, 1600–1850: The Puritan and Evangelical Traditions* (New York: Routledge, 1999), p. 153.

19. Palmer qtd. in *"You Have Stept Out of Your Place,"* p. 121.

20. Lee's text reprinted in William L. Andrews, ed., *Sisters of the Spirit: Three Black Women's Autobiographies of the Nineteenth Century* (Bloomington: Indiana University Press, 1986), quotes on pp. 35–36.

21. Elaw's text reprinted in Andrews, *Sisters of the Spirit,* quotes on pp. 61–63 and p. 82.

22. Gurney qtd. in *Women and Religion in Early America,* pp. 138–39.

23. For more on Eliza Gurney, see Bacon, *Mothers of Feminism,* p. 168.

24. Bacon, *Mothers of Feminism,* p. 175

25. Willard qtd. in *"You Have Stept Out of Your Place,"* p. 124.

26. Eddy qtd. in *"You Have Stept Out of Your Place,"* pp. 268–70; for an extensive recent treatment of Eddy, see Beryl Satter, *Each Mind a Kingdom: American Women, Sexual Purity, and the New Thought Movement, 1875–1920* (Berkeley: University of California Press, 2001).

27. Kathryn Kish Sklar, *Women's Rights Emerges within the Antislavery Movement, 1830–1870: A Brief History with Documents* (Boston: Bedford/St. Martin's, 2000), pp. 5–6.

28. "Pastoral Letter" reprinted in Sklar, *Women's Rights,* pp. 119–21.

29. "Seneca Falls Declaration of Sentiments and Resolutions" reprinted in *Through Women's Eyes: An American History with Documents,* 3rd ed., ed. Ellen Carol DuBois and Lynn Dumenil (Boston: Bedford/St. Martin's, 2005), pp. A18–A21.

30. On the founding of Shakerism, see Lawrence Foster, *Religion and Sexuality: The Shakers, the Mormons, and the Oneida Community* (Urbana: University of Illinois Press, 1984), especially chap. 2, "They Neither Marry nor Are Given in Marriage: The Origins and Development of Celibate Shaker Communities." On Lee's androgynous vision, see Rosemary Radford Ruether, "Women in Utopian Movements," in *Women and Religion in America: Vol. 1, The Nineteenth Century,* ed. Rosemary R. Ruether and Rosemary S. Keller (San Francisco: Harper and Row, 1981), pp. 46–53.

31. Anna White, *Shakerism* (1904), reprinted in Ruether and Keller, *Women and Religion,* p 64.

32. Whitney qtd. in *Religion and Sexuality,* p. 212.

33. Joseph Smith's "Revelation on the Eternity of the Marriage Contract" reprinted in Ruether and Keller, *Women and Religion,* pp. 69–70.

34. Lindley, *"You Have Stept Out of Your Place,"* p. 80.

35. Lindley, *"You Have Stept Out of Your Place,"* p. 197.

36. Goldberg, "Breaking New Ground," p. 206 and p. 214.

37. Nun qtd. in *Women and Religion,* p. 136; on convents and education, see also Lindley, *"You Have Stept Out of Your Place,"* pp. 217–19.

38. Mary Ewens, "The Leadership of Nuns in Immigrant Catholicism," in Ruether and Keller, *Women and Religion*, p. 101.

39. Ewens, "Leadership of Nuns," p. 102.

40. Lindley, "*You Have Stept Out of Your Place*," pp. 219–20.

41. Goldberg, "Breaking New Ground," pp. 206–7.

42. Sister St. Francis Xavier qtd. in *Women and Religion*, p. 137.

43. Information on Gratz in Lindley, "*You Have Stept Out of Your Place*," pp. 231–32.

44. Specific items of reform presented in Lindley, "*You Have Stept Out of Your Place*," pp. 233–34.

45. Hannah Solomon excerpted in Ruether and Kellers, *Women and Religion*, pp. 189–92.

SUGGESTED READING

Bacon, Margaret Hope. *Mothers of Feminism: The Story of Quaker Women in America.* New York: Harper, 1986.

Boylan, Ann M. *Sunday School: The Formation of an American Institution, 1790–1880.* New Haven, Conn.: Yale University Press, 1990.

Braude, Ann. *Radical Spirits: Spiritualism and Women's Rights in Nineteenth-Century America.* Bloomington: Indiana University Press, 2001.

Brekus, Catherine Anne. *Strangers and Pilgrims: Female Preaching in America, 1740–1845.* Chapel Hill: University of North Carolina Press, 1998.

Cott, Nancy F. *The Bonds of Womanhood: "Women's Sphere" in New England, 1780–1835,* 2nd ed. New Haven, Conn.: Yale University Press, 1997.

Douglas, Ann. *The Feminization of American Culture.* New York: Knopf, 1977.

Foster, Lawrence. *Religion and Sexuality: The Shakers, the Mormons, and the Oneida Community.* Urbana: University of Illinois Press, 1984.

Frey, Sylvia R., and Betty Wood. *Come Shouting to Zion: African-American Protestantism in the American South and British Caribbean to 1830.* Chapel Hill: University of North Carolina Press, 1998.

Gedge, Karin E. *Without Benefit of Clergy: Women and the Pastoral Relationship in Nineteenth-Century American Culture.* New York: Oxford University Press, 2003.

Grimshaw, Patricia. *Paths of Duty: American Missionary Wives in Nineteenth-Century Hawaii.* Honolulu: University of Hawaii Press, 1989.

Hill, Patricia. *The World Their Household: The American Woman's Foreign Missionary Movement and Cultural Transformation, 1870–1920.* Ann Arbor: University of Michigan Press, 1985.

Juster, Susan. *Disorderly Women: Sexual Politics and Evangelicalism in Revolutionary New England.* Ithaca, N.Y.: Cornell University Press, 1994.

Kern, Kathi. *Mrs. Stanton's Bible.* Ithaca, N.Y.: Cornell University Press, 2001.

Lindley, Susan Hill. "*You Have Stept Out of Your Place*": *A History of Women and Religion in America.* Louisville, Ky.: Westminster John Knox Press, 1996.

McMillen, Sally. *To Raise Up the South: Sunday Schools in Black and White Churches, 1865–1915.* Baton Rouge: Louisiana State University Press, 2001.

Westerkamp, Marilyn. *Women and Religion in Early America, 1600–1850: The Puritan and Evangelical Traditions.* New York: Routledge, 1999.

4

‍‌‌‌⌇‌‌‍

Education and the Professions

After the American Revolution, the traditional role of women as mothers was central to the educational goals of the new nation, as mothers were the first and primary educators of young children. In the nineteenth century, however, women took on new educational roles as students themselves and as schoolteachers. At the turn of the nineteenth century, the spread of public or common schools made it possible for more girls to attend school for the first time. As more girls entered school, the demand for women's continued education beyond the lower grades sparked the founding of the first all-female seminaries and then colleges in the first half of the nineteenth century. Even promoters of women's education, however, continued to emphasize that education should be in service to women's primary roles in the home. As reformer Catharine Beecher explained in her 1841 *A Treatise on Domestic Economy for the Use of Young Ladies at Home and at School,* "The proper education of a man decides the welfare of an individual; but educate a woman, and the interests of a whole family are secured."[1] Still, the nineteenth century saw women's roles shift from being the educated mothers of future citizens, to schoolteaching as a predominantly female occupation, to women's presence in the highest levels of university and professional education and administration.

Beginning in the 1790s, and into the first decades of the nineteenth century, a new emphasis was placed on education to impart new American cultural and political values to the next generation. Women had always been responsible for the moral and religious training of children in the home, but although they were denied their own rights at citizens in the creation of a new nation, women's roles as mothers took on new political meaning and their education became the subject of national debate. In 1790, Judith Sargent Murray, a prolific magazine essayist and New England intellectual, published an article, "On the Equality of the Sexes," in which she challenged the belief that there were inherent or natural intellectual differences between men and women. If there were such differences, Murray argued, it was only because of women's lack of education, and that woman, "an intellectual being," needed greater "ideas, than those which are suggested by the mechanism of a pudding, or the sewing of the seams of a garment[.]"[2] Murray was an early voice for a woman's right to an education as self-development, introducing what would become one of the main issues of the nineteenth-century women's rights movement.

The idea of "republican motherhood," that is, emphasizing women's role in educating children as future citizens, opened up the debate and the educational opportunities for white women, as the importance of education for women could no longer be denied.[3] Thomas Jefferson planned the studies of his own daughters according to the expectation that they would eventually fulfill adult roles as planter's wives. He explained that girls needed "a solid education which would enable them to become mothers to educate their own daughters & even to direct the course for sons should their fathers be lost or incapable or inattentive."[4] To this end, their daily schedule included French lessons, music, drawing, and reading literature and political theory, as well as instruction by their mother in housekeeping and needlework. Although Jefferson's daughters, like most young women of the late eighteenth and early nineteenth century, were educated at home, the new emphasis on the importance of women's education justified more formal training, and many "ladies' academies" were founded in the 1780s, 1790s, and early 1800s.

LADIES' ACADEMIES

Whereas boys needed education as career training, the primary goal for early nineteenth-century parents sending their daughters to female seminaries or academies was, as for someone like Jefferson, that education prepare young women for roles as wives and mothers. Young ladies' academies or seminaries offered high-school equivalent educations, but this training and legacy inspired the next generation to establish the first women's colleges with the goal of providing a more rigorous academic curriculum, similar or equal to that offered in men's colleges. Increasingly, middle- and upper-class parents sent their daughters as well as sons to school, expecting both academics and social training.

Many Northern women born at the turn of the nineteenth century attended seminaries and went on to become the generation of prominent teachers, writers, and reformers of the mid-century, although some of the most important intellectuals of that generation, such as Elizabeth Cady Stanton or Margaret Fuller, still had no formal education but received rigorous educations at home from their fathers. For white middle-class women born in the next generation of the 1810s and 1820s and beyond, however, educational options increased greatly as the century progressed. Seminaries gradually expanded their curriculum and higher-level women's colleges were established to match the more rigorous academics of men's colleges.

Before the Civil War, women's higher education meant high-school level educations at one of hundreds of women's-only seminaries established before 1860. Beneficiaries of such educations, some women in the first decades of the nineteenth century took a central role in expanding the justifications and the opportunities for women's education by founding their own schools. Tutored primarily at home, Emma Hart Willard became a teacher at age 15, and, even after her marriage, ran a boarding school in her home. She sought to continue her own education by studying the college textbooks of her nephew and resolved that women should have access to the same information and knowledge. Willard sought public acceptance and funding for her educational plan, and to that end, in 1818 self-published "An Address to the Public, Particularly to Members of the Legislature of New York, Proposing a Plan for Improving Female Education." The state legislature rejected her proposal, but when the merchant city of Troy offered free land for her to build a school, Willard moved her family there and founded her school in 1821.[5]

The ripple effect of a Troy education was felt throughout the coming decades as graduates of Willard's school went on to found and teach at other institutions. Mary Lyon, a student at Troy, established Mount Holyoke in Massachusetts in 1837, which, in turn, became the model for other schools and for an expanded curriculum for women. Many Troy graduates went on to become teachers in New England and beyond. Graduate Urania Sheldon became head of the Utica Female Academy in New York, but Troy women also created schools and spread their influence farther south, such as Caroline Livy, who established an academy in Rome, Georgia, and Almira Lincoln Phelps, whose Patapsco Female Institute in Maryland, a border state, was attended by many Southern women.[6]

Although historians seem to pay the most attention to the important role of these early female seminaries and academies in the Northeast, by 1860 the South had actually established more women's colleges than the North. All Southern states except Florida had at least one women's college before the Civil War, and most states had several. In North Carolina, there were more women's colleges than men's, and the women's schools established between 1830 and 1860 throughout the South were committed from their beginnings to offering female students a rigorous education comparable to men's. Before Radcliffe College became the model for a women's adjunct to Harvard University much later in the century, the Alabama Female Institute had arranged by the 1830s for students to take courses at the all-male University of Alabama. The Georgia Female College, now known as Wesleyan University, was established in 1836 and is considered to be the first full-course women's college. In the early 1840s, the college advertised that "the object of the founders of the College was to give our daughters as good a disciplinary education as was offered by the best colleges for our sons."[7]

Others were inspired by the model of female academies and colleges to found schools to meet their own community needs and goals. The Cherokee people had pursued a strategy of assimilation into white society, a strategy that did not shield them from involuntary removal from the Southeast by the U.S. government in the 1830s. That strategy meant that many Cherokee families had integrated themselves into white society in the first half of the nineteenth century and had achieved a certain economic and educational level. The Cherokee Female Seminary was opened in 1851 and run by educated and middle-class mixed-blood tribal members. The school prided itself on offering a "white" education well into the twentieth century and students compared their school with white seminaries in the Northeast. As a student named Edith explained in the student paper, the *Cherokee Rose Buds* in 1854, "the taste, refinement, and progress of civilization" now shown by the Cherokee people was because of such educational advancements.[8]

EDUCATION REFORMERS

The spread of female academies and seminaries had a society-wide impact on women's roles. Because of women's expanded education, by 1840 female literacy in New England had reached nearly 100 percent, compared to around 50 percent at the time of the American Revolution.[9] However, even some of the most vocal proponents of women's education, such as Sarah Josepha Hale, whose own daughters attended Emma Willard's Troy Female Seminary, believed that "we should solicit education as a favor, not exact it as a right."[10] As more women received an education, however, they were subsequently more likely to reach outside their "sphere" of influence, to marry later, or to forego marriage and motherhood altogether in favor of public careers as teachers or reformers. A study of Mount Holyoke College during its early years found that the median age of marriage for graduates was 26, compared to 21 among the population at large, and that as many as 19 percent of graduates never married at all.[11] As the century progressed and educated women began to see expanded roles for themselves, many began to demand and expect education as a right, not as a favor granted to potential mothers.

Early female academies and colleges created the first generation of formally educated young women, women with expanded expectations about

Female graduates of Oberlin College, Ohio (1855). Oberlin was the first four-year college to admit both women and men as well as black and white students. At the time this young black woman posed with her white classmates, the United States was embroiled in the heated debates over slavery that would lead to the Civil War in just a few years. (Oberlin College Archives.)

their duties not only to their families, but to society at large. This was reflected in Mount Holyoke's stated mission in 1839 of educating women for the "great task of renovating the world." The era of radical social and political reform also resulted in the founding of the first coeducational (both men and women) and first interracial classes offered at Oberlin College in Ohio beginning in 1833. Although this was a new opportunity for white women and for African Americans, the college maintained a separate curriculum for men and women. A "Female Department" employed women teachers and administrators (most of whom were trained at female seminaries and academies on the East Coast) to oversee a more literary, less rigorous, course of study for early women students. Even after the program was expanded to provide equal undergraduate educations for men and women, women were prevented from entering graduate and professional study programs. Still, by 1860, Oberlin College had produced more than 300 women graduates with bachelor's degrees, inspiring other institutions to either go coeducational or to establish women's full-course colleges.[12]

By the 1850s, gaining access to education and to the professions were major issues for the emerging women's rights movement. After the Civil

War, educational reformers and women's rights activists had moved beyond arguing for women's need for an education in order to fulfill their roles as mothers and teachers, and explicitly connected the issues of education to women's pursuit of a vocation, or profession. In her 1867 text, *The College, the Market, and the Court; or, Woman's Relation to Education, Labor, and Law*, Caroline Dall argued that it was not enough for reformers to focus on women's presence in "facilities of school education," when women were then systematically excluded from entering the professions and putting those educations to any practical use. In an 1849 essay titled "Reforms," Dall had outlined women's need for "a finished education" and "a livelihood" as two main issues of the emerging women's right movement.

As with many reformers, Dall's reform agenda arose from the obstacles she faced in her own life, for even though Dall was a white middle-class woman from Boston, unlike many of her generation she had not had "a finished education." Additionally, like most women throughout the century regardless of their education, she was prevented from pursuing the "livelihood" of her choice. Dall was a student of theology and history and had hoped to become a minister, but even in her liberal Christian church, women were not allowed to be regular preachers. In *The College, the Market, and the Court,* Caroline Dall reminded readers that although women had greater access to education than at any time throughout history, "The right to education . . . *involves* the right to a choice of vocation; that is, the right to a choice of the end to which those faculties shall be trained."[13]

WHITE WOMEN AS TEACHERS

Schoolteaching became one of the few employments open for young women with education, and many of the nineteenth-century's most prominent reformers and writers began their careers as teachers or private tutors. The effect of educating more girls and young women at seminaries and colleges, and simultaneously limiting or closing off their access to other professions, was that a pool of educated, eager, and available young teachers was created just as the number of students attending school necessitated their services. Although the male schoolteacher was most common in the first half of the century, by the 1860s, teaching had become fully recognized as a female profession. In Massachusetts, for example, where the common school movement spread to provide schools in even remote rural locations and female seminaries dotted the landscape, as many as one-quarter of native-born white women worked as teachers before the Civil War. Their presence in the profession continued to increase so that, by the 1870s, nearly three-quarters of the teachers in New England were female.[14]

"The New School-Mistress," *Harper's Weekly* (September 20, 1873). In the early 1800s, the typical schoolteacher (as well as the typical student) would have been male. By midcentury, however, teaching school was a predominantly female occupation and seen as an extension of women's maternal role. (Library of Congress, Prints & Photographs Division, LC-USZ62-104627.)

Some reformers continued to argue that education could support, rather than undermine, women's traditional roles. Reformer Catharine Beecher's greatest influence was, somewhat paradoxically, as promoter of both women's education and domesticity. She founded the Hartford Female Seminary in 1823 and went on to write numerous articles, and the full-length *A Treatise on Domestic Economy* (1841), on women's proper roles as wives and mothers. Beecher argued that the fulfillment of those roles began with a proper education and that American women had a duty to receive an education so that they could become responsible teachers of the young, whether as mothers or as schoolteachers. She focused not only on women's role as mothers, however, but also advocated teaching as a "true and noble" profession for single women and encouraged women to leave factory work and pursue teaching instead. As she wrote to a friend in 1830, at a time when the female schoolteacher was not yet the norm, "To enlighten the understanding and to gain the affections is a teacher's business . . . is not *woman* best fitted to accomplish these important objects?"[15]

Even as more women became available as teachers, and even as some reformers were emphasizing teaching as an extension of women's maternal role, school districts were sometimes reluctant to hire a woman for what was perceived as a man's job, especially where most of the students were boys. In this case, it was not the intellectual but the physical differences between men and women that were emphasized. It was believed that male teachers could hold better discipline over male students; as one superintendent explained, a woman should not be a teacher "for the same reason that she cannot so well manage a vicious horse or other animal, as a man might do."[16]

Even if they were hired, women teachers faced extreme pay discrimination, even for the same jobs. In Connecticut in the mid-1830s, male teachers received a salary of $14.50 per month, compared to the $5.75 per month received by their female colleagues.[17] Civil War nurse and founder of the American Red Cross Clara Barton had begun her career as a teacher. Barton was not against women volunteering their services without pay, but as a schoolteacher, she declared that "I may sometimes be willing to teach for nothing, but if paid at all, I shall never do a man's work for less than a man's pay."[18]

Many women bypassed the common schools and founded their own schools for girls or taught privately in their homes. Either way, women forced their way into the profession and by 1870, the tables had turned and a child's teacher was just as (or more) likely to be female than male. By that date, women made up more than half of the nearly 200,000 schoolteachers in the United States. Even male officials had eventually been won over by the argument that women were, in fact, better suited as teachers as they were "the natural guardians of the young," as explained by Governor William Seward of New York.[19] Thus, by the end of the century, schoolteaching came to be dominated by women, with the same justification that it was suited to their particular natures and roles as with other occupations, such as textile mill work, social reform work and, later, nursing. Women initially encountered opposition to pursuing any occupation that took them out of the home, but each of these eventually came to be seen as primarily "women's work."

Gaining an education and finding regular employment were merely the first challenges facing schoolteachers, however. Although in the urban Northeast schoolteaching soon constituted a distinct professional class among white middle-class women, in rural and frontier areas the job posed unique challenges. Many teachers in the South had been trained in the Northeast, as even educated Southern white women did not find it acceptable to pursue paid work, in particular, teaching. North Carolina had more female teachers than any other region in the South, yet only 8 percent of its teachers were women, compared to women's ever-increasing dominance in the schools of New England.[20] In the sparsely populated and underfunded regions of the South, Midwest, and West, the one-room schoolhouse might have to suffice for up to 60 students to one teacher. The challenge of disciplining, much less teaching, that many students of widely varying ages was one that many teachers commented upon.

Teachers recruited to remote areas usually boarded with families of their students, leaving some teachers vulnerable to being taken advantage of for other services. Mahala Drake of Iowa reported back to her own family that, after teaching all day, her landlords expected that she would help with household chores, such as sewing or childcare. Elizabeth Blackwell taught in Kentucky, and, in addition to harsh conditions in her schoolroom, she did not have a private room in the house she lived in but was expected to share a bedroom with several other family members.[21] (See also Chapter 7, "The West.")

The need for teachers in the developing West coincided with the increased competition for jobs among educated women in the Northeast who were looking to be of use in the world. Catharine Beecher was the founder of the National Popular Education Board, whose goal was to send teachers trained at East Coast schools, such as Mount Holyoke in Massachusetts and Burlington Female Seminary in Vermont, to Western towns in need of teachers and schools. Beecher was concerned about children on the frontier not having the same access to a common school education that was quickly becoming the standard throughout the East. Worse, in some places, the only schools were those operated by Catholic nuns, so Beecher and others sought to increase the Protestant influence in those areas. (See also Chapter 3, "Religion.") Sarah Josepha Hale promoted the mission of the National Popular Education Board in her *Godey's Lady's Book* in the gold rush year of 1849, pointing out that "the gold will prove a curse and not a blessing" to the West and the nation if American children are not properly educated.[22] Young women themselves were drawn in by this almost missionary appeal to teachers but also by the need for employment.

BLACK WOMEN AS STUDENTS AND TEACHERS

A more democratic vision of education meant that not only women, but nonelites, the poor, immigrants, and African Americans all eventually benefited from the spread of educational options in the early nineteenth century, although in an uneven manner. By the 1850s, nearly 75 percent of white children in the North attended some school, compared to less than one-third of white children in the South.[23] The spread of the common school movement was hampered in the South, in part, because of the wide geographical distance between communities and plantations, and many white children continued to be tutored at home. In the black community, access to education was a different kind of struggle, as the education of blacks was strictly forbidden in the South before the Civil War, and racism in the North posed a barrier to the education of even free black children. Both black and white women reformers and teachers fought to expand educational opportunities for black children as well as adults throughout the nineteenth century.

In the pre–Civil War South, slaves were prevented by custom and by law from acquiring the basic tools of literacy, much less receiving a full education. Former slave Hannah Crasson remembered how reading or even possessing books was a serious offense on her white master's plantation: "The white folks did not allow us to have nothing to do with books. You better not be found trying to learn to read. Our marster was harder down on that than anything else. You better not be catched with a book."[24] Ellen Betts, a former slave from Louisiana, shared a similar experience about her master's attitude toward slave learning: "If Marse catch a paper in your hand he sure whip you. . . . Marse don't allow no bright niggers around. If they act bright he sure sell them quick. He always say: 'Book learning don't raise no good sugarcane.'"[25] In this case, Betts's master made clear that education interfered with the economic productivity of his plantation, whether it be in terms of slaves spending time reading, or, more likely, the fear that literacy and knowledge could lead to resistance and even attempted escapes.

Such fears were, in fact, grounded in reality, as more than a few slaves found ways around the prohibition and either learned from other slaves, or, sometimes, even from whites. Although slaves faced extreme physical punishment or the emotional punishment of being sold away from their families, whites who taught slaves to read might be prosecuted criminally by white courts. A white woman, Margaret Douglass, was found guilty by a Virginia court of teaching a young slave girl "to read the Bible," defined by the court as "one of the vilest crimes that ever disgraced society."[26] (See also Chapter 6, "Slavery and the Civil War.")

The first schools for free African Americans in the North were established in the 1790s. Former slave Catherine Ferguson opened her School for the Poor in New York in 1793 and had both black and white students. Schools founded by black educators and reformers were more likely to be interracial as well as to teach boys and girls together, so that black women did not have their own separate academies to the same extent as white women of the same generations did. Only large cities were able to establish and maintain separate black schools. Segregation and inferior resources led some middle-class black families in cities to educate their children at home or open their own private schools. In Cincinnati, Ohio, the public schools did not admit black students, but in 1832 black and white abolitionists worked together to establish a school where white women taught classes attended by black children and adult women.[27]

A young, free black woman named Sarah Harris was emboldened to apply to a white school in Canterbury, Connecticut, in the early 1830s. The teacher, Prudence Crandall, was a white antislavery Quaker who recalled that Harris was "a colored girl of respectability" who clearly stated her case: "'Miss Crandall, I want to get a little more learning, enough if possible to teach colored children, and if you will admit me to your school, I shall be under the greatest obligation to you.'" Sarah continued politely, however, that she would "'not insist on the favor.'"

Sarah Harris's family had ties to the abolitionist community, and she had already attended an integrated public school with some of the white girls who had gone on to Crandall's academy. Crandall admitted Harris to the school, but after receiving threats from a local women's group, and perhaps sensing a greater social point to be made, Crandall went further and specifically recruited more black students by placing an ad in the radical abolitionist paper, the *Liberator,* for a school "for young Ladies and little Misses of color." The larger community, however, was not ready for such change in black women's educational or social roles. The *Norwich Republican* newspaper charged that Crandall was attempting "to foist upon the community a new species of gentility, in the shape of sable belles . . . to cook up a palatable morsel for our white bachelors. . . . In a word, they hope to force the two races to amalgamate." The entire town rose up against the school and eventually the harassment, the attacks on the school building, and fear for the safety of the students all forced the school to close in 1834. The original black student, Sarah Harris, did ultimately realize her goal of securing an education and becoming a teacher.[28]

As with middle-class white women, teaching became one of the most significant employments of free black women in the North before the Civil War. Black women as teachers was a challenge to the idea that African Americans in general were not capable of education. Because of such beliefs, free black women had to struggle not only for their own education, but in deciding to become teachers, they committed themselves to the struggle for the education of the entire race. Despite racism and segregation in the North and the outright prohibition against educating blacks in the South, committed women created opportunities to teach black children.

In slaveholding areas, teachers took great risks in running schools, sometimes doing so secretly. Catharine Deveaux hid her school for the children of friends and neighbors in Savannah, Georgia, from the white community for 27 years. Between 1828 and 1831, Ann Marie Becroft ran a school for black girls in Washington, D.C., that was sponsored by the Catholic Church before becoming a nun herself, the Catholic Church being one of the primary providers of education for poor, immigrant, and black children.[29] (See also Chapter 3, "Religion.")

The commitment of black teachers to educating the race continued through the century, for even after freedom was secured with the end of the Civil War, the education of African American children remained a struggle against racism and poverty well past the end of the nineteenth century. Because slaves were not allowed to read or write, most freedpeople at the close of the Civil War were illiterate. Education was one of the first goals for the newly freed people and one pursued vigorously by former slaves. Both black and white women assisted in this effort in the last decades of the century by working as teachers in Southern schools for black children, their efforts resulting in nearly 9,000 teachers being sent to the South and some 600,000 African Americans enrolled in schools by 1870.[30] Black women trained in Northern schools who went south to teach during the war usually followed alongside or not far behind Union troops, and, therefore, even before the war had ended, there were numerous schools established throughout the Southern states.

Although many Northern white women came south during the Civil War and Reconstruction periods, many blacks preferred that teachers be recruited from within their own community. Former slave Harriet Jacobs, best known for the 1861 publication of her autobiography detailing her own escape from slavery, *Incidents in the Life of a Slave Girl,* spent time working in Union camps to help slave refugees with medical care, raising money for clothing and supplies, and reporting to Northern abolitionist papers on conditions in Southern camps. At one freedmen's school, Jacobs was involved in insisting that black teachers be hired. She explained that she did not "object to white teachers but I think it has a good effect upon these people to convince them their own race can do something for their elevation. It inspires them with confidence to help each other."[31]

One of the most famous and well-recorded wartime educational and social experiments was the Port Royal Experiment in the South Carolina Sea Islands, where Southern slaveholders fled their homes and deserted their plantations in 1862. In an effort to save the crops and to employ the thousands of former slaves who remained, the federal government took over the area, and, among other projects, recruited Northern teachers to establish schools for black children and adults. Among the first to arrive was Charlotte Forten, a free black from Philadelphia who already held the distinction of being the first black teacher of white children in Salem, Massachusetts, where she had also been active in the antislavery movement.

Forten and two other Philadelphians, white teachers Laura Towne and Ellen Murray, taught a full academic course to nearly 100 children on the Sea Islands during the day, and basic literacy skills to working adults in the evenings. Forten remembered that the children "listened very attentively," and she felt her presence there provided more than just academics, believing "it is well that they sh'ld know what one of their color c'ld do for his race. I long to inspire them with courage and ambition (of a noble sort), and high purpose." She sought to inspire them with lessons in black history, but, undoubtedly, it was Forten's very presence that modeled the "courage and ambition (of a noble sort)" she desired for her students. Charlotte Forten published several essays titled "Life on the Sea Islands" in the *Atlantic Monthly* in 1864, telling of her success and further promoting the idea that freedpeople needed and were capable of education.[32]

Black teachers became pillars of the community, not only because of their work in the classroom, but also because they were educated members of the community who could serve as mentors and advisors for freedpeople trying to build new lives. There was a downside, however, to being a visible and successful member of the community, for in providing a service that many Southern whites felt blacks were not entitled to, teachers and their schools were sometimes subject to intimidation and violence. This was in addition to the difficult working conditions, decrepit buildings, lack of textbooks, and low pay. The special need and calling of African American teachers, however, was addressed in Fanny Jackson Coppin's 1879 address to a graduating class of future teachers: "You can do much to alleviate the condition of our people. Do not be discouraged. The very places where you are needed most are those where you will get least pay. Do not resign a position in the South which pays you $12 a month as a teacher for one in Pennsylvania which pays $50."[33]

WOMEN'S HIGHER EDUCATION AFTER THE CIVIL WAR

The education of African Americans in the South required the training of more black teachers and by 1868, already 15 colleges had been established just for that purpose. Educational opportunities for both black and white women were greatly expanded after the Civil War, and followed the pattern of westward expansion and population growth. In the last decades of the nineteenth century, there was a proliferation of "normal" schools or colleges that specifically trained teachers and therefore attracted a large number of female students. In the 1860s and 1870s, the educational commitment of the federal government focused not only on the South, but on the new land-grant colleges of the Midwest and Far West as well. The spread of public colleges and teacher training schools had an enormous impact on the upward mobility of all women—black, white, Native American, and immigrant women alike.

Between the 1860s and the 1880s, the women's colleges later referred to as the "Seven Sisters" were all founded or expanded their programs to offer bachelor's degrees: Vassar in New York (founded in 1861); Wellesley in Massachusetts (founded in 1870); Smith in Massachusetts (founded in 1871); Radcliffe in Massachusetts (founded in 1879); Bryn Mawr in Pennsylvania (founded in 1885); Mount Holyoke in Massachusetts (founded in 1837 but expanded as a full college in 1888); and Barnard in New York (founded in 1889). New coeducational schools were also established, such as Boston

University in 1873. This explosion of higher education options for women in the Northeast coincided with the establishment of numerous coeducational federal "land-grant" colleges in the late nineteenth century. Colleges founded in Midwestern and Western areas such as Illinois, Nebraska, Minnesota, Kansas, and California began to admit female students beginning in the 1860s and 1870s. Because of the coeducational land-grant colleges and the founding of numerous all-female colleges, by the end of the century, women made up 40 percent of the total college graduates in the United States.

Although the sex-segregated colleges of the East assured some critics of women's higher education that at least neither men nor women would be morally or academically compromised by attending classes with members of the opposite sex, some continued to protest the potential costs of women's education. Many simply believed that women were not capable of completing the same course of studies that men did. Once it became apparent that they were capable, some critics expressed concerns that women's health, even their ability to become mothers, could be compromised by their intellectual work. Several members of the medical profession, including most famously Dr. Edward Clarke, who published a treatise titled *Sex in Education; or a Fair Chance for the Girls* in 1873, argued that intellectual work drained women of their reproductive energies. The controversy created by critics of women's higher education had a direct impact on women's own sense of their capabilities and of the prudence of pursuing an education. Reformer M. Carey Thomas, an 1877 graduate of the coeducational Cornell University in New York, later reflected, "We did not know when we began whether women's health could stand the strain of education. We were haunted in those days by the clanging chains of that gloomy specter, Dr. Edward Clarke's *Sex in Education.*"[34] Women writers, reformers, and physicians responded to Clarke's work by pointing out that if such critics were truly concerned with women's bodies, they should consider that the real culprit was lack of attention to women's overall health and diseases, not education. Some colleges responded by paying particular attention to women's physical education, instituting women's sports and health education into their curricula to ensure that college women remained physically strong enough to pursue their later roles as wives and mothers.[35]

After the Civil War, the education of black women began in earnest, as it had earlier with white women, through female seminaries and teacher training schools and then, finally, in regular colleges and universities. The Atlanta Baptist Female Seminary was founded in 1881 and later became Spelman College. Like earlier seminaries for white women, such schools initially provided what amounted to a high-school level education or a specific teacher training curriculum. Other full-course colleges and universities eventually opened their doors to women, such as Howard University,

Four young women at Atlanta University (1899). Educational opportunities for African American women expanded greatly after the Civil War with the founding of schools such as Atlanta University, an important training school for black teachers and librarians. (Library of Congress, Prints & Photographs Division, LC-USZ62-114272.)

which was established in Washington, D.C., in 1867, but did not graduate its first woman with a B.A. degree until 1901. The majority of the relatively small number of African Americans who received bachelor's degrees by 1900 graduated from already established integrated schools, such as Oberlin College in Ohio, which alone accounted for a full one-quarter of the undergraduate degrees held by black women in the nineteenth century.

By the end of the century, the reinstitution of white supremacy as well as sheer economic necessity meant that most all-black colleges focused more on vocational training and less on academics. The Hampton Institute, founded in Virginia just a few years after the Civil War, provided teacher training as well as other vocational courses. The school was a revolutionary experiment and opened its doors not only to African Americans, but to Native Americans as well beginning in 1878. Omaha Indian Susan La Flesche attended Hampton before going on to graduate from medical college and become the first Native American woman doctor.

Many African Americans migrated west after the Civil War, escaping Jim Crow laws and the violence and intimidation of the Ku Klux Klan. Black teachers established schools to minister to the needs of children on the frontier, and, in these new towns, sometimes black schools were the first or even the only educational institutions. More than 50,000 blacks migrated into Kansas alone in the 1870s and 1880s, and, in towns like Nicodemus, children worked on farms most of the year but were able to attend school in the winter and study, where teacher Francis Fletcher taught them "arithmetic, literature, moral values, and hygiene," using books donated by a former slave.[36]

By the end of the century, middle-class black women became active as race reformers, and the education of the children, rather than adult women, was at the center of their concerns. For the black women's club movement, education was an issue arising from the needs of their own communities; they not only promoted new schools, but investigated existing schools for black children and reported on changes needed in facilities, black teacher's salaries, and on the problems with segregated and unequal higher education. By the 1890s reformers were working to create after-school care programs, playgrounds, and vacation schools, all issues to accommodate working mothers, who were a given in most black communities. (See also Chapter 2, "Work.")

Just as the general population spread west, so did education; while reformers such as Catharine Beecher emphasized the role of women as teachers sent to establish schools for white and black children, other educational reformers and missionaries focused on the education of Native American children for futures as U.S. citizens. Religious organizations set up boarding schools, often run and taught by white women, separating Native American children from their families and cultures, teaching them English and Christianity as well as academics. Zitkala-Sa (later known as Gertrude Simmons Bonnin) was born in 1872 on a Sioux Indian reservation in South Dakota to a Native American mother and a white father, who abandoned the family before her birth. When she was eight years old, Quaker missionaries came to the reservation to persuade Sioux parents to send their children to boarding school. Zitkala-Sa recalled how, as a child, she felt this would be a great adventure, and, against her mother's wishes, she left to attend school in Indiana, where she learned English as well as the ways of white Americans. She later attended college and became a teacher herself at an Indian school in Pennsylvania, an experience that prompted her eventual criticism of such efforts and that she wrote about in her 1900 essay, "An Indian Teacher among Indians."[37]

The 1862 Morrill Act set aside land for territories and new states to build public educational institutions. Territorial citizens were more likely to send daughters as well as sons to such schools, which usually specialized in vocational, agricultural, and, for women, domestic science programs, more so than liberal arts. These programs were more suited to the economic roles of people in the agricultural West, where men could

"Educating the Indians—A Female Pupil of the Government School at Carlisle Visits Her Home at the Pine Ridge Agency," *Frank Leslie's Illustrated Newspaper* (March 15, 1884). The lives of Native Americans in the nineteenth century were dramatically changed by education, by Christianity, and by the reservation system. The young woman in this image returns to the reservation not only educated but also "Americanized," as evidenced by the style of her dress. (Library of Congress, Prints & Photographs Division, LC-USZ62-100543.)

learn to be farmers and women could learn to be farm wives. Like earlier reformers who emphasized that women's education could and should assist them in the fulfillment of family roles, professors of home economics, such as Lou Allen Gregory at Illinois Industrial University, argued that college courses for women "must recognize their distinctive duties as women—the mothers, housekeepers and health keepers of the world—and furnish instruction which shall fit them to meet these duties."[38]

EDUCATION OF IMMIGRANT WOMEN

Whereas education was a route to the professions for white women, and a symbol of freedom and route to upward mobility for black women, it was also a means of "Americanization" for immigrant children and women in the last decades of the nineteenth century. Between 1880 and 1902, millions of new immigrant groups, southern and eastern Europeans, most of them Jews or Catholics, came to the United States seeking a better life. Many of them encouraged the education of sons, but eventually, daughters as well were able to take advantage of new opportunities and new roles for women in America. Russian-Jewish immigrant Mary Antin recalled how important education was to her father, and to her, and the special role that female teachers as mentors played in her life. She remembered her early school days in her autobiography, *The Promised Land,* published in 1912:

> My half-hours with Miss Dillingham were full of delight for me, quite apart from my new-born ambition to become a writer. What, then, was my joy, when Miss Dillingham, just before locking up her desk one evening, presented me with a volume of Longfellow's poems! It was a thin volume of selections, but to me it was a bottomless treasure. I had never owned a book before. . . . And so Miss Dillingham, who was my first American friend, and who first put my name in print, was also the one to start my library.

She went on to explain how her perception of herself and of women's roles was changing because of her education:

> About the middle of the year I was promoted to the grammar school. Then it was that I walked on air. For I said to myself that I was a *student* now, in earnest, not merely a school-girl learning to spell and cipher. I was going to learn out-of-the-way things, things that had nothing to do with ordinary life—things to *know*.[39]

The Irish had begun immigrating to the United States in large numbers in the 1840s, and their numbers continued to increase. By the end of the century, however, the second generation and second wave of Irish women were able to escape menial work as domestic servants (an occupation held primarily by black women after the Civil War) and factory workers (positions now filled by the new European immigrants) and acquire an education, first in the Catholic school movement that spread throughout the Eastern United States and then to college for training as teachers or nurses, following similar patterns as native-born white women. (See also Chapter 2, "Work.")

But it was the rare daughter of an immigrant family who had access to a formal college education before the end of the nineteenth century. It was in the first two decades of the twentieth century that their numbers began to swell and second-and even third-generation women achieved upward mobility through education. By 1907 Boston University welcomed applications from the "newer elements in the population" and by 1911, nearly 24 percent of American female college students were the daughters of immigrants, compared with black women who by that time were just 0.3 percent of female college students.[40] At the turn of the century, however, the typical female college student was a native-born Protestant white woman, leading some critics to warn of "race suicide" as America's immigrant population swelled by the millions and native-born white women were delaying (or foregoing altogether) marriage and motherhood in pursuit of education and careers.

One of those possible careers soon became, ironically, the education of poor immigrant and black women and children. In 1889 reformer Jane Addams assembled some of her other college-educated women friends and opened the first settlement house in Chicago to serve the poor Italian community there. The white reformers at Hull House offered courses on academic subjects such as history, literature, and English to the local immigrant community, as well as classes on domestic topics such as American-style cooking, housekeeping, infant care, and sewing. Undoubtedly, the intentions of reformers were to assist poor families in meeting some of their basic needs, and, in the case of immigrants, facilitating their assimilation into American culture through education, but that education was focused primarily on immigrant women's roles as mothers.[41]

WOMEN AND THE PROFESSIONS

By the 1870s, Northern women's access to higher education extended to include the establishment of the first all-female universities, but also to the opening of other schools to female students. Turn-of-the-century white women reformers were more likely to be college graduates than their counterparts of earlier generations and than black women at any time. Whereas the justification for women's education in the early 1800s was to make them better wives and mothers, by the end of the century, female college graduates were the most likely to avoid women's traditional roles in marriage and motherhood. Although more and more women were either postponing or forgoing marriage altogether, they found few public roles open to them to which they could apply their educations and earn an independent livelihood. (See also Chapter 2, "Work.") Jane Addams, in founding Hull House, created a vocation for herself and several of her contemporaries, and, in general, paved the way for social work to develop as a female-dominated profession in the twentieth century.

Colleges and universities provided opportunities for women not only as students, but as teachers and administrators as well. Alice Freeman had been one of the first female graduates of the University of Michigan and became the first woman college president in the United States in 1882, when she became president of Wellesley College, a position she resigned, however, in 1888 after her marriage to Harvard professor George Palmer. She returned to the University of Michigan in the 1890s as dean of women.[42] Women also took a greater role in the last decades of the century in influencing issues of pedagogy, not only related to the higher education of women, but to children's education as well. Elizabeth Palmer Peabody, born in 1804, was a generation too early for full access to women's colleges or to the professions. She was rigorously educated at home and was a self-taught student of theology who was excluded from the profession of her choice, the ministry. In her early career, the never-married Peabody turned to one of the few occupations available to a woman of her social class and level of education by founding and teaching in private schools. After the Civil War, Peabody's interest in education and her reform spirit led her to focus especially on improving the education of young children. She was responsible for establishing the first American kindergarten in 1860, based on her readings in German educational philosophy.[43]

Besides the ministry, in which women made relatively few gains (see also Chapter 3, "Religion"), two professions that educated women pursued with great energy and some success in the nineteenth century were the law and medicine. In these fields, in particular, the 1870s and 1880s saw several "firsts" for women. Women's entrances into these male strongholds in the nineteenth century were still minimal, but paved the way for continued struggles well into the twentieth century regarding access to education and professional recognition.

In 1868, Myra Bradwell founded the *Chicago Legal News* and began writing a regular column for the paper on "Law Relating to Women." Bradwell advocated the vote for women and provided news on and advertisements for working female lawyers, most of whom practiced without being admitted to the bar or even possessing a law degree. The first woman to receive a law degree in the United States was Ada Kepley, who graduated from the Union College of Law (now Northwestern University) in Chicago in 1870, and that same year, the first woman judge was appointed, Esther McQuigg Morris, also in the West, in a small town in Wyoming. Despite these individual stories, at the end of the century women were still denied admission to law schools; in 1898, two women, Ellen Spencer Mussey and Emma Gillett, founded the Washington (D.C.) College of Law (now part of American University), specifically to train female students who might be denied admission elsewhere.

Access to education was the first hurdle and professional certification the next. The same year she began her paper, Myra Bradwell herself applied to, but was rejected by, the Illinois Bar. Bradwell was rejected because she was a woman, but probably also because she was married. Strides were slowly being made, however, primarily owing to the efforts of Bradwell and other women who did not give up pushing for admittance to law schools and the bar. After being denied admittance to the state bar, Bradwell brought a lawsuit against Illinois, in which the U.S. Supreme Court in 1873 upheld a state's right to deny women professional status as bar-certified lawyers. But at the state level, another young female lawyer, Alta M. Hulett, drafted a bill in 1872 forbidding general employment discrimination based on sex, a bill approved by the Illinois legislature, thus opening the way for Hulett herself to become the first woman to join the Illinois bar.

During the 1870s, African American women also made their first strides into the legal profession. In 1872 Charlotte Ray, a graduate of Howard University, was the first woman to join the bar in Washington, D.C. Receiving an education and professional accreditation were only the first steps, however. Being able to practice the profession was another struggle, especially for a black woman, and Ray eventually gave up her practice because of the prejudice that prevented enough clients from seeking her services. She moved to New York, where she became a schoolteacher, the career she had originally pursued before turning to the law. Like many other female lawyers, Ray also became very active in the suffrage movement, focusing on women's need for the vote as a route to changing the laws about their exclusion from the professions. Mary Ann Shadd Cary was another graduate of Howard University Law School who became a Washington, D.C., lawyer and focused her efforts on suffrage in the 1880s, founding the Colored Women's Progressive Franchise Association. In 1897, however, it was an African American attorney who made another important "first" in the legal and educational professions, when Lutie A. Lytle began teaching at Central Tennessee College of Law, becoming the first female law professor in the nation.[44]

Whereas the law was a traditionally male domain, some women reformers in the mid-nineteenth century began to push for women's entrance into the medical profession by pointing out that caregiving and knowledge of medicines had traditionally been part of a woman's sphere of duty. As part of the abolitionist and women's rights movements of the 1850s, reformers protested the ill treatment of women and children by the medical profession as well as doctors' monopoly on scientific information. Both Lucy Stone and Elizabeth Cady Stanton, prominent women's rights activists, criticized male doctors for their presumptuous knowledge and misdiagnosis of diseases. In 1852 Lucy Stone remarked that, "My brother's little children are both dead—killed we think by the Drs. I do believe they kill more than they cure." In her writings, Elizabeth Cady Stanton concurred on the "ignorance of physicians" and encouraged women themselves to study the latest scientific developments in the areas of family and reproductive health. The argument

"New York City—Medical College for Women, East Twelfth Street and Second Avenue—The Anatomical Lecture-Room," *Frank Leslie's Illustrated Newspaper* (April 16, 1870). Critics charged that anatomical studies were too indelicate for female students, but by midcentury women seeking to become doctors demanded the same education as men, and several medical colleges for women were established. (Library of Congress, Prints & Photographs Division, LC-USZ62-2053.)

that women were more natural and capable caregivers led to the argument that female doctors would be more capable when it came to women's health and diseases, in particular. Abolitionist reformer Sarah Grimké argued that "the medical profession opens more than all other things a highway of improvement to woman," meaning that it provided not only an occupation but increased knowledge about women's bodies. Still, Grimké relied on traditional ideas about women's roles in her belief that female physicians brought something different to medical care because no woman doctor could "justly fulfil her mission as a physician without a love spirit."[45]

Englishwoman Florence Nightingale, to whom many American women looked for inspiration in the medical field, also associated medical caregiving with women as she herself had written in 1860 that "Every woman is a nurse." In part because of such beliefs, and in part because of women's volunteer service and relief efforts during the Civil War, nursing emerged as a new female profession in the last decades of the nineteenth century. The first nursing training schools opened in 1873, and by the late 1890s, there were 35 nursing schools in the country, including at least four programs specifically for black women. Many nurses were available for hire in private homes, but as health care, including childbirth, increasingly shifted to a hospital model, nurses provided an essential source of inexpensive labor for busy urban medical centers.[46]

Although nursing was accepted as an extension of women's traditional caregiving roles, opposition to women doctors was in part an attempt by male physicians to keep women out of the elite professions, but it was also opposition to coeducation. The first woman to earn a medical degree in the United States was Elizabeth Blackwell, who graduated from the all-male Geneva Medical College in New York. Blackwell later recalled the personal reasons she sought to become a doctor in the first place: "My friend died of a painful disease, the delicate nature of which made the methods of treatment a constant suffering to her. She once said to me: '. . . If I could have been treated by a lady doctor, my worst sufferings would have been spared me.'"[47] Specifically, critics of women's medical education argued that it was simply improper for men and women to attend anatomy courses or view patient examinations together. The creation of all-female medical colleges was one solution for their education. Female doctors were expected to primarily attend to female patients, and pregnancy and childbirth were specifically seen as proper areas of medical specialization for women. The same year Blackwell completed her medical education at Geneva, the Boston Female Medical College was established for the express purpose of training women to assist other women in childbirth, and to offer such training in a single-sex environment.

The number of female doctors in the nineteenth century remained small, and their employment options, even if they did manage to get a medical education, were few. These physicians banded together to conduct their work and to assist and employ each other where possible. Marie Zakrzewska was another of the few women who received a medical degree before the Civil War, graduating from Cleveland's Western Reserve College in 1856. Zakrzewska opened her office next to that of Elizabeth Blackwell, and, in 1857, joined Elizabeth and Emily Blackwell in founding the New York Infirmary for Women and Children with the goal of providing health services to women and children. The New York Infirmary also became an important training ground and place of employment for other female physicians. Both Blackwell and Zakrzewska fought to expand women's medical training beyond just obstetrics, and, to this end, eventually each went on to found hospitals in New York and in Boston, respectively.

Marie Zakrzewska was among those medical reformers who promoted black women's entrance into the medical and nursing professions after the Civil War. As black women gained access to education in all-black and in coeducational colleges and universities that proliferated after the

Civil War, they began to make an entrance into the professions, including medicine. In 1864, before the war had even ended, Rebecca Lee Crumpler became the first black woman doctor when she graduated from the New England Female Medical College. Crumpler began her work as a nurse but was encouraged to attend medical school. After becoming a doctor, she dedicated herself to helping former slaves in the South and to advancing women's knowledge of their own bodies and health, publishing in 1883 her own *Book of Medical Discourses in Two Parts*. In the decades between the Civil War and the end of the century, more than 100 black women became doctors. Nearly one-third of these had been graduated from Howard University Medical School alone. Employment discrimination, especially in white hospitals, North or South, meant that many black female physicians opened independent practices, often in their own homes.[48]

Native American women as well, initially brought into the white educational system under dubious circumstances, were in some cases able to complete higher educations and enter the professions, such as medicine. Although church-run boarding schools aimed at destroying Native tribal and cultural ties, in some cases, these schools facilitated the higher education of a few who were able to take skills and knowledge back to serving the Native American community. Omaha Indian Susan La Flesche was taken, along with her sister, to attend mission and government schools and continued on to graduate from Women's Medical College of Pennsylvania in 1889, becoming the first Native American woman doctor. She returned to the Omaha reservation in Nebraska to work there as a physician, attending to the needs of her own people.[49]

Hospitals such as the New England Hospital for Women and Children not only treated women, but also trained and employed primarily women as doctors and nurses. Women still continued to demand access to the men's colleges, which had superior teachers and resources. The field of medicine was ultimately one in which women's presence was not a continuous story of integration and progress, as by the end of the century, there was something of a backlash and closing in the ranks of the medical profession. The exclusivity of medical education was insured by reducing the number of medical schools in the United States and requiring postgraduate-level courses in medicine for the first time, resulting in a dramatic decrease in the number of female medical students.

The early strides that had been made by women such as Blackwell or Zakrzewska were not repeated in the following years. Whereas an astounding 19 all-female medical schools had been founded by 1890, by the end of that decade, only 8 of those remained.[50] Most medical schools still excluded women, who found it increasingly difficult to acquire the education or the professional affiliation needed, and their numbers in the field began to quickly decrease. Nevertheless, women continued to push into the twentieth century and beyond, demanding the right to an education and to employment in their desired fields.

NOTES

1. Beecher quoted in Jeanne Boydston, *The Limits of Sisterhood: The Beecher Sisters on Women's Rights and Woman's Sphere* (Chapel Hill: University of North Carolina Press, 1988), p. 133.

2. Murray quoted in Sheila L. Skemp, ed., *Judith Sargent Murray: A Brief Biography with Documents* (Boston: Bedford/St. Martin's, 1998), p. 179.

3. On "republican motherhood," see Linda Kerber, *Liberty's Daughters: The Revolutionary Experience of American Women, 1750–1800,* rev. ed. (New York: Cornell University Press, 1996).

4. Jefferson quoted in Kimberley Tolley, *The Science Education of American Girls: A Historical Perspective* (New York: Routledge, 2003), p. 24.

5. Information on Willard from Barbara Solomon, *In the Company of Educated Women: A History of Women and Higher Education in America* (New Haven, Conn.: Yale University Press, 1985).

6. On Troy graduates, see Anne Firor Scott, "The Ever-Widening Circle: The Diffusion of Feminist Values from the Troy Female Seminary, 1822–1872," in *Making the Invisible Woman Visible* (Urbana: University of Illinois Press, 1984).

7. Christie Anne Farnham, *The Education of the Southern Belle: Higher Education and Student Socialization in the Antebellum South* (New York: New York University Press, 1994), pp. 17–18.

8. See Devon Mihesuah, *Cultivating the Rosebuds: The Education of Women at the Cherokee Female Seminary, 1851–1909* (Urbana: University of Illinois Press, 1993), quote on p. 41.

9. Michael Goldberg, "Breaking New Ground, 1800–1848," in *No Small Courage: A History of Women in the United States,* ed. Nancy F. Cott (New York: Oxford University Press, 2000), p. 195.

10. Hale quoted in Gail Collins, *America's Women: 400 Years of Dolls, Drudges, Helpmates, and Heroines* (New York: HarperCollins, 2003), p. 106.

11. Solomon, *In the Company of Educated Women,* p. 31.

12. Information cited in Catharine Clinton and Christine Lunardini, eds., *The Columbia Guide to American Women in the Nineteenth Century* (New York: Columbia University Press, 2000), p. 44.

13. Dall quoted in Tiffany K. Wayne, *Woman Thinking: Feminism and Transcendentalism in Nineteenth-Century America* (Lanham, Md.: Lexington Books, 2005), p. 90.

14. Thomas Dublin, *Transforming Women's Work: New England Lives in the Industrial Revolution* (Ithaca, N.Y.: Cornell University Press, 1994), pp. 205–7.

15. Beecher quoted in Kathryn Kish Sklar, *Catharine Beecher: A Study in American Domesticity* (New York: Norton, 1976), p. 97. Italics in original.

16. Collins, *America's Women,* p. 107.

17. Collins, *America's Women,* p. 107.

18. Elizabeth Brown Pryor, *Clara Barton: Professional Angel* (Philadelphia: University of Pennsylvania Press, 1987), p. 23.

19. Collins, *America's Women,* p. 107.

20. Collins, *America's Women,* p. 110.

21. Collins, *America's Women,* p. 110. See also Polly Welts Kaufman, *Women Teachers on the Frontier* (New Haven, Conn.: Yale University Press, 1984).

22. Hale qtd. in *Women Teachers,* p. 8.

23. S. J. Kleinberg, *Women in the United States, 1830–1945* (New Brunswick, N.J.: Rutgers University Press, 1999), p. 65.

24. Crasson quoted in Darlene Clark Hine and Kathleen Thompson, eds., *A Shining Thread of Hope: The History of Black Women in America* (New York: Broadway Books, 1998), p. 73.

25. Betts qtd. in *America's Women,* p. 144.

26. Hine and Thompson, *Shining Thread of Hope,* p. 74.

27. Kleinberg, *Women in the United States,* pp. 65–66.

28. Crandall qtd. in *America's Women,* pp. 161–65; see also Susan Strane, *A Whole-Souled Woman: Prudence Crandall and the Education of Black Women* (New York: Norton, 1990).

29. Hine and Thompson, *Shining Thread of Hope,* pp. 123–24.

30. Harriet Sigerman, "Laborers for Liberty: 1865–1890" in Cott, *No Small Courage,* p. 301.

31. Hine and Thompson, *Shining Thread of Hope,* pp. 135–36.

32. Forten qtd. in *Shining Thread of Hope,* pp. 137–39; see also Willie Lee Rose, *Rehearsal for Reconstruction: The Port Royal Experiment* (Athens: University of Georgia Press, 1999).

33. Hine and Thompson, *Shining Thread of Hope,* p. 160.

34. Carey quoted in Rosalind Rosenberg, *Beyond Separate Spheres: Intellectual Roots of Modern Feminism* (New Haven, Conn.: Yale University Press, 1983), p. 12.

35. For more on the debate and controversy, see Patricia A. Vertinsky, *The Eternally Wounded Woman: Women, Doctors, and Exercise in the Late Nineteenth Century* (Urbana: University of Illinois Press, 1994).

36. Hine and Thompson, *Shining Thread of Hope,* p. 173.

37. Zitkala-Sa/Bonnin discussed and writings excerpted in Linda Kerber and Jane Sherron de Hart, eds., *Women's America: Refocusing the Past,* 6th ed. (New York: Oxford University Press, 2003), pp. 282–85; see also Ruth Spack, *America's Second Tongue: American Indian Education and the Ownership of English, 1860–1900* (Lincoln: University of Nebraska Press, 2002).

38. Gregory quoted in Susan Strasser, *Never Done: A History of American Housework* (New York: Owl Books, 2000), p. 203.

39. Antin excerpted in Kerber and de Hart, *Women's America,* pp. 293–94.

40. See Solomon, *In the Company of Educated Women,* p. 76.

41. See Victoria Bissell Brown, *The Education of Jane Addams* (Philadelphia: University of Pennsylvania Press, 2004); see also Julia Grant, *Raising Baby by the Book: The Education of American Mothers* (New Haven, Conn.: Yale University Press, 1998).

42. See Ruth Bordin, *Alice Freeman Palmer: The Evolution of a New Woman* (Ann Arbor: University of Michigan Press, 1993).

43. See Bruce Ronda, *Elizabeth Palmer Peabody: A Reformer on Her Own Terms* (Cambridge, Mass.: Harvard University Press, 1999).

44. See J. Clay Smith, ed., *Rebels in Law: Voices in History of Black Women Lawyers* (Ann Arbor: University of Michigan Press, 2000).

45. Reformers quoted in Chris Dixon, *Perfecting the Family: Antislavery Marriages in Nineteenth-Century America* (Amherst: University of Massachusetts Press, 1997), pp. 137–38.

46. Overview of nursing and Nightingale quoted in Barbara Melosh, "Every Woman Is a Nurse: Work and Gender in the Emergence of Nursing," in *"Send Us a Lady Physician": Women Doctors in America, 1835–1920,* ed. Ruth J. Abram (New York: Norton, 1985), pp. 121–28.

47. Blackwell quoted in Ruth J. Abram, "Will There Be a Monument?: Six Pioneer Women Doctors Tell Their Own Stories," in Abram, *"Send Us a Lady Physician,"* p. 72.

48. See Darlene Clark Hine, "Co-Laborers in the Work of the Lord: Nineteenth-Century Black Women Physicians," in Abram, *"Send Us a Lady Physician,"* pp. 107–20.

49. See Jeri Ferris, *Native American Doctor: The Story of Susan La Flesche Picotte* (Minneapolis, Minn.: Carolrhoda Books, 1991).

50. Hine, "Co-Laborers in the Work of the Lord," in Abram, *"Send Us a Lady Physician,"* p. 108.

SUGGESTED READING

Abram, Ruth J., ed. *"Send Us a Lady Physician": Women Doctors in America, 1835–1920.* New York: Norton, 1985.

Farnham, Christie Anne. *The Education of the Southern Belle: Higher Education and Student Socialization in the Antebellum South.* New York: New York University Press, 1994.

Freeberg, Ernest. *The Education of Laura Bridgman: First Deaf and Blind Person to Learn Language.* Cambridge, Mass.: Harvard University Press, 2001.

Harris, Barbara. *Beyond Her Sphere: Women and the Professions in American History.* Westport, Conn.: Greenwood, 1978.

Horowitz, Helen. *Alma Mater: Design and Experience in the Women's Colleges from Their 19th-Century Beginnings to the 1930s.* Amherst: University of Massachusetts Press, 1993.

Kaufman, Polly Welts. *Women Teachers on the Frontier.* New Haven, Conn.: Yale University Press, 1984.

Mihesuah, Devon. *Cultivating the Rosebuds: The Education of Women at the Cherokee Female Seminary, 1851–1909.* Urbana: University of Illinois Press, 1993.

Solomon, Barbara. *In the Company of Educated Women: A History of Women and Higher Education in America.* New Haven, Conn.: Yale University Press, 1985.

Strane, Susan. *A Whole-Souled Woman: Prudence Crandall and the Education of Black Women.* New York: Norton, 1990.

5

‒⊗⊗⊘‒

Politics and Reform

The nineteenth century was the era of reform, and, even though the ideology of domesticity defined limited public roles for women, America's women were central to the major political, legal, social, and moral reform efforts of the century. In fact, women were not only central, but envisioned themselves as having a unique role as women in bringing about social harmony. The Boston Female Antislavery Society defined in 1840 the special role American women might play in shaping their society: "How many times have nations been saved by their women when every other hope seemed extinct; and so it may be with America, if we will have it so."[1]

The transformation of labor and of the household brought on by industrialization in the early nineteenth century had particular significance for changing gender roles, for women's roles in the household, and, therefore, for women's participation in public life. The separation of skilled from unskilled and of shop from household labor impacted the structure of the home and family life. As men's work moved away from the household, into small businesses or professional offices, the daily experiences and work lives of men and women of the middle classes were separated as well. Contemporaries and historians have referred to this as an ideology of "separate spheres," which emerged at this time to explain the perceived differences between the public world of men and the private world of women.

Ironically, the isolation of women in the home and the intense moral and economic authority granted to women in the management of their homes opened up a new era of female collectivity and public activity. Despite the solitariness of domestic life, women, as they always had, continued to attend church, where they interacted with other women in the community. Women's roles as the guardians of children and the home gave them new authority in addressing problems outside the home as social and moral reformers. Eventually, efforts to change society led women to question the social, political, and legal limitations on their own lives and to demand a greater public role as America's women.

MORAL REFORM

White women expanded upon their role as moral guardians of the home to reform themselves, women of other classes and locations, and eventually to address larger social problems, such as prostitution, alcoholism, poverty, crime, and disease. These social problems only a decade or so previous would have been less prominent features of American society, and they would certainly not have been appropriate concerns of America's wives and mothers.

With a religious motivation toward perfectionism (striving to be Christlike), many of the earliest reform associations focused inward on improving the individual. For middle-class women, this meant improving themselves as mothers. The first "maternal association" was organized in Portland, Maine, in 1815, and numerous others were established in the coming decades throughout New England and New York. In maternal associations, women met together to discuss childrearing ideas, with older, or at least more experienced, women providing assistance to new mothers on "how best to train up our children." Such associations were usually church-based, assisting mothers in the religious education of their children. The associations quickly became more like support groups on a range of parenting issues, with each member expected to "suggest to her sister members such hints as her own experience may furnish, or circumstances seem to render necessary."[2]

Concern about the moral health of the family led to concern about other families and the community at large. Wives of merchants and lawyers gathered together under names like the Female Missionary Society, not to be missionaries themselves, but to raise funds to send young male missionaries into frontier areas where people might not be reached by the town-centered revivals then sweeping Northern cities. Middle-class white women concerned about the religious training of their own children and of the children of immigrants and workers as well were largely responsible for the emergence of a Sunday School movement in the early decades of the century, creating almost 50,000 Sunday schools in the United States by the 1820s. (See also Chapter 3, "Religion.")

Free black women also used the church as a springboard to female collectivity and activism. More so than the maternal associations of white women, the most popular self-help societies in Northern African American communities were the mutual relief societies or benevolent associations (characteristic of many urban immigrant communities as well). Both men and women of the working and middle classes organized such charitable organizations in the early nineteenth century. As precursors to the protections eventually offered by life or disability insurance policies, early benevolent or relief societies were established by churchwomen in order to collect and distribute food, clothing, and sometimes cash for the poor, sick, orphaned, or widowed. Between 1821–1829 the Philadelphia-based Daughters of Africa claimed some 200 women (themselves mostly poor and working class) as members, who raised money and channeled it back into the community in the form of payments to the sick who could not work or loans to families for funeral expenses.[3] Other organizations had names such as the African Female Benevolent Society of Newport, Rhode Island, or the Colored Female Religious and Moral Society of Salem, Massachusetts.

In the 1830s, both black and white women focused on their own improvement by forming literary societies to educate themselves. Whereas white women focused on improving their education in order to more effectively perform their duties as wives and as mothers who must educate their children, black women perceived a different importance and justification for their own education, that of combating racism. As the Female Literary Association of Philadelphia described their mission in 1831: "As daughters of a despised race, it becomes a duty . . . to cultivate the talents entrusted to our keeping, that by so doing, we may break down the strong barrier of prejudice."[4] These women reformers worked to combat racism, and therefore the philosophical justification for slavery, by proving themselves to be intelligent beings. One "Miss Jennings," speaking at an 1837 meeting of the Ladies' Literary Society in New York, emphasized that "the mind is the greatest" of black women's powers "and great care should be taken to improve it with diligence. Neglect will plunge us into deep degradation . . . while our enemies will rejoice and say, we do not believe (the colored people) have any minds; if they have, they are unsusceptible of improvement."[5] Whether explicitly or implicitly, women's charitable and literary societies, both black and white, with their emphasis on women's moral authority, laid the foundations for women's prominent role in the emerging antislavery movement.

The religious and spiritual renewal of the era combined with women's expanded vision of their role in protecting the welfare of women and children throughout society. From maternal or literary associations of likeminded women from a specific community, reformers soon reached out to other women unlike themselves, such as widows, immigrants, and even prostitutes. The New York Female Moral Reform Society was founded in 1834 and the Boston Female Moral Reform Society the following year, in

1835. These organizations collectively claimed thousands of members and the moral reform movement quickly became national in scope, spawning the need for a national organization, the American Female Moral Reform Society, with its own publication, the *Advocate of Moral Reform*. By the 1840s, moral reform had moved from local church-based activities to a national movement involving women reformers in new types of political strategies and activism.

Spanning the entire century, and into the twentieth century, the American temperance movement used varying strategies at different times in its history. The motivations and tactics of reformers in the pre–Civil War decades differed from their late nineteenth-century and early twentieth-century counterparts, even when they identified the problems as the same. Temperance activity began in the antebellum period in the larger context of other reform movements, where it was linked explicitly with ideas about the moral superiority of women and the religious enthusiasm of the 1820s and 1830s. The American Society for the Promotion of Temperance was founded in 1826 and in 1833 the first national temperance convention was held. Focusing on the perceived sinfulness and loss of self-control caused by a rapidly changing society, temperance advocates saw alcohol use and abuse as one of several problems introduced into American society by urbanization and industrialization, along with prostitution, poverty, and an increase in crime. Indeed, alcohol abuse was often portrayed as at the root of these other problems, and, therefore, as a foundational reform. It was a problem that affected not only drinkers, but the family and community as well by threatening the safety and morality of women and children.

With stories of abusive or deserting husbands and financially ruined households, groups such as the Female Total Abstinence Society in 1838 urged that all women stand "united in a holy phalanx to arrest an evil which has poured its bitterest causes upon the head of women."[6] Women made up half or more of temperance society membership throughout the century. They relied heavily on a message of self-control, mandatory abstinence among their own members, and on "moral suasion" as a strategy; that is, attempting to convince individuals of the immorality of their actions. Married women formed associations and threatened to withhold sexual services if their husbands did not give up the drink, and, drawing on an emerging women's rights discourse, demanded the "right" of every woman to have a sober husband.

Temperance reform was not limited to middle-class women's groups only, as a working-class organization, the Washingtonians, brought former alcohol abusers into the crusade to tell their stories of degradation, despair, and redemption. Washingtonian members included many men from the artisan and lower classes and inspired parallel female Martha Washington societies. Presenting themselves as concerned with woman's legitimate interests in religion, charity, and the health of the family, female reformers

"Woman's Holy War. Grand Charge on the Enemy's Works,"
Currier & Ives (1874). Temperance, or the antialcohol movement, was seen primarily as a women's campaign for the protection of home and family. The temperance movement relied on
increasingly militant strategies after the Civil War, reflected in
this image of a female army destroying barrels of liquor "In the
Name of God and Humanity." (Library of Congress, Prints &
Photographs Division, LC-USZ62-683.)

slowly expanded their sphere of influence into the public realm outside
their own families, concerning themselves with the activities and habits of
other men besides their husbands.

The temperance movement grew to become perhaps the largest reform
movement of the century with hundreds of thousands of supporters and
members. In 1874 the Women's Christian Temperance Union (WCTU)
was formed to bring together reformers in various states. The WCTU
clearly and forcefully presented temperance as a women's issue because,

as stated at one of their national conventions, "women are among the greatest sufferers from the liquor traffic."[7] With the goal of the WCTU nothing less than the elimination of the national liquor industry, they targeted not only users of alcohol, but producers, retailers (saloons and bars), and, most important, legislators. Although Maine had established a state-level prohibition in 1851, the work of women reformers through the WCTU was responsible for propelling the alcohol issue into the twentieth century and eventually achieving national prohibition in 1919 with the 18th Amendment to the U.S. Constitution (subsequently repealed in 1933).

From the temperance movement emerged one of the most active and dynamic reformers of the century, Frances Willard, president of the Women's Christian Temperance Union from 1879 until her death in 1898. Willard was a former teacher and president of a women's college who, even before her work with the WCTU, advocated a wide range of political and social reforms related to women. She brought to the WCTU a policy of "Do Everything," establishing WCTU departments committed not only to temperance, but also marriage equality, dress reform, child labor reform, education reform, and woman suffrage. She explained the wide-reaching scope of the temperance movement in terms of an overarching view of women's roles as reformers in society: "Were I to define in a sentence, the thought and purpose of the Women's Christian Temperance Union, I would reply: *It is to make the whole world HOMELIKE.*"[8] Under Frances Willard's direction, the late nineteenth-century suffrage and temperance campaigns were often linked because, like many other female reform leaders, Willard soon recognized women's need for political power in order to accomplish their reform goals.

ABOLITIONISM

Antebellum moral reform causes brought women increasingly into the public realm as speakers and lecturers on a range of topics, combining a spiritual imperative toward individual and social progress with secular or political concerns. The first female lecturers were nineteenth-century reformers who, like female preachers, justified their presence at the podium or on the stage in spiritual terms. In the early 1830s, women such as Maria Stewart, a free black believed to be the first American woman to lecture in public, and sisters Sarah and Angelina Grimké, white women raised in the South who came to the North to become prominent abolitionists, emphasized that God had called them in their special duty as women to speak out on the wrongs of slavery.

Maria Stewart emerged as part of the same tradition explaining the proliferation of black female preachers in the early nineteenth century, but her lectures included a broader, more explicitly political message. Like black women preachers of the era (see also Chapter 3, "Religion"), Stewart explained to an audience in Boston in 1832 how she felt called by God to speak out as a woman against slavery and oppression in all forms: "Methinks I heard a spiritual interrogation—"Who shall go forward, and take off the reproach that is cast upon the people of color? Shall it be a woman?"—And my heart made this reply—"If it is thy will, be it even so, Lord Jesus!" Stewart addressed black women specifically to rise up from "beneath a load of iron pots and kettles" and take on a larger public role for the sake of the entire race: "O, ye daughters of Africa, awake! Awake! Arise! No longer sleep nor slumber, but distinguish yourselves. Show forth to the world that ye are endowed with noble and exalted faculties."[9]

Sarah and Angelina Grimké came from a South Carolina white slaveholding family and moved north after converting to Quakerism. Like Stewart, the sisters also couched their arguments for an expanded public role for women in terms of God's mandate for Christian women to reach out and help their enslaved "sisters." Angelina Grimké's 1837 "An Appeal to the Women of the Nominally Free States" reminded Northern women that their duty was not to their families alone, but that they "have high and holy duties to perform in the work of emancipation—duties to themselves, to the suffering slave, to the slaveholder, to the church, to their country, and to the world at large, and, above all to their God." Grimké connected the plight of all women with that of the female slave, urging white Northern women into the antislavery cause by reminding them that, under slavery, women were prevented from fulfilling their roles as wives and mothers. As long as slavery existed within the United States, this was "a country where women are degraded and brutalized, and where their exposed persons bleed under the lash . . . torn from their husbands, and forcibly plundered of their virtue and their offspring. . . . They are our countrywomen—*they are our sisters.*"[10]

The Grimké sisters sparked controversy as much over the fact that they were women speaking in public as over their antislavery message. In order to work against slavery, they ultimately had to campaign for women's right to speak publicly and did so by continuing to argue that women, in particular, had a moral duty to change society. The controversy and criticism surrounding the Grimkés inspired other women to demand their own right to engage in public reform work. In 1837, the same year that Grimké's "Appeal" was published, the Antislavery Convention of American Women met in New York and resolved "that it is the duty of woman, and the province of woman, to plead her cause of the oppressed in our land and to do all that she can by her voice, and her pen, and her purse, and the influence of her example, to overthrow the horrible system of American slavery."[11]

The abolitionist movement continued to grow throughout the 1840s and 1850s along with the other political events and sectional crises that were leading the United States to civil war. But abolitionism was also part of a larger network of women's reform activities in the first decades of the nineteenth century. The abolitionists themselves were individuals largely concentrated in the Northeast, who were often simultaneously involved in multiple reform causes and organizations. Abolitionism shared with other reforms the desire to end social wrongs, the idea of middle-class benevolence in aiding the oppressed and downtrodden, and the spiritual imperative to allow each individual to reach his or her potential as the route to a perfected society.

White women had to fight for their right to speak publicly, but black women, in their public activism, had to confront the forces that sought to keep them quiet both as women and as African Americans. Whereas white women tried to identify with the black female slave in order to articulate their own sense of oppression, free black women struggled to claim their identity as "women" in the first place by pointing out that ideas about "true womanhood," or about women's domestic and moral roles, often did not apply to black women. Sojourner Truth, a former slave from New York, was a well-known speaker throughout the 1850s who articulated the dual oppression of black women. Truth spoke at women's rights conventions organized by white women reformers, but she also pointed out that for black women, suffrage alone would do little to change their lives as long as racism existed. At a speech before an 1851 women's rights convention in Akron, Ohio, Truth highlighted the false idea of completely separate gender roles by emphasizing that black women, especially, often worked as hard as men, and therefore they ought to have the same rights as men:

> I have as much muscle as any man, and can do as much work as any man. I have plowed and reaped and husked and chopped and mowed, and can any man do more than that? I have heard much about the sexes being equal; I can carry as much as any man, and eat as much too, if I can get it. I am as strong as any man that is now.[12]

Whether white or black, women's involvement in the antislavery movement transformed women's own sense of themselves and of their public roles. Through their work in the antislavery movement, women learned how to be political activists, how to organize, and how to pursue new strategies beyond just "moral suasion," such as gathering petitions, lobbying legislatures, writing for and editing newspapers, organizing conventions, and delivering public speeches. Angelina Grimké went from justifying her right and duty to speak in public to becoming the first woman to testify before a government committee. Beginning in the 1830s, women established and led local and state level antislavery societies, lectured at conventions,

"I Sell the Shadow to Support the Substance. Sojourner Truth" (1864). Former slave Sojourner Truth became a popular lecturer on equal rights for blacks and women. She often sold these souvenir photo cards at her lectures to supplement her income. (Library of Congress, Prints & Photographs Division, LC-USZ62-119343.)

and published antislavery tracts. Lydia Maria Child was a well-established author of books and magazines for children and homemakers before she moved into reform work with the 1833 publication of *An Appeal in Favor of That Class of Americans Called Africans.* In 1841 she took over as editor of the New York–based newspaper, the *Antislavery Standard.* Abby Kelley Foster was a Quaker who worked with radical abolitionist William Lloyd Garrison and launched a public speaking career, which she insisted on continuing even after marriage and motherhood. Of course, many women who did not become famous or whose names have not been recorded in the history books were politicized by and contributed to the strength of the antislavery cause through their work in local societies, fundraising, subscribing to antislavery newspapers, and attending abolitionist lectures.

Female reformers brought their special roles and duties as women, and as mothers, to the antislavery movement. Articles in abolitionist newspapers as well as the narratives of former slaves themselves, and, most famously, Harriet Beecher Stowe's *Uncle Tom's Cabin* (published in 1852), all made special appeal to the hearts of Northern women readers as mothers and as keepers of the home. From the poor Eliza escaping in fear as she crossed the icy river with her children in tow, to the heart-wrenching accounts of the physical abuse and deaths of slave children, Stowe's novel highlighted the effect of slavery on families, both black and white, and on women and children, in particular. And perhaps the most compelling theme of Harriet Jacobs's autobiography *Incidents in the Life of a Slave Girl,* was the fact that Jacobs herself was a mother, separated for years from her own children, unable to protect them from slavery. Because of slavery's destruction of the family and its blatant physical abuse of women and of children, antislavery activists clearly urged that abolitionism was a cause all women, black and white, should see as their own. As one lecturer urged, "every woman in the community should raise her voice against the sin, that crying evil that is degrading her sex."[13]

Many women did begin to raise their voices. The 1820s and 1830s saw a proliferation of women's auxiliary antislavery societies in support of the national organizations led by men, but by 1840 there was a split within the abolitionist ranks over women as members of associations, as officeholders, and as public speakers for the cause. William Lloyd Garrison, the founder of the most radical abolitionist newspaper, the *Liberator,* often took revolutionary positions such as supporting full civil and political rights for black citizens, and attacking the U.S. government and churches for allowing slavery to continue, and he was among those who supported the right of women to speak out against slavery and to participate in the movement on equal terms. Quaker reformer Lucretia Mott helped found the Philadelphia Female Anti-slavery Society in 1833 and was one of the delegates, along with Garrison, to the international World Anti-slavery Convention in London in 1840. Also among the delegates was the newly married Elizabeth Cady Stanton. To their surprise, the first debates were not about slavery, but about the female delegates to the convention who, ultimately, were not allowed to speak. Stanton reported in a letter from London to Angelina and Sarah Grimké that, "as the female delegates were not received and were not permitted to take their seats as delegates, [William Lloyd Garrison] refused to take his, consequently his voice was not heard throughout the meeting."[14] Over the next several days of the convention, Elizabeth Cady Stanton and Lucretia Mott decided that more attention needed to be focused on the plight of "oppressed woman." It was not until 1848, however, that they finally met in Seneca Falls, New York to discuss the rights, or lack of rights, of American women.

WOMEN'S RIGHTS

Building upon the previous decades of work in the antislavery movement and on a generation of women trained as activists and leaders, by the 1850s, women's rights had emerged as an identifiable movement separate from the issues and organizations of abolitionism. Although many of the same women lent their voices and energies to both causes, there were reasons explaining the need for a separate movement at this time. First of all, as revealed in the controversies over the Grimkés and over the female convention delegates, not all abolitionists supported women as public reform speakers and some women activists needed a forum from which to address this issue. Second, the abolitionist movement was focused on a single goal—ending slavery—while women's rights activists sought to address a variety of issues affecting women's lives, especially during the radical decade of the 1850s. The association between the two movements, however, meant that Southern white women were not involved in creating the early women's rights movement, a trend that continued to be a problem with the suffrage movement even after the Civil War.

In the days before the Seneca Falls convention, Elizabeth Cady Stanton, Lucretia Mott, and three other women reformers drafted a list of grievances and resolutions to be read at the July 1848 convention. What they came up with was the "Declaration of Sentiments," modeled explicitly after Thomas Jefferson's words in the Declaration of Independence that had, according to the women, guaranteed the political rights of men in the wake of the American Revolution. The women's declaration, however, emphasized that "all men *and women* are created equal"; it replaced the king as tyrant with the not-generic "man"; and it specifically articulated for the first time an organized response against the social, political, and economic restrictions on American women. It included such new and radical demands as women's right to their own property and wages, the unequal power of men in divorce and custody cases, the barring of women from the professions and from higher education, and, most radical of all, the denial of the franchise to women. The convention also drafted a series of resolutions that included the revolutionary concept that women's roles should not be determined by men, but rather by "nature" and by women themselves:

> *Resolved,* that all laws which prevent women from occupying such a station in society as her conscience shall dictate, or which place her in a position inferior to that of man, are contrary to the great precept of nature, and therefore of no force or authority. . . .

> *Resolved,* That woman has too long rested satisfied in the circumscribed limits which corrupt customs and a perverted application of the Scriptures have marked out for her, and that it is time she should move in the enlarged sphere which her great Creator has assigned her.[15]

More than 200 people attended the Seneca Falls convention and 100 men and women signed the Declaration of Sentiments, including William Lloyd Garrison and well-known black abolitionist Frederick Douglass, both of whom picked up on the radical nature of the suffrage demand and promptly supported it in their respective newspapers. Whereas the reform ideas of earlier women such as Maria Stewart or Angelina and Sarah Grimké were based on a religious imperative of moral *duties,* Elizabeth Cady Stanton, Lucretia Mott, and others began with an explicit argument toward a woman's individual *rights* and sparked a public movement toward redefining women's roles in the family and society. Stanton reflected upon her motivations years later in her autobiography:

> The general discontent I felt with woman's portion as wife, mother, housekeeper, physician, and spiritual guide; the wearied, anxious look of the majority of women impressed me with a strong feeling that some active measures should be taken to right the wrongs of society in general, and of women in particular.[16]

After Seneca Falls, other local conventions were held in established centers of reform sentiment in New York, Massachusetts, and Ohio. The first national women's rights convention was held in Worcester, Massachusetts, in October 1850. Presided over by Paulina Wright Davis, an antislavery and women's health reformer, the Worcester convention set the tone for a broad-based movement by asserting its scope as that of womankind's "Education, literary, scientific, and Artistic; Her Avocations, Industrial, Commercial, and Professional; Her Interests, Pecuniary, Civil, and Political; in a word Her Rights as an Individual, and her Functions as a Citizen."[17] Calling upon women themselves to join the conventions and therefore to act upon the resolutions proposed at Seneca Falls just two years earlier, Davis explained that "It is one thing to issue a declaration of rights or a declaration of wrong to the world, but quite another thing wisely and happily to commend the subject to the world's acceptance, and so to secure the desired reformation."[18]

Through their own newspapers, lecture circuits, and conventions, women's rights advocates began to attack the tenets of domesticity that kept their personal and their political interests confined to those of their families and households, and launched an incredibly broad-based critique of American political culture and gender relations. The 1850s was the decade of the radical women's press, with the earliest editors and contributors drawn from the same circle of reformers who were involved in temperance, antiprostitution campaigns, and abolitionism. The *Una* (a literary reform magazine founded and edited by Paulina Wright Davis, president of the Worcester convention), the *Lily* (a temperance and dress reform paper edited by Amelia Bloomer), *Woman's Advocate* (focused on labor), and the *Sybil* (dress and health reform) were among the first papers dedicated to women's issues. (See also Chapter 8, "Literature and the Arts.")

Besides demanding political and social rights, the early women's movement also emphasized barriers to women's physical health through dress and fashion. In the 1850s, women's rights advocates began to promote and some even to wear the "new costume" of full-length baggy trousers with a below-the knee-skirt worn over (also known as the "Turkish dress") as an alternative to women's heavy floor-length dresses, complete with hoops, petticoats, and corsets. Labeled by critics as "bloomers," the costume was not actually invented by Amelia Bloomer, nor was she the first among reformers to wear it in public. Her name was associated with it because she

"Woman's Emancipation," *Harper's New Monthly Magazine* 3, no. 15 (August 1851): p. 424. Critics of the early women's rights movement feared that equality would mean a complete erasure or even reversal of gender roles. The women in this cartoon are wearing bloomers, or "the new costume," while loitering in the streets smoking cigars. (Division of Rare and Manuscript Collections, Cornell University Library.)

was the editor of a women's rights newspaper, the *Lily*, which promoted the costume by distributing patterns for sewing it, with much popularity among its readership. Traditional women's fashions could be harmful to women's health, and it was argued that long skirts swept up dirt and disease in the streets and carried it into homes, while corsets, the worst health hazard, restricted women's breathing and crushed organs. Many complaints focused on the significant restrictions placed on women's physical movement, keeping them from efficiently performing their household chores, thus undermining domesticity.

Such emphases on the external practicalities and health issues of women's dress soon gave way to a broader cultural critique of women's roles. Women's rights advocates cried out against the dictates of fashion that kept women ornamental, for men's pleasure rather than for women's comfort. As with corsets, floor-length dresses kept women constrained to certain roles and limited their freedom to pursue other activities. Elizabeth Cady Stanton wore bloomers, threw out her corset, and cut her hair short in the 1850s. After two years, however, Stanton stopped wearing the costume in public because she feared that the controversy over the outfit distracted the public from the larger demands for women's rights that she was trying to articulate.

The issues raised by the earliest women's movement activists of the 1850s were thus sweepingly broad and forced the American public to begin to reconsider women's roles in both the public and private spheres. Empowered by their ability to have their voices heard in conventions and the press, women's rights activists addressed all aspects of women's lives, from marriage and health, to education and employment, to the law and the vote. In the words of reformer Ernestine Rose, speaking in 1856, the stated goal of feminism was to tear down the "thick and impenetrable fortress of prejudice." Speaker, editor, novelist, and poet Elizabeth Oakes Smith explained in 1852 that the goal of the movement was to "pull down our present outworn and imperfect structure of human institutions" and to "reconstruct it upon a new and broader" foundation.[19] Such a far-reaching plan for the complete social and cultural reorganization of women's roles was perhaps a difficult goal to reach immediately. The ultimate success of the organized movement was primarily in the realm of specific political and legal reforms.

Most women's rights activists, black and white, continued to fight for the abolition of slavery, and, during the Civil War, many built upon their already established public roles as activists in turning their attention to supporting the war effort. (See also Chapter 6, "Slavery and the Civil War.") In May 1863, just a few months after President Abraham Lincoln's Emancipation Proclamation freeing slaves in the rebel states, Elizabeth Cady Stanton and Susan B. Anthony established the National Women's Loyal League with the goal of gathering one million signatures in support of a constitutional amendment to end slavery throughout the United States. Stanton emphasized that even though it was men acting in "the forum, the field and the camp," women had a public role to play in securing the goals of the war as well. She pointed out that in order to secure those goals, women should have a more active role in politics, including the vote; the press criticized this "great uprising of women of the North" for its "most patriotic and praiseworthy motive had been distorted into ... a revolutionary woman's rights movement." Even supportive congressmen were disappointed to see women entering into "the strife of politics," revealing the discomfort with women stepping outside of their expected wartime roles, as Elizabeth Cady Stanton put it, of "nursing the sick and wounded, knitting socks, and making jellies." The league lasted only a short time before the war ended and the goal of emancipation was achieved, but it had attracted more than 5,000 members and presented nearly 400,000 signatures to Congress by August 1864.[20]

In general, the Civil War brought a temporary disruption to the momentum of the women's movement, and many reformers from the abolitionist and women's rights movements believed that the end of slavery and the granting of civil rights for African Americans would result in the simultaneous granting of women's rights as well. Founded immediately after the war, in 1866, the American Equal Rights Association (AERA) was made up of former abolitionists and women's rights activists who planned to continue to work on political and civil rights issues. With the end of the Civil War and an impending constitutional amendment to give black men the vote, however, some women's rights activists became resentful and made racist arguments stating that white women were more deserving of the vote and of political power. At the 1869 meeting of the Equal Rights Association, Susan B. Anthony argued that "If intelligence, justice, and morality are to have precedence in the Government, let the question of woman be brought up first and that of the Negro last." It was reported that the president of the association, Elizabeth Cady Stanton, "argued that not another man should be enfranchised until enough women are admitted to the polls to outweigh those already there.... She did not believe in allowing ignorant Negroes and foreigners to make laws for her to obey." Black women were caught between the two sides, and Frances E. W. Harper, for one, responded to the attitudes of Stanton and Anthony, in particular, by pointing out that not all white women were as virtuous, intelligent, or fair as they would claim. Harper was reported as saying that "If the nation could only handle one question, she would not have the black women put a single straw in the way, if only the men of the race would obtain what they wanted." Three years earlier, at an 1866 women's rights convention, Harper had stood up to white women who argued that their rights should come before those of African Americans: "I do not believe that giving the woman the ballot is immediately going to cure all the ills of life. . . . You white women speak here of rights. I speak of wrongs."[21]

Black and white women's public activism took separate paths and strategies through the last decades of the nineteenth century. The post–Civil War white women's movement became narrowly focused on the vote, not only at the expense of more radical demands about women's economic and social subordination, but also at the expense of allegiances with other subordinated groups that had characterized the movement in the 1850s. White suffragists severed alliances with black allies even though African Americans, the vote for black men notwithstanding, still lacked many basic civil rights in the post-Reconstruction era. Black women also continued to support women's suffrage, but through their own organizations and as part of a broader civil rights commitment to addressing other issues, such as education and antilynching.

WOMAN SUFFRAGE

Although suffrage is probably the issue most identified with nineteenth-century feminism, it remained a radical and even marginal demand until after the Civil War. The issue of suffrage, introduced in 1848 at Seneca Falls as the "sacred right to elective franchise," eventually became the primary focus of the organized white women's movement. The differences of opinion about priorities concerning racial politics led to an eventual split within the women's movement itself. In May 1869, many members of the American Equal Rights Association joined Susan B. Anthony and Elizabeth Cady Stanton in the newly formed National Woman Suffrage Association (NWSA). The NWSA allowed only women as leaders and focused its efforts on securing a constitutional amendment for woman suffrage. As president of the NWSA, Susan B. Anthony began traveling across the country lecturing on the need for such an amendment and establishing NWSA branches.

Susan B. Anthony and other women began to challenge the point that the Constitution did not explicitly forbid women from voting by simply showing up at the polling place and attempting to vote. After Anthony attempted to vote in Rochester, New York, in the presidential election of 1872, she was arrested and put on trial, all according to her plan to challenge the state law in the courts. Unfortunately, she lost her case, was simply fined, and was denied any right to testify on her own behalf or to appeal, an act by the courts that she termed "[t]he greatest outrage History ever witnessed."[22]

Nonetheless, Anthony's actions pushed the suffrage movement on through the final decades of the nineteenth century and inspired women in other districts and states to make similar attempts at voting in order to bring lawsuits against the government. Another NWSA member, Virginia Minor,

"Washington, D.C. The Judiciary Committee of the House of Representatives Receiving a Deputation of Female Suffragists, January 11th—A Lady Delegate Reading Her Argument in Favor of Woman's Voting, on the Basis of the Fourteenth and Fifteenth Constitutional Amendments," *Frank Leslie's Illustrated Newspaper* (February 4, 1871). Activists in the post–Civil War suffrage campaign employed new political strategies, including lobbying Congress directly. (Library of Congress, Prints & Photographs Division, LC-USZ62-2023.)

sued the St. Louis, Missouri, registrar of voters, resulting in the 1874 U.S. Supreme Court decision in *Minor v. Happersett,* which determined that the "Constitution of the United States does not confer the right of suffrage upon any one." In 1878, Susan B. Anthony drafted a woman suffrage amendment to be presented to the U.S. Congress, which simply stated, "The right of citizens of the United States to vote shall not be denied or abridged by the United States or by any State on account of sex. Congress shall have the power, by appropriate legislation, to enforce the provisions of this article."[23] The so-called "Anthony Amendment" was not passed by Congress and finally ratified until 1920.

The same year that Anthony was arrested for entering the male realm of the polling place, another feminist, Victoria Claflin Woodhull, went a step further and declared herself a candidate for President of the United States. Woodhull explained her strategy as one that required "individual independence," rather than a mass women's movement:

> While others of my sex devoted themselves to a crusade against the laws that shackle the women of the country, I asserted my individual independence. . . . While others sought to show that there was no valid reason why woman should be treated . . . as a being inferior to man, I boldly entered the arena of politics and business and exercised the rights I already possessed.

> I therefore claim the right to speak for the unenfranchised woman of the country and . . . I now announce myself as a candidate for the Presidency.[24]

Woodhull's campaign was plagued by criticism, even from other feminists, and she did not receive any recorded votes in the election of 1872.

While the NWSA women worked at filing lawsuits and pushing a federal amendment, a separate group, the American Woman Suffrage Association (AWSA), was founded in 1869, and included among its members many of the former abolitionists interested in promoting black civil rights as well as woman suffrage and other reform issues. There were regional as well as strategic differences between the two groups, as the AWSA was dominated by New England reformers, whereas the NWSA membership was drawn from New York and other areas. The AWSA not only welcomed male members but chose a man as its first president, reformer Henry Ward Beecher. The primary strategy of the AWSA was to gain support for woman suffrage on a state-by-state basis as a route to eventual federal-level change. This strategy meant that state-level affiliates of the AWSA were an important part of the organization, and it was at this level that some African American women also joined in the leadership. For example, Charlotte Rollin had an active role in the South Carolina chapter of the AWSA as secretary and member of the executive committee. Other prominent black reformers, such as Frances E. W. Harper and Josephine Ruffin, were also affiliated with the AWSA.[25]

The NWSA was met with defeat in the Supreme Court and in Congress in the late nineteenth century, but the state-by-state strategy of the AWSA did have some early successes. A few Western territories and states, primarily as an enticement to encourage settlement, passed woman suffrage ballots in the last half of the century. In 1869 Wyoming became the first territory to grant the vote to women, followed by Utah in 1870. The Utah suffrage provision was subsequently challenged and reversed by Congress before full woman suffrage was finally included as part of Utah's admittance as a state in 1896. Only two other states, Colorado and Idaho, granted women the vote in the nineteenth century, encouraging the AWSA activists to continue with the state-by-state strategy into the first decades of the new century, however slow the progress.

Each branch of the postwar suffrage movement had its own periodical as well. The NWSA's paper, *Revolution,* was only published between 1868 and 1870, but the AWSA's more conservative *Woman's Journal* had a long run, from its founding in 1870 to 1917, as one of the most important women's rights papers of the century, eventually incorporating the views of a re-united movement. The beginning of an attempt to bring the two sides of the women's movement back together began in 1888 with plans for celebrating the 40th anniversary of the Seneca Falls convention. A few years

later, in 1890, spearheaded in large part by reformers of the next generation, such as Elizabeth Cady Stanton's daughter, Harriot Stanton Blatch,
and Lucy Stone's daughter, Alice Stone Blackwell, the two organizations
were merged together as the National American Woman Suffrage Association (NAWSA).

Although Elizabeth Cady Stanton served for two years as the first president of NAWSA, at which time Susan B. Anthony took over, eventually it
was younger, more conservative women who set the course for the twentieth-
century suffrage movement. After 1900, the primary focus and strategy of
NAWSA remained on state campaigns rather than on passing a national
amendment, efforts that would continue for another 20 years. Neither
Susan B. Anthony nor Elizabeth Cady Stanton lived to see the passage of
the 19th Amendment granting American women the vote in 1920. Amaz-
ingly, however, one of the original signers of the 1848 Seneca Falls Declaration of Sentiments did. At age 91, Charlotte Woodward Pierce voted in the
November 1920 presidential election.

WOMEN'S CLUB MOVEMENT

In the last decades of the nineteenth century, both black and white
women continued their decades-long activism but negotiated new roles and
new strategies in the post–Civil War context. During the Reconstruction-
era, black women, North and South, considered the meaning of freedom
itself, demanding self-determination in matters both public and private.
Economic self-sufficiency and marriage were particularly important to
former slaves, as they tried to build the foundations of family denied to
them under slavery. Although black men gained at least the abstract political rights guaranteed by the 15th Amendment, prompting white women
to focus more intently on gaining suffrage for themselves, during the final
decades of the nineteenth century, black women were left to fight for their
own political and civil rights.

A mass movement of middle-class black women stepped up to focus on
this postslavery need for black women's self-determination and for protection and "uplift" of the entire black family and race. As white women did
in other contexts, black women entered the political arena and justified
their activism by claiming it an extension of their role as wives and mothers in protecting the home and children. They also drew upon the example
of antebellum free black women reformers to embark upon a campaign
of "racial uplift" in creating charitable organizations and literary societies. A historical legacy of exclusion from white reform movements led to
the need for separate organizations addressing race issues along with, not
separate from, women's issues. The difference between black and white
women's groups, as antilynching activist Ida B. Wells and other black

reformers emphasized, was that black women by necessity must be for ending *all* forms of discrimination.

As well as being excluded from some organizations, black women and their families became targets of new forms of racism in the postslavery South. The Confederacy attempted to reassert itself and its identity after losing the war. An ideology of white Southern womanhood emerged that held up white women as the virtuous ladies who must be protected and valorized. This ideology had a negative and restricting impact on white women, but for black men and women, it meant that they were subjected to new kinds of violence. Once the U.S. government ended Reconstruction efforts in the South, black men, particularly, became vulnerable to mob violence and vigilante justice by racist groups, such as the Ku Klux Klan, who claimed that white women must be especially protected from black men. In the last decades of the nineteenth century, the lynching of black Americans in the South increased every year, peaking at 160 lynchings in 1892 alone. Although the rape of white women by black men was the crime most often cited by whites to justify the lynchings, not all lynching victims had even been accused of rape at the time of their killing, nor does this explanation account for that fact that some black women were also killed.

In the last decade of the nineteenth century, Ida B. Wells was the most outspoken critic of the Southern lynch mobs. Wells had been born into slavery in 1862 and came of age during and benefited from the promises of the Reconstruction era. She attended a school established by the Freedmen's Bureau and worked as a teacher until she lost her job for criticizing the unequal facilities for black and white children. She was politicized by the segregation of the postwar South and won a lawsuit she brought against the railways for maintaining separate black and white seating areas. When some of her close friends were the victims of a lynch mob, she exposed the crimes and condemned Southern white society in the Memphis *Free Press,* where she worked as an editor and writer. After her newspaper office was vandalized, she feared for her own safety as an outspoken public critic of the violence and she was forced to move north, where she remained for many years.

Throughout the 1890s, Ida B. Wells wrote articles and editorials to alert the Northern public to these events, traveled to England to garner support from reformers there, and in 1892 published her shocking report on lynching entitled *Southern Horrors.* She followed up in 1895 with another book, *A Red Record: Tabulated Statistics and Alleged Causes of Lynchings in the United States, 1892–1893–1894.* In all of her writings, Wells rejected the idea that the lynching and intimidation of black men was necessary for the protection of white women. She pointed out that black social mobility and economic independence were the real "crimes" or threats to white

Ida B. Wells (ca 1893–94). Wells was a writer and newspaper editor who launched the antilynching campaign with her pamphlet "Southern Horrors" (1892) and other explicit accounts of racism and violence in the post–Civil War South. (Ida B. Wells Papers, Special Collections Research Center, University of Chicago Library.)

society, and threatened or actual violence was intended to remind blacks of their place in even a postslavery society. Wells controversially suggested, in response to the rape charge, that there could be consensual sexual relationships between black men and white women.[26]

Most white women, especially those already prominent as activists for suffrage or temperance, could not be bothered to support the antilynching campaign, either out of apathy or fear that it would harm their own reform causes. There was also racial pressure from within the white community, as those white women who did attempt to speak or take actions against lynching faced retaliation. Bostonian Lillian Clayton Jewett lent assistance to the family of a South Carolina lynching victim and attempted to launch a national women's antilynching movement. Jewett received personal death threats, was labeled a "South-hater," and was burned in effigy in Richmond, Virginia, public reactions that undoubtedly deterred other white women from joining her in the cause.[27]

Black reformers such as Ida B. Wells were able to get their message out because of two developments in late nineteenth-century American political culture: the growth of a black press in the North and the emergence of a black women's club movement. Wells worked through the black women's clubs, which organized around the same time and in the same ways that white women's clubs were unifying on a national level. After the Reconstruction era, black women reformers organized around issues of civil rights, self-improvement or "racial uplift," and woman suffrage. Local clubs included the Colored Women's League of Washington, D.C., and the Woman's Era Club of Boston, but after black women reformers experienced exclusion from white women's national clubs and conferences, such as being shut out of the ladies' organizing committees for the 1893 World's Columbian Exposition, they sought their own umbrella organization for national effectiveness.

In 1896, the National Association of Colored Women (NACW) was founded with Mary Church Terrell as its first president. Just as white women did, middle-class black women also used the language of domesticity and of their responsibility as women to address issues relevant to their race. "Lifting as We Climb" became the motto of the NACW, and they professed the goal of helping themselves as they helped others. Like the mostly white General Federation of Women's Clubs (GFWC), founded in 1890, the NACW was made up of middle-class Protestants who shared and emphasized women's domestic influence, but race made a difference in the way middle-class gender was experienced. One black woman reformer explained the difference between black and white women's clubs: "Among colored women the club is the effort of the few competent in behalf of the many incompetent. . . . Among white women the club is the onward movement of the already uplifted."[28]

Black women moved outward from the community, as their claim to "making the home better" encompassed a large realm of issues. But, unlike the situation with white women, the problems they addressed were not always those of different or unfortunate "others." The issues addressed by black women were more likely problems in their own neighborhoods. Education was often at the center of their concerns as an important issue in their own communities. Reformers investigated schools for black children and reported on changes needed in facilities, black teachers' salaries, and segregated and unequal higher education. Their solutions included creating after-school care programs, playgrounds, and vacation schools, significantly, all issues to accommodate working mothers,

Mary Church Terrell (ca 1890s). Terrell was a prolific journalist and reformer committed to racial uplift, social justice, and women's rights. She served as the first president of the National Association of Colored Women, founded in 1896 as an umbrella organization for the black women's club movement. (Library of Congress, Prints & Photographs Division, LC-USZ62-84496.)

as black women were more likely to have to continue to work for wages after marriage and motherhood.

In 1890 the General Federation of Women's Clubs (GFWC) served as a national umbrella group, bringing together various white women's organizations such as mother's clubs, educational clubs, temperance societies, protective labor leagues, and other local and state organizations. Although some clubwomen were supportive of suffrage, officially the women's club organizations did not engage in the effort to pass either state- or federal-level amendments. The GFWC focused its members' energies on a wider range of issues related to bettering the lives of women and children, from public health reforms, to community-based projects and services, to establishing schools and libraries, to temperance. The women's club movement marked a shift in the temperance campaign toward the more aggressive strategies that would lead to prohibition within a few decades. The late nineteenth-century reform networks ushered in a new era as women reformers turned away from a strategy of self-improvement to more active engagement in political affairs. As one clubwoman argued, referring to nineteenth-century literary clubs, "Dante is dead. He has been dead for several centuries, and I think it is time that we dropped the study of his *Inferno* and turned our attention to our own."[29]

Although the growth of a black middle class and a larger number of black and white American women attaining college educations meant an expansion of women's participation in public life, women were still barred from many of the professions and late nineteenth- and early twentieth-century women reformers continued to draw upon the ideology of domesticity and female moral authority to justify their involvement in the public world. Women reformers emphasized responsibility and duty rather than rights in an approach referred to as "social" or "municipal" housekeeping. As Jane Addams explained of her generation's work in 1910:

> If a woman would keep on with her old business of caring for her house and rearing her children she will have to have some conscience in regard to public affairs lying quite outside of her immediate household. The individual conscience and devotion are no longer effective.[30]

Jane Addams is often cited as the perfect example of this generation of college-educated women, determined to engage in some useful occupation, but without access to political power or to many of the professions at the end of the nineteenth century. Addams responded, in part, by helping to create a new profession for American women, that of social worker. (See also Chapter 4, "Education and the Professions.") Building on the tradition of women's involvement in reform throughout the century, Addams founded the settlement house movement with the establishment of Hull House in Chicago in 1889. Hull House was a center dedicated to aiding urban immigrants, the poor, women, and children, through providing health services, education and vocational training, child care, and a variety of legal, social, and cultural services. Addams, her coworkers, and settlement workers in other cities made it their business to campaign for clean water, health care, and child labor laws, all in the name of helping other women and children. The idea of the settlement house helped centralize services and women's political involvement at the local level and brought many social service concerns to the attention of government officials, defining reform strategies of the first decades of the twentieth century, which came to be referred to as the Progressive Era.

Women were prominent as social and political reformers and many of the issues addressed throughout the nineteenth century were primarily concerned with women's lives, with relations between the sexes, and with issues of women's moral and political influence on society. Arguments against slavery often revealed anxieties about all women's sexual and economic vulnerability, as well as restrictions on women's public activities and speech. Temperance arguments highlighted the issue of male abuse of women and children. Dress and diet reform were intricately tied to women's right to control their own health and bodies. And the women's club movements ushered in an era of social work and government attention to issues important to local communities. Although they fought tirelessly for

Susan B. Anthony and Elizabeth Cady Stanton (ca 1890s). Anthony (standing) and Stanton (seated) were leaders of the women's rights movement for more than half a century. (Library of Congress, Prints & Photographs Division, LC-USZ61-791 DLC.)

the vote well into the twentieth century, lacking any formal political rights of citizenship, both black and white women had a strong voice in public affairs and debates by claiming social and political reform as an extension of their roles in the home and family, whether in the moral reform campaigns of the early part of the century or the later nineteenth- and early twentieth-century focus on social housekeeping. When American women demanded representation at the Columbian Exposition of 1893, they sought to highlight but also to demand recognition for women's involvement in public life and reform throughout the "century of women."

NOTES

1. Chris Dixon, *Perfecting the Family: Antislavery Marriages in Nineteenth-Century America* (Amherst: University of Massachusetts Press, 1997), p. 58.

2. Mary Ryan, *Cradle of the Middle Class: The Family in Oneida County, New York, 1790–1865* (New York: Cambridge University Press, 1981), p. 90.

3. Bruce Dorsey, *Reforming Men and Women: Gender in the Antebellum City* (Ithaca, N.Y.: Cornell University Press, 2002), p. 65.

4. Dorothy Sterling, ed., *We Are Your Sisters: Black Women in the Nineteenth Century,* rev. ed. (New York: Norton, 1997), p. 110.

5. Sterling, *We Are Your Sisters,* p. 112.

6. Dorsey, *Reforming Men and Women,* p. 134.

7. Mari Jo Buhle, *Women and American Socialism, 1870–1920* (Urbana: University of Illinois Press, 1983), p. 61.

8. Buhle, *Women and American Socialism,* p. 65. Emphasis in original.

9. Maria Stewart, "Religion and the Pure Principles of Morality, 1831" and "Lecture Delivered at the Franklin Hall, Boston, 1832," excerpted in Kathryn Kish Sklar, *Women's Rights Emerges within the Antislavery Movement, 1830–1870: A Brief History with Documents* (Boston: Bedford/St. Martin's, 2000), pp. 80–81.

10. Angelina Grimké, "An Appeal to the Women of the Nominally Free States, 1837," excerpted in Sklar, *Women's Rights,* pp. 100–102. Emphasis in original.

11. "Anti-Slavery Convention of American Women, Proceedings, New York City, May 9–12, 1837," excerpted in Sklar, *Women's Rights,* p. 105.

12. Sojourner Truth, "Speech at Akron Women's Rights Convention, Ohio, June 1851," reprinted in Sklar, *Women's Rights,* pp. 179–80.

13. Dixon, *Perfecting the Family,* p. 30.

14. Elizabeth Cady Stanton, "Letter to Sarah Grimké and Angelina Grimké Weld, London, June 25, 1840," reprinted in Sklar, *Women's Rights,* p. 169.

15. "Report of the Women's Rights Convention, Seneca Falls, N.Y., July 19–20, 1848," reprinted in Sklar, *Women's Rights,* p. 174.

16. Elizabeth Cady Stanton, *Eighty Years and More* (1898), quoted in *Through Women's Eyes: An American History with Documents,* 3rd ed., ed. Ellen Carol DuBois and Lynn Dumenil (Boston: Bedford/St. Martin's, 2005), p. 225.

17. Paulina Wright Davis, "The 'Call' to the Worcester Convention," reprinted in John F. McClymer, *This High and Holy Moment: The First National Woman's Rights Convention, Worcester, 1850* (Orlando, Fla.: Harcourt, Brace, 1999), p. 67.

18. Paulina Wright Davis, "Proceedings of the Woman's Convention, Held at Worcester, 1850," reprinted in McClymer, *This High and Holy Moment*, p. 75.

19. Quotes in Sylvia Hoffert, *When Hens Crow: The Woman's Rights Movement in Antebellum America* (Bloomington: Indiana University Press, 1995), p. 57.

20. Mary Ryan, *Women in Public: Between Banners and Ballots, 1825–1880* (Baltimore: Johns Hopkins University Press, 1990), pp. 152–54.

21. Frances Ellen Watkins Harper, "Speech at the Eleventh Woman's Rights Convention, New York, May 1866"; and "Equal Rights Association, Proceedings, New York City, May 1869," in Sklar, *Women's Rights*, pp. 196–99 and pp. 200–203, respectively.

22. Lynn Sherr, *Failure Is Impossible: Susan B. Anthony in Her Own Words* (New York: Random House, 1995), p. 109.

23. On Anthony's congressional amendment campaign, see Sherr, *Failure Is Impossible*, pp. 91–105.

24. Barbara Goldsmith, *Other Powers: The Age of Suffrage, Spiritualism, and the Scandalous Victoria Woodhull* (New York: Knopf, 1998), p. 212.

25. On black women's participation in AWSA and other organizations, see Rosalyn Terborg-Penn, *African American Women in the Struggle for the Vote, 1850–1920* (Bloomington: Indiana University Press, 1998).

26. See Jacqueline Jones Royster, ed., *Southern Horrors and Other Writings: The Anti-Lynching Campaign of Ida B. Wells, 1892–1900* (Boston: Bedford/St. Martin's, 1997).

27. Rebecca Edwards, *Angels in the Machinery: Gender in American Party Politics from the Civil War to the Progressive Era* (New York: Oxford University Press, 1997), p. 144.

28. Fannie Barrier Williams, "The Club Movement among Colored Women" (1900), quoted in Paula Giddings, *When and Where I Enter: The Impact of Black Women on Race and Sex in America* (New York: Morrow, 1984), p. 98.

29. Dorothy Schneider and Carl J. Schneider, *American Women in the Progressive Era, 1900–1920: Change, Challenge, and the Struggle for Women's Rights* (New York: Doubleday, 1993), p. 99.

30. Jane Addams writing for the *Ladies' Home Journal* (January 1910), quoted in Anne Firor Scott, *Natural Allies: Women's Associations in American History* (Urbana: University of Illinois Press, 1992), p. 141.

SUGGESTED READING

Bordin, Ruth. *Women and Temperance: The Quest for Power and Liberty, 1873–1900.* New Brunswick, N.J.: Rutgers University Press, 1990.

Dixon, Chris. *Perfecting the Family: Antislavery Marriages in Nineteenth-Century America.* Amherst: University of Massachusetts Press, 1997.

Dorsey, Bruce. *Reforming Men and Women: Gender in the Antebellum City.* Ithaca, N.Y.: Cornell University Press, 2002.

DuBois, Ellen Carol. *Feminism and Suffrage: The Emergence of an Independent Women's Movement in America, 1848–1869.* Ithaca, N.Y.: Cornell University Press, 1999.

Edwards, Rebecca. *Angels in the Machinery: Gender in American Party Politics from the Civil War to the Progressive Era.* New York: Oxford University Press, 1997.

Fischer, Gayle V. *Pantaloons and Power: Nineteenth-Century Dress Reform in the United States.* Kent, Ohio: Kent State University Press, 2001.

Ginzberg, Lori. *Women and the Work of Benevolence: Morality, Politics, and Class in the Nineteenth Century*. New Haven, Conn.: Yale University Press, 1992.

Gordon, Ann D., Joyce A. Berkman, and John H. Bracey, eds. *African American Women and the Vote, 1837–1965*. Bloomington: Indiana University Press, 1998.

Hansen, Debra Gold. *Strained Sisterhood: Gender and Class in the Boston Female Anti-Slavery Society*. Amherst: University of Massachusetts Press, 1993.

Hoffert, Sylvia. *When Hens Crow: The Woman's Rights Movement in Antebellum America*. Bloomington: Indiana University Press, 1995.

Jeffrey, Julie Roy. *The Great Silent Army of Abolitionism: Ordinary Women in the Antislavery Movement*. Chapel Hill: University of North Carolina Press, 1998.

Ryan, Mary. *Women in Public: Between Banners and Ballots, 1825–1880*. Baltimore: Johns Hopkins University Press, 1990.

Terborg-Penn, Rosalyn. *African American Women in the Struggle for the Vote, 1850–1920*. Bloomington: Indiana University Press, 1998.

Varon, Elizabeth. *We Mean to Be Counted: White Women and Politics in Antebellum Virginia*. Chapel Hill: University of North Carolina Press, 1998.

Venet, Wendy Hamand. *Neither Ballots nor Bullets: Women Abolitionists and the Civil War*. Charlottesville: University Press of Virginia, 1991.

Wayne, Tiffany. *Woman Thinking: Feminism and Transcendentalism in Nineteenth-Century America*. Lanham, Md.: Lexington Books, 2005.

Yee, Shirley. *Black Women Abolitionists: A Study in Activism, 1828–1860*. Knoxville: University of Tennessee Press, 1992.

Yellin, Jean Fagan. *Women and Sisters: The Antislavery Feminists in American Culture*. New Haven, Conn.: Yale University Press, 1989.

Yellin, Jean, and John Van Horne, eds. *The Abolitionist Sisterhood: Women's Political Culture in Antebellum America*. Ithaca, N.Y.: Cornell University Press, 1994.

6

—⚭—

Slavery and the Civil War

In perhaps the best-known female slave narrative of the nineteenth century, *Incidents in the Life of a Slave Girl* (published in 1861), former slave Harriet Jacobs lamented, "Slavery is terrible for men; but it is far more terrible for women. Superadded to the burden common to all, they have wrongs, and sufferings, and mortifications peculiarly their own."[1] The very purpose of Jacobs's story was to emphasize what those "peculiar" burdens of women were: namely, that slave women were expected to perform many of the same tasks as men in the field and in white households, but women were also subjected to sexual exploitation by white masters, including the expectation that they would reproduce the slave workforce.

Although slavery existed in all of the American colonies before the Revolution, the Southern colonies in particular were founded for the purpose of profitmaking through slave agricultural labor, a system propelled in the nineteenth century by the geographical expansion of the new United States as well as technological advances, such as the invention of the cotton gin in 1793. The North did not need slavery in the same way, for its family farms and merchants were not engaged in large-scale commercial agriculture. However, well into the nineteenth century, profitable Northern industries such as the textile mills, which employed large numbers of young white women, were dependent upon and fueled by the cotton boom in the slave South. By 1804 all of the Northern states had abolished slavery, although some were in the process of doing so only through gradual emancipation so that there were still some legal slaves in the North. In 1808 the international slave trade was abolished, but the United States continued to see heavy growth in the domestic slave population, primarily because of the reproductive work of slave women. The spread of the cotton economy into new territories and states after 1800 brought new opportunities for white pioneers but often had a disastrous effect on the slave community, separating spouses and families, as children and young male laborers were sold farther west.

African and African American men and women had been enslaved for 200 years and had, from the beginning, resisted their enslavement. But it was not until the early nineteenth century that an organized movement of free blacks as well as whites arose to begin the public fight to end slavery. Both black and white women took a prominent role in the abolitionist movement (see also Chapter 5, "Politics and Reform"), which helped propel the nation toward civil war and ultimately secured the freedom of nearly four million African Americans. After the war women continued to work as reformers and as teachers committed to helping the newly freed people.

The war itself affected women, both North and South, black and white, as individuals and as members of families. Both Northern and Southern women responded as patriots, lending their support and assistance to their side's cause by weaving blankets for soldiers, feeding and clothing troops, economizing at home with scarce resources, volunteering as nurses, and managing farms and businesses while men were away. For Southern white women this meant the added responsibility of overseeing slaves and plantations in the absence of men. And in some cases, white women both North and South played unofficial roles with the military as spies and even as soldiers disguised as men. As one Southern woman put it, the onset of war was "an entire disruption of our domestic relations."[2]

SLAVE WOMEN

In the colonial period there were generally more African men than women imported as slaves and by the mid-eighteenth century there were still more men in the overall American slave population. But by 1800 the sex ratio was more evenly balanced because of the natural increase of the slave population. Neither male nor female slaves had any control over the most basic aspects of their lives. Both were subject to harsh physical labor, malnourishment, cruel punishments, and separation from their families. But there were many gendered differences to the slave experience as well. One of the earliest laws regulating slavery spoke to the particular circumstances of slave women. A 1662 Virginia statute established that, unlike the English common law upon which most of the colonial legal system depended, the status of Africans in colonial America, whether slave or free, would be determined by the status of the mother:

> Whereas some doubts have arisen whether children got by any Englishman upon a Negro woman should be slave or free, Be it therefore enacted and

declared by this present grand assembly, that all children borne in this country shall be held bond or free only according to the condition of the mother.[3]

This statute guaranteed that any slave children born on a particular farm or plantation automatically increased the property value of the owner. More devastating, it legally sanctioned the rape and sexual exploitation of black women and institutionalized their status as breeders. Defining the "children got by an Englishman upon a Negro woman" as slaves also allowed one of the most unfathomable cruelties of the system, in that many white men made the decision to sell their own children as slaves, a story repeated over and over throughout the history of slavery.

Women, just as men, experienced a variety of conditions and hardships as slaves. They could live and work on small farms, on large plantations, or in cities. They could be owned by benevolent masters or by cruel ones, reside in one place their entire lives or be subject to sale and separation from their families. Slaves also performed a variety of tasks, as the demands and conditions of slavery varied in different regions of the South and were based on cycles and specific tasks associated with different agricultural products, whether cotton, sugar, or rice. There were, however, some basic commonalities defining the experience of enslaved women as a whole.

Young slave girls began their lives in a world where tasks and family life itself were separated by age and sex. Their mothers were often sent right back to the fields or the white households immediately after giving birth and most slave babies were taken care of by elderly slave women. In turn, young slave girls and boys might spend some time helping take care of infants, running errands, or tending animals before themselves being turned into field laborers and assistants. After reaching a certain age, most slave girls and women were integrated into networks of other women from whom they learned to negotiate the demands of daily life. From these other women, young girls learned not only how to perform the specific tasks assigned to them on the plantation, but also how to cook, spin, sew, and take of each other when they were sick. Mary Island, a slave born in Louisiana, recalled her experience:

> My mama died when I was two years old and my aunty raised me. She started me out washing dishes when I was four years old and when I was six she was learning me how to cook. While the other hands was working in the field I carried water.... When I got to be seven years old I was cutting sprouts almost like a man and when I was eight I could pick one hundred pounds of cotton.[4]

Once a girl became a teenager she might be able to choose a mate, if she was lucky. More likely she had little say in determining her own sexual life and could be subject to rape and exploitation by the master or be forced to "marry" another slave. Texas slave Laura Smalley recounted stories she had heard: "You know, jus' like a big fine looking woman, big fine looking man, you know, old boss wants, you know, children from them, you know. They just fasten them up in the house or somewhere, you know, and go off and leave them in there. Wan' to breed them like they was hogs or horses something like that I say."[5] A woman who did not bear children could be forced by her master to have sexual relations with different men, and, if she still did not conceive, she might be sold off to perform other work. Although some masters approved of slaves choosing their own marriage partners, primarily as a way of keeping their workers happy, whites also had an economic interest in producing slave children. (See also Chapter 1, "Marriage and Family Life.") It was for all of these reasons that former slave Harriet Jacobs lamented giving birth to a daughter: "When they told me my newborn babe was a girl, my heart was heavier than it had ever been before."[6]

All slaves were important investments, but an attractive woman could garner sometimes twice as much as even the most robust male laborer on the slave auction block. Any slave woman of childbearing age could be valued and sold for her reproductive abilities or potential, and any woman was at all times at risk of sexual exploitation by white men, but "fancy girls" constituted a separate market in the slave trade. These were women, young and often lighter-skinned, who were valued not as laborers or even potential breeders, but as prostitutes for their sexual services to the wealthiest white men, with reports of such women sold for as much as $5,000 at auction. As Harriet Jacobs explained the plight of the Southern bondwoman in the nineteenth century, "If God has bestowed beauty upon her it will prove her greatest curse. That which commands admiration in the white woman only hastens the degradation of the female slave."[7]

White slaveholders treated slaves primarily according to economic interests, but they also saw their female slaves according to the racial and gender assumptions of the time. Owners had different expectations in assigning responsibilities based on age, ability, and sex. At cotton-picking time everyone, including children and the elderly, worked in the fields. A male slave from South Carolina remembered: "Women worked in de field same as de men. Some of dem plowed jes' like de men and boys. Couldn't tell 'em apart in de field, as dey wore pantalets or breeches."[8] Besides working in the field, women might be used as housekeepers, nannies for white children, laundresses, cooks, personal servants, caregivers for slave children (usually elderly women), or sexual mistresses for the master. In addition, slave women often had the added responsibility for their own families or for other slaves on the same plantation, which meant spending their evenings preparing food, tending children, mending clothes, and trying to maintain clean living quarters. Some of the cruelest masters expected slave women to do extra work for them in the evenings under threat of punishment, such as recounted by the Georgia slave who explained, "When the work in the fields was finished women were required to come home and spin one cut a night."[9]

Most Southern women, black or white, were aided in childbirth by rural midwives, and many white women were attended as well by black midwives. Enslaved midwives enjoyed a more privileged status than possible for other slaves and possessed a skill that they could pass on to younger slave women. A skilled midwife served not only her own plantation but was frequently called upon and hired out to other plantations, and so she was an especially valuable addition to a slaveholder's income. One black midwife, Mildred Graves, later recalled that her master had even allowed her to keep a portion of the fee for herself, although her master did profit from her skills:

> I was always good when it come to the sick, so that was mostly my job. I was also what you call a midwife, too. Whenever any of the white folks around Hanover was going to have babies they always got word to Mr. Tinsley that they want to hire me for that time. Sure he let me go—'twas money for him, you know.[10]

Although older children or elderly slaves were sometimes assigned to care for babies and toddlers, many slave mothers had no choice but to take their young children right along with them into the fields or the kitchen.

Serving as a cook or housekeeper was also a more privileged position for slave women in that it at least potentially gave them some independence and control over their work and also gave them greater access to food on a regular basis. The demands of household management in the nineteenth century, however, meant that the domestic slave was often expected to live in the white household rather than in separate slave quarters and therefore be available to the white family at all times, day or night. Harriet Jacobs told the story of her Aunt Nancy who "slept on the floor in the entry, near Mrs. Flint's [her mistress] chamber door, that she might be within call."[11] Aunt Nancy was forced to continue sleeping there even after her own marriage. The importance of household slaves to the white family did not necessarily protect them from physical abuse. Indeed, that proximity sometimes increased their vulnerability, especially to the sexual advances of white men, and, subsequently, the humiliation, jealousy, and sometimes violence of the white mistress.

SLAVE WOMEN'S RESISTANCE

In many instances female slaves resisted and outright refused both sexual exploitation and demands for their labor by running away, responding with violence, feigning illness, or sabotaging both white efforts to control them and white economic interests. From the beginning, slave men and women actively resisted their enslavement, but sometimes in different ways. On the earliest slave ships, through what became known as the middle passage or journey across the Atlantic, Africans were often separated by sex, and, according to a 1789 report on slave transport, females were not always shackled as were the men. One trader noted that "we couple the sturdy Men together with Irons; but we suffer the Women and children to go freely about." Of course, going "freely about" was not quite the case, as there were many documented instances of women being abused, physically and sexually, by the ship's European crew members, and, shackled or not, all slaves were given little or no food or water on the long journey. Europeans also worked under the assumption that women would be more docile, although evidence exists that women did participate and perhaps even incite shipboard insurrections. In 1785 the captain of a slave ship was attacked by a group of women who tried to throw him overboard. The captain was rescued by his crew but some of the women, rather than risk punishment or an uncertain future as slaves, further resisted by starving themselves to death.[12]

The trans-Atlantic slave trade was abolished in 1808, although instances of illegal trading continued into the mid-nineteenth century. Beyond revolt on the middle passage, however, there was daily resistance on many levels to plantation slavery in the United States. Women's forms of resistance reflected the particular types of work that they did, the physiological fact that they were female and could therefore menstruate and become pregnant, and their responsibility for caring for children. According to newspaper ads for runaway slaves, there were consistently more male than female runaways. One reason offered for this fact is that slave women were more likely to stay on the plantations if they had children, as they did not want to leave them behind and it was too difficult and dangerous to attempt to run away or revolt with children in tow. In some cases entire families attempted to run away together, but in others only the father or other men escaped alone, planning to return or send for the others at a later date. Like men, however, slave women might also run alone, separated from children and family. Although the majority of runaways ads were for men, there were still a significant number for women in any major newspaper of the day. Some historians have pointed out that the definition of "running away" must be expanded, as in some cases women were more likely to run away temporarily to visit family on other plantations, for example.[13] In *Incidents in the Life of a Slave Girl*, Harriet Jacobs recounted her experience of escaping slavery by going only as far as her nearby grandmother's house, where she hid out in a crawl space above the kitchen for seven years before finally escaping to the North.

In 1850 the U.S. Congress passed the Fugitive Slave Act, making it more difficult for slaves to find refuge in the Northern states by requiring law enforcement, the courts, and citizens to assist in the return of fugitive slaves to the South. Harriet Tubman, herself an escaped slave from Maryland, was probably the best-known "conductor" on the Underground Railroad, a network of individuals and safe-houses that guided thousands of enslaved African Americans through the now-dangerous Northern states to the freedom of Canada. Tubman was personally responsible for helping several hundred slaves, including her own siblings and parents, reach freedom. As a result of her actions, she was wanted in Southern states where officials offered as much as $40,000 for her capture.

Other women played silent but vital roles in the Underground Railroad, sometimes assisting fugitive slaves without leaving their homes. Women created elaborate quilts that communicated clues and instructions for slaves escaping to the North. Patterns and colors on the quilts might indicate which direction to travel or highlight specific landmarks to reach, such as the "Crossroads" pattern, which usually referred to Cleveland, Ohio, as a meeting place. The spacing of the stitching or the size of the squares could be counted to indicate how many miles between safe houses. Black women would hang their quilts in their windows to be aired out, as was often done, and in this manner, the fugitive slaves could easily view them. In the case of quilts along the Underground Railroad, women's traditional domestic work took on a more subversive political role or meaning.[14]

Women also resisted the conditions and demands of slavery through direct physical confrontation with white slaveowners. One woman recounted the story of her own mother, a slave named Chloe Ann, whose master "tried to whop her with a cowhide, and she'd knock him down and bloody him up. Then he'd go down to some of his neighbor kin and try to get them to come help him whop her. But they'd say, 'I don't want to go up there and let Chloe Ann beat me up.' I heard Wash tell his wife they said that."[15] One of the most extraordinary stories of exploitation, violence, and resistance in the nineteenth century was that of a Missouri slave named Celia, who was raped by her master on the very day he purchased her in 1850 when she was only 14 years old. Over the next few years Celia was repeatedly sexually abused by her master and gave birth to several children by him. Her master provided her with her own separate cabin on his property, undoubtedly so that he could have access to her away from the eyes of his own grown children, but the private cabin ultimately allowed her to exact her own revenge. The only reason Celia's story is recorded in history is because she resisted her conditions by killing her white master, dismembering him, and burning parts of the body in her fireplace, acts for which she was ultimately put on trial and executed.[16]

"The Modern Medea—The story of Margaret Garner," *Harper's Weekly* (May 18,·1867). Garner was a fugitive slave who killed two of her children rather than have them returned to slavery. Her story inspired Toni Morrison's 1987 novel, *Beloved*. (Library of Congress, Prints & Photographs Division, LC-USZ62-84545.)

One of the ways slave women resisted rape and forced breeding was by refusing to bear children for white masters or refusing to allow their own children to become enslaved. The use of birth control, including abortion, was one way that women attempted to maintain some control over their bodies. Slave women did not necessarily act alone in these forms of resistance, but were often aided by other women with knowledge of medicines or herbs as well as instructions on specific methods. It is difficult for historians to ascertain precise numbers on how many slave women engaged in such practices, just as it was difficult for white owners to prove that such methods of sabotage had been used by their own slaves. But reports abounded of slave women who failed to produce any children during years of bondage but who went on to have several children after they were freed.[17]

Another subtle form of resistance that impacted white economic interests, but that could not always be proved, was feigning illness in order to avoid work. An overseer at President James Polk's plantation reported on the illnesses and missed work of a slave named Maria over the course of a year. Maria was "in a very bad condishon every thre or fore weeks," sometimes a month at a time, so that she was reported as "likely not to be able to do any service." Maria was finally deemed incapable of field service and brought into the house to learn weaving, where the overseer then reported that she "aperes to enjoy as good helth at present as any person." Maria not only escaped punishment for her actions but was successful in negotiating the conditions of her enslavement by simply refusing to do certain types of work.[18]

Access to the white household allowed for very particular types of resistance. White families knew that they were vulnerable because of the trust they instilled in cooks, housekeepers, and nannies of their own children. A house servant named Delia later almost humorously recalled, "How many times I spit in the biscuits and peed in the coffee just to get back at them mean white folks."[19] White masters were afraid of being poisoned by slaves in the kitchen and of kitchen slaves who sabotaged their masters by stealing or simply destroying food and other provisions. Women resisted slavery in a variety of ways, but despite the cruelties and indignities of slavery, African American women endured and survived the roles imposed upon them as slaves and as women.

PLANTATION MISTRESS

Before the Civil War, Southern white women occupied a precarious and paradoxical position in the American slave system. On the one hand, they were not slaves, and the gender ideology of the nineteenth-century plantation South meant that white women were seen as frail, feminine, and morally superior. On the other hand, they were members of the slaveholding class and the reality of most Southern white women's lives of the nineteenth century was defined by violence as much as by hard work. Southern white women of all classes managed farms, homes, children, and sometimes slaves. Like their Northern counterparts, they were responsible for tasks such as organizing the household, food production, attending to the medical needs of their families, and educating their own children. (See also Chapter 2, "Work.")

Women of the slaveholding class had little choice in the matter of slavery as it existed in their own households, although they certainly could choose how to respond to individual slaves. Many white women were privately critical of slavery, and, in particular, of its effect on white women, who were often tormented over illicit relationships between their own husbands and female slaves. Numberless white women endured this indignity quietly, while others took their anger and humiliation out on the slaves themselves. Others wrote privately about the degradation of white womanhood, a theme which emerged in diaries, letters, and even women's fiction of the time. One of the most famous Civil War–era diarists, Mary Chesnut of South Carolina, criticized the activities of white men and the blindness of white women to what was going on in their own homes. Chesnut reflected on the shame that pervaded white Southern society so that "the mulattoes one sees in every family partly resemble the white children. Any lady is ready to tell you who the father is of all the mulatto children in everybody's household but her own."[20] Mary Chesnut reported that a male overseer once remarked that, regardless of what they could say or do publicly, most Southern white women were "abolitionists in their hearts—and hot ones, too."[21]

Some white women were critical not so much of slavery, but of individual slaves who were deemed lazy and demanding, and of the "exactions and dictations of the black people . . . which now seem almost too extraordinary to relate," as one mistress complained. An Alabama mistress declared she "would be willing to spend the rest of my life at the North, where I never

"Ladies Whipping Girls" (1834). This illustration appeared in a book by prominent antislavery activist George Bourne, entitled *Picture of Slavery in the United States of America.* The image was intended to shock readers by revealing how slavery degraded not only the black woman but the white woman as well. (Library of Congress, Prints & Photographs Division, LC-USZ62-30825.)

should see the face of another Negro"—hardly an abolitionist sentiment. Besides accounts of the hardships and complaints of managing slaves, the writings of plantation wives overwhelmingly reveal a life of geographical isolation and of restrictions based on an ideology of white womanhood that kept them confined to domestic concerns. One Virginia woman wrote after moving to a large estate that she was "absolutely as far removed from every thing . . . as if I was in a solitary tomb."[22]

Given such isolation from other white families and friends, many white women depended upon the friendship and company of their female slaves and certainly many formed lifelong bonds with their servants, cooks, and nannies. Others, however, lived in fear of the slaves in their midst. Mary Chesnut's cousin was smothered by a slave, leading Chesnut's sister, Kate, to be wary of her own house servant: "Does she mean to take care of me— or to murder me?"[23] White women were also capable of inflicting physical punishment on their slaves, and, in some cases, such actions were demanded of them in their role as slave managers when their husbands were away. Other women took on this new role quite reluctantly and still others admitted they were not up to the task, emotionally or physically, of controlling a slave labor force alone, especially slaves who knew the nation was in the midst of a war over their very freedom. One Alabama woman wrote to the governor of her state, requesting an exemption from service for her husband, pleading that "Where there are so many negroes upon places as upon ours, it is quite necessary that there should be men who can and will controle them." Another woman decided she could manage quite well as she knew how to "get along with negro men," a necessary skill because she had determined "I shall not farm myself."[24]

CIVIL WAR

Once war broke out, women were called upon to support the war, either from afar or within their own backyards, in addition to continuing to carry out their duties in their own households. For many women throughout the South, as well as some women in the North, the war hit too close to home when their towns and neighborhoods became the battlefield. Women and children could be caught in the crossfire, with soldiers demanding food, stealing horses and supplies, and injured soldiers needing help. Many women were willing to give assistance where needed. One plantation mistress in Louisiana was so wearied by not only troops, but also poor white families going from town to town looking for food and shelter, that she set up two rooms in her house specifically for the use of strangers.[25] Other women were forced into service; in some instances, they were literally brought onto the battlefield to nurse the sick or to provide other assistance to troops coming through town. Others were simply attempting to go about their lives, running farms and raising children, such as 20-year-old Jennie Wade of Gettysburg, Pennsylvania, who was kneading dough in her own kitchen when a bullet from the outside ensuing battle came through the wall and hit her in the back, killing her instantly.[26]

For many women whose husbands were enlisted to fight, their wartime roles expanded to include maintaining family businesses and farms. The war became personal and close to home for 30-year-old Elizabeth Thorn, mother of three and pregnant again in 1863. Thorn had spent the war running her own household, feeding generals and troops on demand, and doing her husband's work of running the family business, the town cemetery, while he was away on a Union campaign. Elizabeth was responsible for general upkeep as well as gravedigging and other tasks associated with interment while her husband was gone. She was finally forced to evacuate as the fighting closed in on the family compound, and returned later only to find that her own home had been destroyed, her gardens and animals ransacked by Union soldiers for food, even her furniture had been stolen. Under these conditions, in the immediate aftermath of the battle at Gettysburg, a pregnant Thorn, along with her father and a few hired friends, dug nearly 100 graves for Union soldiers in need of proper burial. Thorn later told a reporter, "Those hard days always told on my life."[27]

Although local women with no formal medical or volunteer experience attended many soldiers, throughout the North women began to organize hospitals and relief societies to officially support the war effort. The Civil War resulted in the shift in nursing, in particular, from a formerly male to a predominantly female occupation, with as many as 2,000 Northern women serving the Union cause during the war. Women were now in a role that took them out of the home and onto the front lines of the sick and dying as well as into new executive roles. For many volunteers, such as Louisa May Alcott, who worked as a nurse in Washington, D.C., and published a fictional account of her experiences, *Hospital Sketches*, in 1863, wartime service was an extraordinary and temporary experience, but other women made new careers out of nursing. Dorothea Dix, a former teacher and prison and asylum reformer, emerged as a leader of this new army of female nurses in her role as Union Superintendent of Nurses. Concerned about the propriety of women working so closely with male soldiers, Dix set up strict regulations for recruiting volunteers, requiring that nurses be more than 30 years old and "plain looking women." The government eventually paid female nurses under Dix $12 per month at a time when male nurses were paid three times that amount.

The women of one of the largest relief organizations, the United States Sanitary Commission, founded in 1861 to attend to the health needs of soldiers on the battlefield, took pride in their "executive talents" put to use in organizing food and medical supplies to be sent to troops in the field.

Women and children at a Union camp near Washington, D.C. (1862). The Civil War was often a family affair as women joined husbands or brothers in camp or came from nearby towns to offer assistance to soldiers in the field. (Library of Congress, Prints & Photographs Division, LC-USZC4-7983.)

Mary Livermore recalled her numerous roles and duties within the Chicago chapter of the Sanitary Commission:

> I ... delivered public addresses to stimulate supplies and donations of money; ... wrote letters by the thousand ...; made trips to the front with sanitary stores ...; brought back large numbers of invalid soldiers ...; [and] detailed women nurses.[28]

Livermore used her wartime experience to launch a public service and re-form career after the war, as did Clara Barton, a nurse and organizer of relief efforts for the Union army during the war who later founded the American Red Cross in 1881 to carry on her mission of bringing assistance and supplies to those in need.

Confederate women also collected and brought food, medicine, and comfort to rebel prisoners and hospital inmates in border cities such as Washington, D.C., and Baltimore, Maryland. Juliet Opie Hopkins organized a hospital in Richmond, Virginia, where one admirer declared "if you had been a man, you would have been a commanding general." As it was, Hopkins volunteered her time and was not acknowledged by the Confederate army at all. Not all men were as ready to accept women's contributions, especially their new supervisory roles. As one critic wrote in a newspaper editorial, "In their proper sphere, [women] are most valuable auxiliaries; but when they presume to direct or control the physician, their services may well be dispensed with."[29]

Critics or others with reservations about women stepping outside of her "proper sphere" could not counter the desperate need for women's labor, nor their own desire to make a patriotic contribution, during the Civil War. Women also took on more public roles through organizing, either in support of the war or in protest to specific policies. During the war, women entered the public sphere of the streets and town halls as wives and mothers, emphasizing the costs and the significance of the war for American families. As the *New York Herald* reported on women's presence in one particular "Immense Demonstration" to support the Union cause in the summer of 1862, women, even though they are not in battle, "share[d] the danger and privations of war."[30]

Many Northern abolitionists as well as women's rights activists simply expanded their already established public roles as reformers to lend their support to the Union cause. Susan B. Anthony and Elizabeth Cady Stanton established the National Women's Loyal League in 1863 to push for a constitutional amendment to end slavery. The league specifically sought to provide a role for activist women interested in supporting and contributing to the war effort beyond the typical women's roles of "nursing the sick and wounded, knitting socks, and making jellies." Stanton emphasized that the war concerned women just as much as men, and the group created some controversy when Stanton and other members were publicly critical of President Lincoln's hesitance in pursuing emancipation. The newspapers reported on this "great uprising of the women of the North," who, by the end of the war, had collected nearly 400,000 signatures that they presented to Congress.[31]

Whereas Northern middle-class women displayed their patriotism through organizing and relief efforts, the war had a very different meaning for working women in the North as poorer and immigrant men were drafted into service with the Union army. The New York City draft riots in the summer of 1863 incited public outcries from many Irish and working-class women who protested the drafting of their men, which left their families in economic hardship. The *New York Herald* newspaper went so far as to blame women for the violence of other rioters, explaining, "The female relatives of the conscripts mingled their wildest denunciations against the conscription law, and thus gave the people a 'cavalier' motive to enact the terrible scenes."[32]

Women in both the North and the South found paid work in temporary positions that would have been unavailable and even considered unsuitable for women before the war. Both Union and Confederate governments hired women for clerical positions and women took such jobs in the name of patriotic duty. Although their labor was needed and they were actively recruited during the war, the presence of women in the workforce created tensions, and, in one case, controversy within the federal government itself. In 1864 a Congressman from New York accused the Patent Office filled with young women of becoming a place of "orgies and bacchanals," resulting in a scandalous investigation into "the reputation of three hundred females," which included the false accusation that one woman had even had an abortion to cover up her actions.[33] Young women working in clothing and munitions factories faced damage to their reputations as well as life-threatening dangers. A deadly explosion in a Washington munitions assembly factory employing more than 100 women workers, mostly single Irish women, killed 23 and wounded several others, and similar accidents happened in other cities as well.[34]

For African American women the war brought the promise of freedom. As soon as war broke out, some slaves sought to escape to the North or to join Union forces as they swept through the South. As early as August 1861, the U.S. Congress gave the Union army authority to seize "all property in aid of rebellion," including slaves. After the Emancipation Proclamation of January 1, 1863, African American men could enlist in the Union army as soldiers, but many formerly enslaved women also joined Union camps, working as cooks, laundresses, seamstresses, and nurses. Susie King Taylor was one such woman who worked in a variety of roles with the Union's first black regiment and later recounted her story in *Reminiscences of My Life in Camp with the 33rd U.S. Colored Troops, Late 1st South Carolina Volunteers.* King Taylor had been born a slave, but had received an education and was freed early in the war. She worked for the Union army, first as a laundress and then as a nurse and a teacher for escaped slaves living behind Union lines during the war. She even taught several soldiers enlisted with the black regiments to read and write. All of King Taylor's work for the Union army was as a volunteer; as she recalled, "I was very happy to know my efforts were successful in camp, and also felt grateful for the appreciation of my services. I gave my services willingly for four years and three months without receiving a dollar." King Taylor realized what an important role she had taken on and wrote her autobiography precisely because, years after the war, she realized that, "There are many people who did not know what some of the colored women did during the war."[35]

Even before the war ended, Northern women, white and black, followed closely behind the armies to provide relief to devastated and poverty-stricken Southern black communities and to assist in the transition from slavery to freedom. Women rushed in as missionaries and teachers to teach reading and writing as preparation for freedom. Approximately 4,000 women were responsible for establishing and running schools for freedpeople in the South throughout the 1860s and early 1870s. Charlotte Forten was a free black from Philadelphia who worked as an abolitionist and a teacher before the war. After the Civil War broke out, Forten went to South Carolina to teach escaped and former slaves, publishing her accounts as "Life on the Sea Islands" in the *Atlantic Monthly* in 1864. Forten wanted to teach children and adult slaves and to provide a role model, stating, "It is well that they sh'ld know what one of their own color c'ld do for his race. I long to inspire them with courage and ambition (of a noble sort), and high purpose," emphasizing the postwar themes of black women's work as "race reformers."[36] Many of these female teachers continued with their educational and reform work in the South through the end of the century, such as another Philadelphia teacher, Laura Towne, who went to South Carolina in 1862 and remained in the South for 40 more years as a teacher, temperance advocate, and public health reformer.

Working closely with the military as nurses, teachers, and in other positions led some women to make themselves available as spies during the war. One of the Confederacy's most famous female spies, Maria Isabella "Belle" Boyd, began her work as a nurse in Virginia but was employed because of her skills on horseback to travel and spy on the Union army and to carry information between Confederate officials. She was only 17 years old when the Union newspapers called her "the Siren of the Shenandoah" for her aid to Stonewall Jackson. She hid messages back and forth in her shoes, baked into bread, or hidden inside fruit, and was captured, imprisoned, and released on several occasions. Her account of her exploits, *Belle Boyd in Camp and Prison,* was published in 1865 at the end of the war.[37] Another Southerner, Elizabeth Van Lew, placed her loyalty with the Union cause, however, and used her connections to employ her own former slave, Mary Elizabeth Bowser, as a spy. These two women conspired in having Bowser work from the very top, in Jefferson Davis's office at the Confederate White House, where she stole information from his desk and Van Lew then passed the messages on to the North.[38]

Besides their work as spies, it is estimated that as many as 400 women dressed as men and served as soldiers. Some employed this strategy in order to accompany husbands and spouses into battle, while others enlisted and fought on their own out of a desire to serve. Such women used male names and many were successful at keeping their disguises for long periods of time before being discovered because of injury or death. Female spies and soldiers were celebrated by the press both during and after the war, and many subsequently published accounts of their wartime experiences. Sarah Emma Edmonds was one of the few women, however, who, having served as a nurse, spy, and soldier by the name of "Frank Thompson," was ultimately officially recognized by the Union army, and, in 1884, began to receive a military pension.[39]

RECONSTRUCTION

The end of the Civil War brought freedom for some four million African American men and women, but it left a generation of people struggling to rebuild their lives, economically and socially, including reconnecting with families separated by slavery and by war. As one Freedmen's Bureau official noted of what was often described as the "wandering" of black people after the war, "Every mother's son seemed to be in search of his mother; every mother in search of her children." Former slave Annie Burton recalled how her own mother had escaped from slavery before the war but returned to the plantation in 1865 to gather her children from a white mistress who still refused to give them up. The mother, knowing that they were legally free, was forced to physically remove them from the plantation:

> [M]y mother took Henry in her arms, and my sister carried me on her back. We climbed fences and crossed fields, and after several hours came to a little hut which my mother had secured . . . the master's sons rode up and demanded that the children be returned. My mother refused to give us up. Upon her offering to go with them to the Yankee headquarters to find out if it were really true that all negroes had been made free, the young men left, and troubled us no more.[40]

The postwar era of Reconstruction brought economic hardship as well, as black families sought to establish themselves in the Southern economy and in the only occupation most of them had ever known, farming. In some cases, former slaves began sharecropping simply because they continued to work the same land owned by the same master they had under the slave system. One former slave from Louisiana explained in a matter-of-fact way how the work remained the same, but how their roles had shifted from master-slave to landowner-tenant:

> [Master] come home and told us the War was over and we was all free. The Negroes didn't know what to make of it, and didn't know where to go, so he told all that wanted to stay on that they could just go on like they had been and pay him shares. About half of his Negroes stayed on and he marked off land for them to farm and made arrangements with them to let them use their cabins, and them have mules and tools. . . . But about half went on off and tried to do better somewheres else.[41]

Some slaves undoubtedly avoided working the fields for white landowners, a situation they found too reminiscent of slavery days. A Mississippi woman was moved to ask after the war, "Is I free? Hasn't I got to get up before daylight and go into the field to work?" Another who had stayed on with her former owners bitterly realized, "[D]ere wusn't no difference in freedom cause I went right on working for Miss."[42]

Nevertheless, sharecropping allowed black women, in particular, to have some control over their work lives, and, more important, over their own homes. Despite the hardships and the economic inequalities, sharecropping meant that families worked together, and the opportunity of tending to her own children in her own home was one that no former slave woman took for granted. Many preferred fieldwork to working in white households whenever possible, escaping the potential for sexual exploitation by white men that had prevailed under the slave system. Years after the Civil War, one black woman vowed, "There is no sacrifice I would not make . . . rather than allow my daughters to go in service where they would be thrown constantly in contact with Southern white men, for they consider the colored girl their special prey."[43] Many black women were eventually forced by economic necessity to do domestic work for white families but, even then, they preferred day-work to living-in so that they could return to their own homes and families at the end of the day. (See also Chapter 2, "Work.")

Southern white women were also economically devastated by the war. They had disproportionately lost their husbands and sons to the war, as well as their farms, and, in many cases, their slaves. Gertrude Thomas recalled that with the end of the war, "We were reduced from a state of affluence to comparative poverty, so far as I am individually concerned to utter beggary for the thirty thousand dollars Pa gave me when I was married was invested in Negroes alone."[44] Some whites appealed to the Freedmen's Bureau for economic relief, even though that agency had been established to aid former slaves. Widows had to depend only on themselves to rebuild their farms and livelihoods. One Virginia woman resorted to driving the plow herself, pulled by her two young daughters, as the family no longer owned any livestock.[45]

Black and white middle-class women were inspired by the war to continue their reform efforts into the Reconstruction era and to fulfill the promise of true "freedom" begun by the abolition of slavery. Women, including many former abolitionists, were central to the work of the Freedmen's Bureau, including Josephine Griffing, a white abolitionist and women's rights advocate, who was influential in getting the Freedmen's Bureau Bill passed in the first place in 1865, and who believed that women had a special role in the "care and education of these freedmen" that the government should recognize and support. Griffing herself organized mass numbers of volunteers, many of them women, to work for the agency, which provided education and employment assistance, did fund-raising for school buildings, and distributed food and confiscated and abandoned Confederate lands to former slaves.[46]

In 1872 the Freedmen's Bureau terminated as an office of the federal government and funding to such projects was ended. By that time, however, it had enlisted nearly 9,000 volunteer teachers, half of them women and many of whom continued on in their work, even without government assistance. Washington, D.C., schoolteacher Emma V. Brown declared that, in their service to the black community, she and her colleagues "have a little Freedmen's Bureau of our own." Like Griffing, Brown was convinced that women, especially black women, now had a significant role to play on the national scene, concluding, "I don't think women have ever before had so glorious an opportunity to do something—They have always been such insignificant creatures—so dependent."[47] By the end of the century, the political work of black women reformers, in particular, during the Reconstruction era gave rise to a national "club movement," which organized around postwar issues from black civil rights and antilynching to public health and education reform. (See also Chapter 5, "Politics and Reform.")

NOTES

1. Harriet Jacobs, *Incidents in the Life of a Slave Girl, Written by Herself,* ed. Jean Fagan Yellin (Cambridge, Mass.: Harvard University Press, 2000), p. 77.

2. Drew Gilpin Faust, *Mothers of Invention: Women of the Slaveholding South in the American Civil War* (Chapel Hill: University of North Carolina Press, 1996), p. 74.

3. Virginia statute quoted in Linda Kerber and Jane Sherron DeHart, *Women's America: Refocusing the Past,* 6th ed. (New York: Oxford University Press, 2004), p. 67.

4. Mary Island quoted in Ira Berlin, Marc Favreau, and Steven F. Miller, eds. *Remembering Slavery: African Americans Talk about Their Personal Experiences of Slavery and Emancipation* (New York: New Press, 1998), p. 95.

5. Laura Smalley qtd. in *Remembering Slavery,* pp. 298–99.

6. Jacobs, *Incidents in the Life of a Slave Girl,* p. 77.

7. Jacobs, *Incidents in the Life of a Slave Girl,* p. 28.

8. George Fleming qtd. in *Remembering Slavery,* p. 78.

9. Slave quoted in Deborah Gray White, *Ar'n't I a Woman?: Female Slaves in the Plantation South* (New York: Norton, 1985), p. 122.

10. Mildred Graves quoted in Darlene Clark Hine and Kathleen Thompson, eds., *A Shining Thread of Hope: The History of Black Women in America* (New York: Broadway Books, 1998), p. 77.

11. Jacobs, *Incidents in the Life of a Slave Girl,* p. 143.

12. Slave insurrection recounted in White, *Ar'n't I a Woman?,* p. 63.

13. Hine and Thompson, *Shining Thread of Hope,* p. 92.

14. See Jacqueline L. Tobin and Raymond G. Dobard, *Hidden in Plain View: A Secret Story of Quilts and the Underground Railroad* (New York: Doubleday, 1999).

15. Lulu Wilson qtd. in Hine and Thompson, *Shining Thread of Hope,* p. 90.

16. Melton A. McLaurin, *Celia, a Slave: A True Story of Violence and Retribution in Antebellum Missouri* (Athens: University of Georgia Press, 1991).

17. On birth control, abortion, and infanticide as resistance, see White, *Ar'n't I a Woman?*, pp. 84–87, and Hine and Thompson, *Shining Thread of Hope*, pp. 98–100.

18. Maria's story recounted in White, *Ar'n't I a Woman?*, pp. 81–82.

19. Delia qtd. in Hine and Thompson, *Shining Thread of Hope*, p. 92.

20. Chesnut qtd. in Hine and Thompson, *Shining Thread of Hope*, p. 50.

21. Chesnut quoted in Gail Collins, *America's Women: 400 Years of Dolls, Drudges, Helpmates, and Heroines* (New York: HarperCollins, 2003), p. 185.

22. Collins, *America's Women*, pp. 184–86.

23. Collins, *America's Women*, p. 189.

24. Faust, *Mothers of Invention*, pp. 56–57.

25. Charles Roland, *Louisiana Sugar Plantations during the Civil War* (Baton Rouge: Louisiana State University Press, 1997), p. 63.

26. Margaret S. Creighton, *The Colors of Courage: Gettysburg's Forgotten History: Immigrants, Women, and African Americans in the Civil War's Defining Battle* (New York: Perseus Books, 2005), pp. 120–22.

27. Creighton, *The Colors of Courage;* on Thorn, see p. 35, p. 154, and p. 158.

28. Livermore quoted in *Through Women's Eyes: An American History with Documents*, 3rd ed., ed. Ellen Carol DuBois and Lynn Dumenil (Boston: Bedford/St. Martin's, 2005), p. 232.

29. Faust, *Mothers of Invention*, pp. 93–94.

30. Mary Ryan, *Women in Public: Between Banners and Ballots, 1825–1880* (Baltimore: Johns Hopkins University Press, 1990), pp. 141–42.

31. Ryan, *Women in Public*, pp. 152–53.

32. Ryan, *Women in Public*, p. 148.

33. Collins, *America's Women*, p. 197.

34. Ernest B. Furgurson, *Freedom Rising: Washington in the Civil War* (New York: Knopf, 2004), pp. 303–5.

35. Patricia W. Romero, ed., *Susie King Taylor, Reminiscences of My Life: A Black Woman's Civil War Memoirs* (New York: Markus Wiener, 1988), quotes on p. 52 and p. 141.

36. Hine and Thompson, *Shining Thread of Hope*, p. 139.

37. Larry G. Eggleston, *Women in the Civil War: Extraordinary Stories of Soldiers, Spies, Nurses, Doctors, Crusaders, and Others* (Jefferson, N.C.: McFarland, 2003); see chap. 20, "Maria Isabella Boyd: Confederate Spy," pp. 92–96.

38. Catherine Clinton and Christine Lunardini, eds., *The Columbia Guide to American Women in the Nineteenth Century* (New York: Columbia University Press), p. 84.

39. See Laura Burgess, ed., *An Uncommon Soldier: The Civil War Letters of Sarah Rosetta Wakeman, alias Private Lyons Wakeman, 153rd New York State Volunteers* (New York: Oxford University Press, 1995).

40. Hine and Thompson, *Shining Thread of Hope*, p. 150.

41. Berlin, Favreau, and Miller, *Remembering Slavery*, pp. 232–33.

42. Noralee Frankel, *Freedom's Women: Black Women and Families in Civil War Era Mississippi* (Bloomington: Indiana University Press, 1999), p. 77.

43. DuBois and Dumenil, *Through Women's Eyes*, p. 281.

44. DuBois and Dumenil, *Through Women's Eyes*, p. 280.

45. Carol Hymowitz and Michaela Weissman, *A History of Women in America* (New York: Bantam, 1978), p. 151.

46. Griffing discussed in Carol Faulkner, *Women's Radical Reconstruction: The Freedmen's Aid Movement* (Philadelphia: University of Pennsylvania Press, 2003).

47. Faulkner, *Women's Radical Reconstruction,* p. 32.

SUGGESTED READING

Clinton, Catherine. *The Plantation Mistress: Woman's World in the Old South.* New York: Pantheon Books, 1982.

Clinton, Catherine, and Nina Silber, eds., *Divided Houses: Gender and the Civil War.* New York: Oxford University Press, 1992.

Edwards, Laura. *Gendered Strife and Confusion: The Political Culture of Reconstruction.* Urbana: University of Illinois Press, 1997.

Faulkner, Carol. *Women's Radical Reconstruction: The Freedmen's Aid Movement.* Philadelphia: University of Pennsylvania Press, 2003.

Faust, Drew Gilpin. *Mothers of Invention: Women of the Slaveholding South in the American Civil War.* Chapel Hill: University of North Carolina Press, 1996.

Fox-Genovese, Elizabeth. *Within the Plantation Household: Black and White Women in the Old South.* Chapel Hill: University of North Carolina Press, 1988.

Frankel, Noralee. *Freedom's Women: Black Women and Families in Civil War Era Mississippi.* Bloomington: Indiana University Press, 1999.

Gaspar, David Barry, and Darlene Clark Hine, eds. *More Than Chattel: Black Women and Slavery in the Americas.* Bloomington: Indiana University Press, 1996.

Leonard, Elizabeth D. *Yankee Women: Gender Battles in the Civil War.* New York: Norton, 1994.

Schultz, Jane E. *Women at the Front: Hospital Workers in Civil War America.* Chapel Hill: University of North Carolina Press, 2004.

White, Deborah Gray. *Ar'n't I a Woman?: Female Slaves in the Plantation South.* New York: Norton, 1985.

7

The West

The push westward was one of the defining characteristics of U.S. society in the nineteenth century, and one that defined the nation's politics, economy, and race relations. Westward movement had an enormous impact on the lives of American women—Anglo American women, European and Asian immigrant women, slave women, and Native American women alike, although each in different ways. For white women and new immigrant groups, moving into the western territories and states meant leaving family, but in search of new opportunities and new possibilities. For enslaved women, westward movement was involuntary, going where masters moved or sold them, from the Eastern Seaboard into the cotton fields of Texas, or to newly available lands in California on the eve of the Civil War. For Native American women, the westward movement of whites and the final "opening" and settlement of the frontier meant displacement and change.

From the European perspective, North America had always been a frontier society, even as that frontier was constantly shifting. For early colonists, Maine, Connecticut, or western Pennsylvania represented the farthest frontiers of settlement through the eighteenth century. By the turn of the nineteenth century, the European American population of the new United States was still largely concentrated east of the Appalachian Mountains, with the frontier by 1800 reaching only to Ohio in the North or Mississippi in the South. The nineteenth century opened with a new political purpose for the United States, based on Thomas Jefferson's vision of the nation's growth and expansion. This vision led Jefferson to make the Louisiana Purchase in 1803, doubling the geographical size of the United States at that time, and facilitating efforts to push white exploration and settlement to the Pacific Coast. The frontier soon moved rapidly over the course of just a few decades, so that by the mid-nineteenth century, white Americans had traveled and settled in large numbers throughout the Midwest, Southwest, and into the Oregon and California territories.

The massive movement of European Americans westward in the nineteenth century changed the economy and culture of the United States, so much so that it is accurate to characterize the Civil War, which broke out in 1861, as the North and South fighting over the West. Although abolitionists had spent decades decrying slavery as a moral and human rights problem, the nation was finally pushed to war in the 1860s in the midst of debates over whether and to what extent slavery would exist in the western territories and in any new states admitted to the Union. The Missouri Compromise of 1820 was a temporary solution to the strategy of balancing the number of free and slave states, but sectional politics, fueled by the hunger for western lands, accelerated the problem through the 1850s.

Underlying the political drama over control of the West were the many stories of the regular people who participated in and were impacted by the great movement across the continent in the nineteenth century. There were, in fact, many different frontiers over the course of the century—from early outposts engaged in the business of extracting and trading resources, to lone homesteads, to full-fledged pioneer settlements and new towns. Women's roles on each of these frontiers differed, resulting in many women's histories that make up the story of westward movement and settlement.

NATIVE AMERICAN WOMEN

From the first colonies in the early 1600s, European settlement of North America meant a constant push into lands already occupied by Native peoples, a struggle that continued throughout the nineteenth century. For three centuries, American Indians confronted disease, the decimation of their cultures, removal from their homelands, and military action by the United States. The final push came with the creation of the new U.S. government and the removal of other European interests from the majority of the continent. By the end of the 1830s, all eastern nations had been pushed west of the Mississippi and the rise of the reservation system characterized life in the West. By the end of the century, the reservations themselves, as well as government allotments to individual Indian families, were becoming smaller and smaller as European American settlement reached all the way to the Pacific Coast. Whether Native peoples chose to resist or to accommodate the westward push of white settlement, women had a central role in the survival of Native cultures and people, as well as in negotiating the terms and success of white exploration and settlement.

Native women fulfilled different roles in relation to the westward expansion of the United States, including sometimes as facilitators and mediators between white explorers and Native peoples. The story of a Shoshone woman, Sacagawea, made its way into American popular culture not through her own words but through the accounts recorded in the journals of William Clark and Meriwether Lewis, agents of Thomas Jefferson's Corps of Discovery expedition. Taken captive as a child, Sacagawea was purchased by a French fur trader who became her husband and with whom she had a son. She joined the expedition of William Clark in 1804, and he described her simply as the "Indian woman who has been of great service to me as a pilot throughout this country," a role that was used to justify subsequent U.S. treatment of "unfriendly" Indians. Sacagawea also assisted the men with finding food, making leather clothes, and medical care. At one point when she herself fell ill, Meriwether Lewis recorded his "concern for the poor object herself, then with a young child in her arms," but also his anxiety about "her being our only dependence for a friendly negociation [sic] with the Snake Indians on whom we depend for horses."[1] These brief journal accounts reveal more about the expedition's feelings toward Sacagawea rather than providing any substantial information about her life, but at least there are hints about her role in the legendary exploration.

At the time of Sacagawea's presence in the Lewis and Clark expedition, official U.S. Indian policy was focused on "civilizing" or Americanizing Native peoples, as Thomas Jefferson included Native peoples in his vision of a nation of independent family farmers. That policy, therefore, focused in large part on gender roles, as Jefferson and his agents believed that if Native Americans adopted white gender roles, they would have less need for land and there would be reduced conflict between whites and Native peoples. Specifically, Jefferson pleaded that Native men should give up hunting in exchange for farming and settled property ownership, and Native women should give up farming and traditional public or political roles to focus on domesticity:

> Let me entreat you, therefore, on the lands now given you to begin to give every man a farm; let him enclose it, cultivate it, build a warm house on it, and when he dies, let it belong to his wife and children after him. . . . If the men will take the labor of the earth from the women they will learn to spin and weave and to clothe their families. . . you see what a brilliant aspect is offered to your future history, if you give up war and hunting.[2]

Although every tribal group was different, many Native American women did traditionally derive economic and social power from their roles as the primary providers of food and cultivators of the land. In addition, Native women were more likely than white women to hold positions of spiritual leadership and, sometimes, political leadership as well. Thus, for those groups who accommodated under Jefferson's policy, an emphasis on men as heads of households and farmers meant a major shift in gender roles, and in women's potential power within those societies.

The U.S. policy of "civilizing" Native Americans was initially seen, by both white and Native men, as affecting primarily women, who were expected to give up their roles as farmers in traditional Cherokee society and engage in domestic tasks such as textile production, introduced to Native women by whites after the American Revolution. In the early 1800s, a white man who had married a Cherokee woman reported that "the females have made greater advances in industry than the males, they now manufacture a great quantity of cloth; but the latter have not made proportionate progress in Agriculture."[3] Cherokee men's reluctance to become small family farmers, as well as the fact that some Cherokee women, even married women, managed to retain control over their land or property, are evidence that the most "civilized" tribes were involved in a compromise only. Combining old and new beliefs and ways, many Cherokee women continued to farm, conduct business, and even own property. As many as one-third of Cherokee names listed as heads of households at the time of removal in 1835 were women.[4]

Those who resisted accommodation completely in favor of retaining their own culture, religion, and economic ways risked military confrontation with the United States. And, as became clear by the 1830s, even the five most "Civilized Tribes" of the Southeast—the Cherokee, Creek, Choctaw, Chickasaw, and Seminole—were eventually forced off their homelands. Many of these had spent the previous decades adapting to white society. Native American women had adopted domestic roles related to house and garden, men had taken up farming and business, and some Native families even owned African American slaves at the time of removal. Nonetheless, they were forced out to make room for white settlement and prospecting by President Andrew Jackson in a series of moves, culminating in the final 1838 "Trail of Tears" from the Southeast all the way to the Oklahoma Territory. The final removal was violent for many families, as a former soldier and interpreter recalled:

> Men working in fields were arrested and driven to stockades. Women were dragged from their homes by soldiers whose language they could not understand. Children were often separated from their parents and driven into the stockades with the sky for a blanket and earth for a pillow.[5]

Just a decade after white Georgians were pushing the Cherokee and other Southeastern tribes west of the Mississippi, the California gold rush forced the U.S. government to regulate settlement into the Far Western territories and states, resulting in ever-increasing warfare and tensions. Since colonial times, the meeting of Natives and whites on the frontier sometimes resulted in intermarriage and in the captivity of whites, stories of which continued to shock white society well into the 1800s, as the frontier of white settlement made its final push on Native lands. (See also Chapter 1, "Marriage and Family Life.") Even more shocking were cases of white women who chose to remain with their captors rather than return to their original families. Cynthia Ann Parker was born in frontier Illinois and moved to Texas with her family as a young child. In 1836, when she was just nine years old, Comanches raided the family compound and killed several family members. Most of the women and children, including Cynthia, were spared and taken captive. Over the next few years, all of the Parker captives were ransomed and released, except teenaged Cynthia, who chose to stay with her Comanche adoptive family. She took a new name, Preloch, and married a Comanche warrior who had been a leader in the attack on her family, bearing three children with him. In a U.S. military raid on the Comanche in 1860, she was separated from her husband and sons and she and her young daughter were returned to her white family in Texas. Both Parker/Preloch and her daughter died of illness soon after.[6]

Intermarriage was one way of establishing political and cultural ties between the two sides, and Indian women were central as mediators, peacemakers, and interpreters for both military and business negotiations. Born in Canada, Blood Indian Natawista traveled with her father into U.S. territory on business and at the age of 15 wed a white man, the head of a fur trading post. She often accompanied her husband on trading business and on his later survey expeditions for the railroads. Natawista played an important role as cultural mediator and probably interpreter for such projects as the railroads, which required negotiating for rights to travel and build the railroads through Native American lands. After 20 years of marriage, however, Natawista left her husband and returned to her Blood homeland and family.[7]

Of course, serving as a mediator, or even marrying a white man, were exceptional, not typical, experiences for women. Although their culture and traditional ways continued to change because of white settlement and policy, much about most Native American women's day-to-day lives remained the same, and, as with white women on the frontier, their lives revolved around the work of childrearing and household chores. Pretty-Shield, a Crow woman born in 1858, later remembered how the late nineteenth-century Plains Indians still practiced arranged marriages and explained the roles of the two sexes thus:

> We women had our children to care for, meat to cook and to dry, robes to dress, skins to tan, clothes, lodges, and moccasins to make. Besides these things we not only pitched the lodges, but took them down and packed the horses and the travois [a cart for pulling supplies], when we moved camp.

The final blow for these nomadic people and change to those traditional roles came, however, at the very end of the century, when "white men began to fence the plains so that we could not travel."[8]

Some Native women as well as white women spoke out publicly against U.S. Indian and Western policy, detailing the effects of westward expansion on Native culture and family life. Sarah Winnemucca's Paiute family was among those forcibly relocated from their homes in Nevada to a reservation in Washington in 1878. Just a few years later she published an account of their experiences in *Life among the Piutes: Their Wrongs and Claims* (1883), in which she recalled the harsh conditions and maltreatment of Native Americans by the United States. Just as some white pioneers described their fear of savage Indians, Winnemucca described the fear and rumors among her people that white people "were killing everybody and eating them," and remembered that the first white emigrants to come into Paiute country "came like a lion, yes, like a roaring lion, and have continued so ever since."⁹

Sarah Winnemucca Hopkins (ca 1880s). Winnemucca, also known as Thocmetony or Shell Flower, was the daughter of a Paiute chief and a lecturer and reformer who sought to raise awareness about the effect of white settlement on Native Americans in the Far West. This photo of her in full traditional dress was taken around the time that her auto-biography, *Life among the Piutes: Their Wrongs and Claims*, was published in 1883. (Nevada Historical Society.)

At first, Sarah's grandfather, once the chief of the Paiute nation, convinced his people to trust the whites and to migrate to California. Once they were removed all the way to Washington, however, Sarah described the harsh conditions, including the freezing cold and lack of adequate shelter or supplies: "Oh, how we did suffer with cold. . . . There was no wood, and the snow was waist-deep, and many died off just as cattle or horses do after traveling so long in the cold."[10] Sarah Winnemucca used her own experience to draw attention to the plight of Native Americans in the Far West in the last decades of the nineteenth century. Besides publishing her autobiography, she also traveled extensively, going to Washington, D.C., to speak out against U.S. treatment of Native peoples and against the reservation system in the West.

White author and reformer Helen Hunt Jackson also used her voice and her writing talent to draw attention to the plight of Native Americans. In her hugely popular 1884 fictional account of the displacement of American Indians, *Ramona,* as well as in her 1881 treatise, *A Century of Dishonor: A Sketch of the United States Government's Dealings with Some of the Indian Tribes,* Jackson produced a scathing critique of U.S. Indian policy and attempted to bring the problem to the attention of the white American public. She criticized the white frontiersman and the U.S. government working together to trample the claims and rights of indigenous people in the West:

> So long as there remains on our frontier one square mile of land occupied by a weak and helpless owner, there will be a strong and unscrupulous frontiersman ready to seize it, and a weak and unscrupulous politician, who can be hired for a vote or for money, to back him.[11]

Helen Hunt Jackson and other activists for the Indian cause promoted the allotment of land parcels to individual Indian families as an alternative to the degrading reservation system, but the 1887 Dawes Severalty Act, which set up the system of allotments, did not ensure the survival of Native families, either economically or culturally. The U.S. government reserved the most fertile farmlands for white settlers; additionally, allotments disrupted Native gender roles by designating men as heads of households and landowners. In the end, the allotment system at the end of the century threatened to undermine women's traditional sources of power, as well as traditional communal existence, just as Jefferson's "civilizing" policy did in the first part of the century by promoting the European model of men as farmers and women as keepers of the home. But as a group of Hopi women protested in 1894, "The family, the dwelling house and the field are inseparable because the woman is the heart of these, and they rest with her."[12]

The cases made by activists such as Sarah Winnemucca or Helen Hunt Jackson were bolstered by the tragic events at Wounded Knee Creek, South Dakota, in December 1890. In the process of forcibly marching more than 300 Sioux men, women, and children to a temporary campsite before removing them to Nebraska, the U.S. army began firing into the crowd. Louise Weasel Bear was there and remembered, "We tried to run, but they shot us like we were a buffalo."[13] At least 150 Lakota Sioux were killed that day, and perhaps more than 100 more who fled subsequently died because of the harsh winter conditions. Wounded Knee came to represent a violent and emblematic end to a century of tensions between Native Americans, white settlers, and the U.S. government.

Whereas Native peoples battled the U.S. government on one level, at the day-to-day level, they encountered the actual white settlers who pushed westward, facilitated by the larger battles and policies. Although many white pioneers feared encountering Native Americans, many white women diarists and letter writers often discussed their roles as guides and providers of food to near-starving travelers. In 1853, Amelia Knight revealed something of the role of Indian women meeting with white travelers along the overland trail and wishing to trade: "This afternoon we passed a large village of Sioux Indians . . . some of the women had moccasins and beads, which they wanted to trade for bread. I gave the women and children all the cakes I had baked."[14]

Once whites settled into their new homes, white women and Native women were sometimes brought together through common experiences as women, sharing knowledge of medicines, food preparation, and childcare. One white woman in California recorded that a local Native woman presented her mother with "beautiful baskets and elaborate moccasins worked with beads and feathers" upon the birth of a child. In some cases, white settlers and Native women found themselves interacting simply as neighbors, as one woman recalled making regular visits among "the Cherokee ladies." In other instances, however, the relationship was unequal, such as when Native women were employed to help white women with chores and childcare.[15]

Like indigenous women, the story of Mexican women, or Californianas, in the nineteenth century was one of displacement and loss of economic and social power as white settlers poured into the Far West. Mexican women had legal rights to land and property ownership that white women still did not have in the nineteenth century. In the 1830s and 1840s, Mexican women retained legal rights to property holdings, and some of the first white men to the region often married Mexican women, facilitating white control of valuable fertile lands and ranches. One of the richest women in California at the turn of the twentieth century was Arcadia Bandini of San Diego, who married two different white men but was able to hold on to her property rights as she was widowed both times. Some scholars believe that the Bandini family was the model for the wealthy Mexican rancheros who lost their lands and their culture in the last half of the nineteenth century, and the women in particular who lost their traditional sources of power, as portrayed in Helen Hunt Jackson's 1884 novel, *Ramona: A Romance of the Old Southwest.*[16]

Not all Mexican women had such power, however, nor were all unions based on schemes for control of property. Many indigenous and Native Mexican women intermarried or lived with the white men who came and established mining camps and other ventures before the large-scale movement of white women into areas of the Southwest and West. Such relationships rarely enter the historical record, but an 1864 wedding was recorded by a missionary minister in territorial Arizona. A miner named George Clinton and a Native New Mexican woman named Juanita Bachichia lived together and ran a boardinghouse or hotel for miners. Their wedding, the minister reported, "was conducted in an off-hand and truly Western manner. George was in his shirt sleeves and Juanita in her morning gown."[17] Although the presence of a minister in this particular outpost may have both encouraged and facilitated the recording of this marriage (the minister who performed the ceremony, a Reverend Hiram Walter Read, was also responsible for returning census records to the territorial government), surely many other relationships were never legalized or acknowledged in the historical record.

Not all encounters between men of European descent and Native American or Mexican women were always consensual. The opportunity for exploitation of the indigenous people was not just economic, but potentially sexual as well. A letter writer to the *Beacon* newspaper in Red Bluff, California, in 1862 complained that the soldiers who had been brought in for the purpose of protecting white settlers "against Indian depravations" were, in fact, the responsible parties in attacks on the "peaceful and domesticated Indians." In this instance, a group of soldiers "entered the Indian rancheria, with demands for Indian women, for the purpose of prostitution. They were requested to leave and ordered off the place. They answered they would do as they pleased." It was reported that most of the young women hid themselves from the men, but some of the soldiers subsequently "had forced intercourse with old squaws."[18]

EUROPEAN AMERICAN WOMEN

Accounts of European American pioneers usually focus on the decades of the most significant migrations in the latter half of the nineteenth century. White women's experience of westward migration began even earlier, however, in the 1810s and 1820s, with the movement of Southern planter families into the frontier areas of Alabama, Mississippi, Tennessee, and Kentucky. The sons of planters traveled to these areas in search of more land to grow their slave-based wealth, and, in many cases, these men wanted to escape the expectations and limitations of family connections on the East Coast. Women of the planter class, however, did not always have a role in making the decision to go west and often experienced the move as a great loss in terms of family connections. Moving even just 500 miles away was enough for a young man to start a new life, but for his wife to expect never to see her family again. One woman still wrote to her cousin 30 years after moving west, wishing "you were well nigh that I could step over and see you any time I wished, but that privilege is denied me."[19]

Men's writings as well reveal the difficulty of the situation for women. As one man warned his brother who was also considering the migration, "all do not like that move to the west—especially ladies." Another husband lamented that he had taken his wife "away from her family and friends, to a land of strangers, where she finds much to regret." Wives may have had little say or choice in the matter, but relatives left behind sometimes expressed their disapproval. One woman wrote to her son of another friend's son who had gone west, "[T]is strange that the love of money is stronger than the love of a kind and affectionate mother whose heart yearned to look on him." Slave women as well were taken involuntarily and saddened to leave familiar places. Former slave Issabella Boyd had been taken from Virginia to Texas and later recalled, "Every time we look back and think 'bout home it make us sad."[20]

After mid-century, a new wave of Anglo American and new European immigrants found their way westward because of technological advances as well as the encouragement of the government. The development of the railroads resulted in the spread of the agricultural economy and the settlement of Midwestern and Western towns. Additionally, in 1862, the opening of the West was facilitated by the federal Homestead Act, which encouraged individual families to move west and farm in exchange for acreage. White settlers made their way to Wisconsin and Minnesota, on to Utah and Idaho, and eventually all the way to Oregon, Washington, and California. Whereas many young families from Eastern states decided to head west for new opportunities, Midwestern and Far Western settlers at mid-century were just as likely to be foreign-born European immigrants as native-born Easterners. Immigrants primarily from northern and western Europe transplanted their families and their cultures into the new Midwestern farming and business communities they established. By the end of the nineteenth century, more than one-fourth of the entire U.S. population lived west of the Mississippi.

Although histories and legends of the American West often emphasize the lone frontiersmen and the miners, the Indian fighters and the individual explorers, it was primarily permanent settlers who changed the West by claiming land for farming and establishing new villages and towns. This was a West explored and settled by families—men, women, and children, young and old. In the last half of the nineteenth century, thousands of Americans crossed the continent into the Western territories to claim free land and

The Semler family homestead in Nebraska (1886). After the Civil War, increasing numbers of European Americans made the move westward in search of land and opportunities. This family's simple sod house was typical of many isolated homesteads established on the Midwest plains. (Library of Congress, Prints & Photographs Division, LC-USZ62-8277.)

resources and to begin new lives. Among them were thousands of ordinary women who knew that by claiming and settling land in the West, they were part of a uniquely American experiment. Luckily for future generations, hundreds of these women recorded their journeys, experiences, and feelings in diaries and letters back home, providing insight into what roles white women played in the "winning" and settling of the West.

Again, white women were not always eager volunteers for migration and men were more likely to make the economic and personal decision to go west. Although some territories encouraged women to file Western land claims by themselves if necessary, offering a legal and economic opportunity not as easily available to unmarried women in the East, most women who came west were members of families, daughters or wives who had no other choice. Some women eventually made known their feelings, especially after numerous migrations and moves had failed to land them in a settled place they could call home. One Colorado woman stood up to her husband, who apparently wanted to continue following the promise of the frontier, declaring:

> Ernest, you can move on if you have to, but I've dragged two boys and a houseful of furniture just as far as I'm going to. First it was Ohio, then Michigan, then the Peninsula, then Minnesota, Michigan again, then Denver, Weaver, and Creede, and right here I'm going to stay.[21]

Many women left their homes and families reluctantly, uncertain of their futures, but fairly certain that they would never see their families in the East (or what people in the new territories referred to as "the states") again. From the very outset, then, women's experiences and accounts of the journey were different from those of men.

Several themes emerge from women's own writings that illuminate their specific roles on the journey, as well as once they reached their destination. During the journey and once they reached their new location, all adults as well as older children were called upon to do whatever was necessary. Everyone contributed hard labor. Women did what might have once been considered men's work and both men and women did things never expected of them before. Still, there was a clear division of labor among most families during the overland journey itself, with men responsible for hunting, trading, driving and wagon repair, and tending animals. Women kept busy preparing food, washing clothes in the rivers and streams, nursing the sick, and tending small children. Although these roles may not seem to deviate from the expected roles of any farming family, the work was often done under extremely difficult circumstances, with the additional burden of performing work not in a settled home, but while constantly moving on the trail. Martha Morrison Minto recalled that, in addition to the cooking and washing,

> [T]he women helped pitch tents, helped unload, and helped yoking up the cattle. Some of the women did nearly all of the yoking; many times the men were off. One time my father was away hunting cattle that had been driven off by the Indians, and that left Mother and the children to attend to everything.[22]

She went on to explain that even young girls were expected to fulfill the roles of adult women:

> At 13 or 14 we were considered young ladies. . . . The men had a great deal of anxiety and all the care of their families, but still the mothers had the families directly in their hands and were with them all the time, especially during sickness. Some of the women I saw on the road went through a great deal of suffering and trial. . . . It strikes me as I think of it now that Mothers on the road had to undergo more trial and suffering than anybody else.[23]

For some women, however, even basic domestic tasks constituted an out-of-the-ordinary adventure, such as for white middle-class Southern-born Catherine Haun, who recounted with some humor what happened when her group's "woman cook" quit and refused to continue on:

> Our first impulse was that we should have to return, but after a day's delay during [which] our disappointment knew no bounds, I surprised all by proposing to do the cooking, if everybody else would help. My self-reliance and the encouragement of our fellow travelers won the day and our party kept on.

Having been reared in a slave state my culinary education had been neglected and I had yet to make my first cup of coffee. My offer was, however, accepted, and as quantity rather than quality was the chief requisite to satisfy our good appetites I got along very well.[24]

The bearing and care of children was a role that few women in the nineteenth century escaped, including those traveling westward. Diarist Harriet Clarke noted, "As we passed the emigrant trains there were always plenty of babies. We saw many women traveling along with their sun-bonnets on, leading children or carrying a child on their hips."[25] Life did not stop for the overland journey, and, as taxing and dangerous as pregnancy and child-birth were in regular settled life under the best circumstances, numerous accounts tell of pregnancy and birth endured under extreme conditions during the westward journey. Women and infants were exposed to the hardships and logistics of travel, to inclement weather conditions, and to the emotional strain of sometimes being alone, away from family with no designated midwives or other women at all to assist and comfort. Martha Morrison Minto recalled the loneliness: "When my second child was born my husband and I were alone, three miles from any woman or doctor; my oldest child 18 months old—my husband had to do the washing."[26] She took the time to at least record the birth of her child and in her brief account gave hints as to the loneliness and burden on her husband as well.

In other cases, the mother surely did not have time to write in her diary, but other family members, such as an older daughter, might record the challenges of a particular birth on a family:

Three days after my little sister Lettie drank the laudanum and died we stopped for a few hours, and my sister Olivia was born. . . . We were so late that the men of the party decided we could not tarry a day, so we had to press on. . . . We finally made our way through . . . to Oregon. We had been eight months on the road instead of five, we were out of food, and our cattle were nearly worn out. . . . We left the wagons and with my mother on one horse holding her 6 week old baby in her lap, and with one of the little children sitting behind her and with the rest of us riding behind the different men, we started north. . . . There were five of us children. . . . We lived on boiled wheat and boiled peas that winter. My mother got sick, so my Aunt Susan came to live with us and take care of her.[27]

This young woman recorded how her sister's birth fit into a family already dealing with the death of another child and how family life and hardship could not be expected to slow down the wagons, and, in fact, made it more imperative that they continue on in search of food. If children (or anyone) did not survive, as recorded in the account above, they of course had to buried and left behind on the plains or in the mountains, meaning that the remainder of the journey was often overshadowed with grief.

The meaning of the journey itself might differ for women compared to men. Whereas historians have emphasized that men were attracted to the idea of going west because of economic motivation as well as social and familial restrictions on their lives back east, women's accounts place more emphasis on the hardships and sacrifices than on their personal motivations and expectations. Amelia Stewart Knight traveled in 1853 on a journey from Iowa to Oregon that took five months. She was with her husband and seven children, as well as being pregnant again during the entire journey. A mere one week into the journey she recorded in her journal:

> Made our beds down in the tent in the wet and mud. Bed clothes nearly spoiled. Cold and cloudy this morning, and every body out of humour.... Husband is scolding and hurrying all hands ... and Almira says she wished she was home, and I say ditto. "Home, Sweet Home."[28]

Even after the women reached their destination, the challenges of childbirth and raising young children in isolated locations continued. Some women were, of course, excited by the adventure and the promise of success for their families and for themselves. But women, in general, were more likely than men to focus on the costs of the journey and of permanent relocation in familial-relationship terms over any potential individual rewards. The accounts in letters back home of distress over leaving family and of extreme losses on the trail from disease and accidents would have offered an alternative view from the advertisements for land and gold marketed to potential settlers in the East, and, in particular, must have been a disincentive for other women to want to take up the journey. One woman transplanted to California detailed the specific disadvantages when she wrote to her sisters in the 1850s, asking them to imagine living in a place with "no newspapers, no churches, lectures, concerts, or theaters; no fresh books; no shopping, calling nor gossiping little tea-drinkings; ... no daily mail; ... no vegetables but potatoes and onions, no milk, no eggs, no *nothing*."[29]

The West sometimes offered new opportunities for political participation for white women. Western territories and states were the first to pass woman suffrage laws. (See also Chapter 5, "Politics and Reform.") The vote was not the only source of political power, however, and women in the West were sometimes able to hold office and participate in other ways in local government. In 1887 the town of Argonia, Kansas, elected the first female mayor in the nation, Susanna M. Salter. That same year, the town of Syracuse, Kansas, not only elected a woman to the town council, but also elected an all-female council of six. The newspapers encouraged women, empowered with the vote for the first time, to vote for "men of known morality and upright character," but suffrage also allowed women to run for office. Upon the election of the female council, the editor of the local paper assured the townspeople who, despite the results of the election, might be uneasy about this development of female governance that the "ladies elected are intelligent and worthy. Many of them have had extensive experience in business . . . [and] None of them so far as we are informed, with one exception, is a woman suffragist in the common acceptation of the term."[30]

Although the frontier offered space for new negotiations and debates over gender roles, such promising developments were not always long-term. Once white settlement increased, even with the vote, Kansas women were not able to maintain such a prominent role in local politics. The presence of white women in the territories and new states was necessary for the building up of "civilization," but their presence was primarily desired as wives and mothers, keepers of homes and teachers of children; their participation in politics or other public roles was not a necessary condition for the Western project. After the brief experiment in "petticoat rule" in the late 1880s, no other woman in this Kansas county held public office until well into the twentieth century.[31]

BLACK WOMEN

Although many of the numerous diaries and letters of pioneer and Western life were left by white women, the West itself was a place of incredible racial and ethnic diversity, inviting and incorporating indigenous peoples, Anglo Americans, European immigrants, Mexicans, Asian immigrants, and African Americans. Before the Civil War, many African Americans migrated west as the slaves of white settlers. In many instances, once they reached their destinations, slaves were able to negotiate their freedom because of the changed economic circumstances of their white masters, for better or worse, and the different attitudes and laws regarding slavery in Western territories and states.

The first African American slave was brought to California as early as 1825, when a 14-year-old girl named Juana was brought west with her white mistress. When whites flooded into California after 1849, in hopes of finding gold, they brought along slaves who also were able to take advantage of the resources and opportunities provided by the West. Ellen Mason came to California with her master in 1849, and, earning just fifty cents a week, saved enough to buy her own freedom and that of her sister. When California entered the Union as a free state in 1850, many former slaves were able to petition for their freedom there. Biddy Mason was a slave from Mississippi and the mother of three young girls when she herself drove the ox-team taking her master's family first to Utah and then on to California in 1851. After securing her freedom, she began to save money to buy property and accumulated a legendary number of real estate holdings in nineteenth-century Los Angeles.[32] A number of black slaves accompanied the Native tribes forced into Oklahoma on the Trail of Tears in the 1830s. As many as 18 percent of the Cherokee and the Chickasaw who were moved westward were actually African American, and they were also included among the Choctaw and Creek. According to the 1860 census, there were more than 7,000 slaves in the Oklahoma Territory on the eve of the Civil War, and many more freed blacks swarmed into Oklahoma after the war.[33]

Before the Civil War, individual former slaves might take the opportunity the West offered to leave the South on their own and seek out a better life. Clara Brown was freed by her owner in 1859 and made her way from Kentucky to Denver by working as a cook and laundress for prospectors traveling west. In Colorado she ran a laundry service and, by 1864, she owned several properties in a number of Colorado cities. After the Civil War ended in 1865, she returned south in the hopes of reuniting with her family. She eventually reunited with only one of her four children, but she helped numerous other former slaves relocate to Colorado and sponsored their educations. She was so well respected in the Denver community for her business success as well as her charitable work that in 1883 she became the first female member of the Colorado Pioneer Association.[34]

After the Civil War, most black women, like their white counterparts, traveled West in family groups, seeking land ownership and work as independent farmers as an alternative to sharecropping in the South. Some 50,000 African Americans fled to Kansas alone after federal relief efforts of the Reconstruction era failed them. Places such as Kansas and Oklahoma, two of the most popular destinations for freedpeople immediately after the war, offered the possibility of both social and economic freedom through the promise of unlimited fertile land, a promise that had lured white Americans throughout the century and that blacks now had the freedom to pursue. Besides migrating as families, black women were especially encouraged to move west to work as teachers in black communities. Black teachers were especially important, as the Topeka, Kansas, *Tribune* explained in 1880, as they "would introduce an additional number of educated men and women whose presence would greatly benefit our society as well as excite a laudable emulation in our children." Citizens of black towns, such as Nicodemus, Kansas, and Langston, Oklahoma, also placed a high priority on education and founded the first black schools in the West, where black women schoolteachers taught both children and adults.[35] (See also Chapter 4, "Education and the Professions.")

Ultimately, however, the lives of black women in the West were just as diverse as those of white pioneer women and there was no single African American experience of the West, except to say that the West offered more freedom and mobility than the South, either before or after the Civil War. Women worked as farmers and ranchers, teachers, laundresses, cooks, businesswomen, and even stagecoach drivers. One of the most famous female stagecoach drivers was "Stagecoach Mary." In 1887, Mary Fields, a former slave from Tennessee, made her way to Montana to work as a wagon driver for a Catholic girls' school. She was fired after her involvement in a shootout, but she went on to run a restaurant and eventually drive a stagecoach for the U.S. postal service, a position she held until she was 80 years old. "Stagecoach Mary" was perhaps the only black person in Cascade, Montana, at the end of the nineteenth century, and occupied a special position in the town. According to legend, she was the only woman allowed to enter the saloons.[36]

ASIAN AMERICAN WOMEN

The actual number of Asian women in America in the nineteenth century was quite small. Millions of eastern and southern European immigrants were pouring into East Coast cities to work as unskilled factory labor, but the federal government targeted Asians, and in particular Chinese women, as undesirable immigrants. The first wave of Japanese immigrants began in the 1880s and consisted primarily of men who came to the United States as laborers on Hawaiian sugar plantations. Because of U.S. anti-Asian immigration policy, the first Japanese women and families did not emigrate until the 1910s and 1920s. Chinese immigration began several decades earlier, however, although it was again the men who first came to the West and the Southwest to work in the mines, build the railroads, or work as merchants and businessmen. By 1850 there were more than 4,000 Chinese men in San Francisco compared to just 7 women on record. The number of Chinese women in America was so low, primarily because of the Page Law of 1875, which prevented almost any woman, except the wife of a legitimate businessman, from entering the United States, under the assumption that most Chinese women immigrants were prostitutes. The numbers of Chinese immigrants were further slowed with the federal Chinese Exclusion Act of 1882. But emigration laws were also in effect in China itself until 1911, making it illegal for women to leave the country, and the financial and cultural obstacles were such that few women could travel away from home.[37]

The small numbers of Asian women who did arrive in California and other Western areas in the last decades of the nineteenth century were victims of racism and sexism, with many forced into prostitution and slave labor. Few could hope to marry and establish homes of their own, and interracial marriage with white men was illegal. By the end of the century, the overwhelming majority of Chinese in America, as many as 95 percent, were men, and the majority of those were concentrated in San Francisco. The few women who came led lives restricted by economics as well as by patriarchy (both within Chinese and Anglo American culture) and racism.

In nineteenth-century Chinatown, whether wives, daughters, domestic servants for wealthier Chinese families, or prostitutes, Chinese women remained largely confined indoors and isolated from the larger culture. Wives of laborers might have gone out shopping or to work for wages themselves, but the "small-foot" wives of merchants rarely left their homes. One Chinatown wife told a white reporter in 1893, "Poor me! In China I was shut up in the house since I was 10 years old, and only left my father's house to be shut up in my husband's house in this great country. For seventeen years I have been in this house without leaving it save two evenings." She reported that she was jealous of women "who are richer than I, for they have big feet and can go everywhere, and every day have something new to fill their minds."[38]

White Protestant women became particularly interested in reaching out to and rehabilitating Chinese prostitutes. Late nineteenth-century reformers set up mission homes as safe havens, but, once there, Chinese women were expected to follow a strict schedule of activities intended to facilitate their entrance back into western Christian society. The Presbyterian Mission Home in San Francisco worked with police to raid brothels, "rescuing" nearly 1,500 women between 1877 and 1897. The women performed chores, learned English, attended religious education classes, and received assistance in finding Christian spouses, as well as alternative employment.[39]

Nevertheless, there were some Chinese immigrant women who led independent lives, such as Lai Yun Oi, a widow who defied Chinese custom by leaving her husband's family and immigrating to the United States sometime in the late 1870s or early 1880s. Lai Yun Oi was even more unusual in that she managed to become quite successful in the United States on her own, supporting herself at various times in New York and in San Francisco as a seamstress, hairdresser, and businesswoman.[40]

For all women in the nineteenth-century West, life was a struggle. Whether immigrant, migrant, or native, women were central to carving out family and community life on the frontier, in the face of hardship, poverty, isolation, and constant relocation or even dislocation. However, like women in the more settled parts of the United States, most women in the West, regardless of their race, lived in families, bore children, and led daily lives that revolved around preparing food, keeping house, and raising children.

NOTES

1. Theda Perdue, ed., *Sifters: Native American Women's Lives* (New York: Oxford University Press, 2001), p. 61.

2. "President Thomas Jefferson to Captain Hendrick, the Delawares, Mohicans, and Munries, December 21, 1808," excerpted in *Discovering the American Past: A Look at the Evidence, Vol. I to 1877*, 5th ed., ed. William Bruce Wheeler and Susan D. Becker (Boston: Houghton Mifflin, 2002), p. 130.

3. Theda Perdue, "Women, Men and American Indian Policy: The Cherokee Response to Civilization," in *Negotiators of Change: Historical Perspectives on Native American Women,* ed. Nancy Shoemaker (New York: Routledge, 1995), p. 97.

4. Theda Perdue, *Cherokee Women: Gender and Culture Change, 1700–1835* (Lincoln: University of Nebraska Press, 1998), p. 153.

5. Theda Perdue, "Cherokee Women and the Trail of Tears," in *Unequal Sisters: A Multicultural Reader in U.S. Women's History,* 3rd ed., ed. Ellen Carol DuBois and Vicki L. Ruiz (New York: Routledge, 2000), pp. 93–104, quote on p. 99.

6. "Cynthia Ann Parker/Preloch (1827–1870)," in Liz Sonneborn, *A to Z of Native American Women* (New York: Facts on File, 1998), pp. 128–29; see also Margaret Schmidt Hacker, *Cynthia Ann Parker: The Life and the Legend* (El Paso: Texas Western Press, 1990).

7. "Natawista (1825–1893)," in Sonneborn, *A to Z of Native American Women,* pp. 124–25.

8. Pretty-Shield was interviewed and an account of her life published by Frank B. Linderman, *Pretty-Shield: Medicine Woman of the Crows* (1932; repr., Lincoln: University of Nebraska, 2003).

9. Winnemucca quoted in *Through Women's Eyes: An American History with Documents,* 3rd ed., ed. Ellen Carol DuBois and Lynn Dumenil (Boston: Bedford/St. Martin's, 2005), p. 209 and p. 237.

10. Winnemucca quoted in Harriet Sigerman, "Laborers for Liberty: 1865–1890," in *No Small Courage: A History of Women in the United States,* ed. Nancy F. Cott (New York: Oxford University Press, 2000), pp. 330–31.

11. Jackson qtd. in *Through Women's Eyes,* p. 346.

12. DuBois and Dumenil, *Through Women's Eyes,* p. 347; see also Valerie Sherer Mathes, *Helen Hunt Jackson and Her Indian Reform Legacy* (Norman: University of Oklahoma Press, 1997).

13. Sigerman, "Laborers for Liberty," p. 330.

14. Lillian Schlissel, *Women's Diaries of the Westward Journey* (New York: Schocken Books, 1992), p. 207.

15. Glenda Riley, *Women and Indians on the Frontier, 1825–1915* (Albuquerque: University of New Mexico Press, 1984), see pp. 173–77.

16. DuBois and Dumenil, *Through Women's Eyes,* pp. 207–10.

17. Susan L. Johnson, "Sharing Bed and Board: Cohabitation and Cultural Difference in Central Arizona Mining Towns, 1863–1873," in *The Women's West,* ed. Susan Armitage and Elizabeth Jameson (Norman: University of Oklahoma Press, 1987), p. 77.

18. "A Citizen Protests the Rape of Indian Women in California, 1862," in *Major Problems in American Women's History,* 3rd ed., ed. Mary Beth Norton and Ruth M. Alexander (Boston: Houghton Mifflin, 2003), pp. 188–89.

19. Joan E. Cashin, *A Family Venture: Men and Women on the Southern Frontier* (Baltimore: Johns Hopkins University Press, 1991), p. 94.

20. Cashin, *Family Venture,* p. 47 and p. 51.

21. Elliott West, "Beyond Baby Doe: Child Rearing on the Mining Frontier," in Armitage and Jameson, *The Women's West,* p. 184.

22. Schlissel, *Women's Diaries of the Westward Journey,* p. 35.

23. Schlissel, *Women's Diaries of the Westward Journey,* p. 35.

24. Schlissel, *Women's Diaries of the Westward Journey,* pp. 169–70.

25. Schlissel, *Women's Diaries of the Westward Journey,* p. 106.

26. Schlissel, *Women's Diaries of the Westward Journey,* p. 45.

27. Schlissel, *Women's Diaries of the Westward Journey,* p. 51.

28. Schlissel, *Women's Diaries of the Westward Journey,* p.202.

29. West, "Beyond Baby Doe," p. 182.

30. Rosalind Urbach Moss, "The 'Girls' from Syracuse: Sex Role Negotiations of Kansas Women in Politics, 1887–1890," in Armitage and Jameson, *The Women's West,* pp. 253–64; quote on p. 256.

31. Moss, "'Girls' from Syracuse," pp. 253–64.

32. Delilah L. Beasley, *The Negro Trail Blazers of California* (1919; repr. Whitefish, Mont.: Kessinger, 2005), p. 69, p. 71, p. 90, and p. 109.

33. Darlene Clark Hine and Kathleen Thompson, eds., *A Shining Thread of Hope: The History of Black Women in America* (New York: Broadway Books, 1998), pp. 173–74.

34. Hine and Thompson, *Shining Thread of Hope,* p. 176–77.

35. Nell Painter, *Exodusters: Black Migration to Kansas after Reconstruction* (New York: Norton, 1992), p. 50.

36. Hine and Thompson, *Shining Thread of Hope,* p. 175; see also Robert Miller, *The Story of Stagecoach Mary Fields* (Morristown, N.J.: Silver Burdett Press, 1995).

37. Judy Yung, *Unbound Feet: A Social History of Chinese Women in San Francisco* (Berkeley: University of California Press, 1995), p. 18.

38. Yung, *Unbound Feet,* p. 42.

39. Yung, *Unbound Feet,* pp. 34–37; see also Peggy Pascoe, *Relations of Rescue: The Search for Female Moral Authority in the American West, 1874–1939* (New York: Oxford University Press, 1990).

40. Yung, *Unbound Feet,* pp. 49–50.

SUGGESTED READING

Cashin, Joan E. *A Family Venture: Men and Women on the Southern Frontier.* Baltimore: Johns Hopkins University Press, 1991.

Deutsch, Sarah. *No Separate Refuge: Culture, Class, and Gender on the Anglo-Hispanic Frontier in the American Southwest, 1880–1940.* New York: Oxford University Press, 1987.

Jeffrey, Julie Roy. *Frontier Women: The Trans-Mississippi West, 1840–1880.* New York: Hill and Wang, 1979.

Kaufman, Polly Welts. *Women Teachers on the Frontier.* New Haven, Conn.: Yale University Press, 1984.

Klein, Laura, ed. *Women and Power in Native North America.* Norman: University of Oklahoma, 1995.

Pascoe, Peggy. *Relations of Rescue: The Search for Female Moral Authority in the American West, 1874–1939.* New York: Oxford University Press, 1990.

Perdue, Theda. *Cherokee Women: Gender and Culture Change, 1700–1835.* Lincoln: University of Nebraska Press, 1998.

Perdue, Theda, ed. *Sifters: Native American Women's Lives.* New York: Oxford University Press, 2001.

Riley, Glenda. *Women and Indians on the Frontier, 1825–1915.* Albuquerque: University of New Mexico Press, 1984.

Schlissel, Lillian. *Women's Diaries of the Westward Journey.* New York: Schocken Books, 1992.

Shoemaker, Nancy, ed. *Negotiators of Change: Historical Perspectives on Native American Women.* New York: Routledge, 1995.

Sonneborn, Liz. *A to Z of Native American Women.* New York: Facts on File, 1998.

Yung, Judy. *Unbound Feet: A Social History of Chinese Women in San Francisco.* Berkeley: University of California Press, 1995.

Zanjani, Sally. *A Mine of Her Own: Women Prospectors in the American West, 1850–1950.* Lincoln: University of Nebraska Press, 2000.

8

∞∞∞

Literature and the Arts

The expansion of women's access to formal education meant women's increased participation in American literary and intellectual life as writers, editors, and artists. In the first decades of the nineteenth century, a "feminized" or sentimental view of American culture meant that, along with spirituality and family life, literature and the arts were seen as a new part of woman's legitimate sphere of moral and domestic influence. It was not long until feminists began to acknowledge that as a woman proved herself in the literary world, so too she might advance into other arenas of public and cultural life. As author Margaret Fuller observed in her 1845 text, *Woman in the Nineteenth Century:*

> Another sign of the times is furnished by the triumphs of female authorship. These have been great and constantly increasing. Women have taken possession of so many provinces for which men had pronounced them unfit, that though these still declare there are some inaccessible to them, it is difficult to say just *where* they might stop.[1]

In the nineteenth century, women authored books, such as Fuller's, and took on new literary roles as novelists, poets, newspaper editors, journalists, and political writers. Although a female literary tradition that included poetry and diary and letter writing extended back to colonial times, after the American Revolution, the role of American writers in general took on new cultural and political significance as the new nation sought to create its own literary and artistic tradition apart from European influence. Women writers participated in this national project, and, as the nineteenth century opened, their expanded roles in these areas were facilitated by new technologies in bookmaking and distribution. By the 1820s, technological advances in printing and bookmaking, as well as the networks of canals and then the railroads, allowed the widespread distribution of books from growing literary urban centers of the East to inland markets and the creation of new readers and new writers for those markets. Combined with the expansion of women's domestic and moral roles into print, these developments ensured that women had a prominent place in the new "literary marketplace" of the nineteenth century.

Women participated in and influenced all literary trends and artistic genres of the century. Some of the best-selling novelists and most beloved poets of the century were women, such as Harriet Beecher Stowe, Louisa May Alcott, or Emily Dickinson. Other women writers, as well as sculptors and painters, demanded entrance into educational institutions and professional circles in order to practice and make a living at their pursuits. Women wrote on domestic or sentimental themes as well as political topics. Both black and white women reformers used the written word as a strategy for social change, including in the fight to end slavery and to expand political and civil rights to all African Americans and all women.

EMERGENCE OF THE WOMAN WRITER

The first, widely read published authors after the American Revolution were novelists and historians, and women dominated these genres as both writers and readers. From the end of the Revolutionary War through the 1830s, authors were preoccupied with writing the history of the new nation, and, in particular, with a patriotic interest in figures and military events of the revolution. The interest in American history expanded into historical fiction by the 1820s and 1830s with well-known works of the era such as James Fennimore Cooper's *The Pioneers* (1823) and *Last of the Mohicans* (1826). Two women writers who found success in this genre were Lydia Maria Child and Catharine Maria Sedgwick. Child's novel, *Hobomok* (1824), was set in seventeenth-century Massachusetts and dealt with the themes of early relations between the English colonists and Native Americans, including the issue of intermarriage. Sedgwick's *Hope Leslie* (1827) dealt with a similar setting and theme and earned her success and comparison with Cooper. Sedgwick was, in fact, the most celebrated American woman writer of this generation.

Many of the lesser-known female historical romance writers of this era went on to successful literary careers in other genres, including nonfiction and reform writing. By the mid-1830s, distinct gender lines were being drawn between literary genres. Lydia Maria Child and Catharine Maria Sedgwick began their careers as contemporaries of James Fenimore

Cooper writing historical "wilderness" fiction, but Cooper's later works turned to popular tastes for action and adventure on the frontier, while Child and Sedgwick helped create new "feminine" genres such as children's fiction and women's advice and domestic manuals. Child's 1829 work, *The Frugal Housewife,* made her a household name and a national authority on domestic matters, and, although never a mother herself, she also founded the first magazine aimed specifically to children as an audience, *The Juvenile Miscellany* (1826–1834).[2]

By the 1820s American women had also secured a public voice and forum as writers, editors, and readers of women's magazines. In addition to evangelical church journals, the earliest regular magazines aimed at a female audience supported women's roles as Christian mothers and as keepers of the home, with titles such as *Mother's Magazine and Family Monitor, Mother's Monthly Journal,* and *Mother at Home and Household Magazine.* Just as much moral reform literature of the day produced by individual churches and religious organizations, these magazines focused on women's roles in the family, related to not only motherhood and marriage, but also to frugal and efficient housekeeping.[3] Catharine Beecher's 1841 *A Treatise on Domestic Economy* exemplified the era of domesticity as woman's highest calling, an idea that women writers themselves had a major role in promoting.

The single most-influential women's magazine of the nineteenth century was *Godey's Lady's Book,* edited by Sarah Josepha Hale between 1837 and 1877. As women pursued new literary roles, however, Hale was among those critics who warned that writing should not interfere with women's traditional roles as wives and mothers. As editor of the earlier *Ladies Magazine,* Hale advised American women in 1828 that "To make a happy home for her husband and children is far more praiseworthy than to make a book."[4] Hale herself was the widowed mother of five, however, whose children were raised with the help of relatives so that she could pursue a literary career in order to support her own family. In addition to her editorial work, Hale published several books of poetry, fiction, cookbooks, domestic manuals, and even women's history, with her 1853 *Woman's Record; or, Sketches of All Distinguished Women, from "The Beginning" till A.D. 1850.* Like Catharine Beecher, Hale was a highly influential woman with a public career dedicated to convincing women to pursue domestic rather than public roles. These writers advocated female education, but only so far as it aided women in being accomplished wives and mothers. Nonetheless, as writers themselves, they provided models of women with literary roles to play in American culture and society as well, and, in the case of *Godey's Lady's Book,* Hale promoted women's literary work by providing a forum in which women could have their stories, poems, or essays published.

ANTEBELLUM WOMEN WRITERS

The "American Renaissance" of literary culture, roughly 1830 to 1860, was an era of more democratic politics, democratic education, and America finally identifying its own national importance, all themes reflected in literature of the era by both male and female authors. Romantic sentiments of the era promoted the role of the individual in artistic expression and experimentation and the "man of letters" became a cultural identity and profession that, by definition, left women out despite the proliferation of women writers. Despite the success and popularity of female writers, they were sometimes still disparaged, as in Nathaniel Hawthorne's infamous 1855 complaint to his publisher that "America is now given over to a damned mob of scribbling women, and I should have no chance of success while the public taste is occupied with their trash—and should be ashamed of myself if I did succeed."[5] Hawthorne undoubtedly was angered by the existence of female writers as competition and drew not only professional, but gendered, lines between high literature and popular "trash" that appealed to the "public taste," meaning that it was more commercially successful than his own work. Hawthorne's comment did reveal, however, the extent to which women had come to dominate as authors of popular literature by mid-century.

Nathaniel Hawthorne voiced his complaint in 1855, in the midst of a decade in which the most popular novels were, in fact, written by women: Susan Warner's *The Wide, Wide World* (1850), Harriet Beecher Stowe's *Uncle Tom's Cabin* (1852), Maria Cummins's *The Lamplighter* (1854), Fanny Fern's *Ruth Hall* (1855), and the more than 40 novels and short-story collections published by E.D.E.N. Southworth between 1849 and her death in 1899. Literary magazines, and the increase of middle-class women as readers of such magazines, propelled the success of these writers and others who had their stories first serialized in periodicals before publishing them as complete novels. This was true for Harriet Beecher Stowe's best-seller, *Uncle Tom's Cabin,* which was first serialized in the *National Era* magazine, beginning in 1851, before its publication as a novel in late 1852. Louisa May Alcott began writing as a teenager and published her first collection of stories for children in 1855. Her novel of the Civil War, *Hospital Sketches,* was first serialized as a collection of stories in the Boston *Commonwealth.* Alcott became best-known, however, for launching the idea of the domestic novel for children with her best-selling 1868 novel, *Little Women.*

Louisa May Alcott never married and her writing helped support her parents and siblings. Few women who hoped to make a career out of writing could afford to concentrate on only one genre and many of these successful novelists also wrote short stories, poetry, essays, and advice columns. The most financially successful women writers of the period were regular

Louisa May Alcott (ca 1880s). Alcott was a prolific writer of short stories and novels, including the 1868 best seller, *Little Women*. (Schlesinger Library, Radcliffe Institute, Harvard University.)

columnists for the literary magazines. After a round of negotiations on her own behalf, Fanny Fern earned an outrageous $100 per week for a column in the *New York Ledger* (a magazine that also published pieces by E.D.E.N. Southworth as well as popular male writers such as Henry Wadsworth Longfellow and Charles Dickens) after Fern proved herself with the success of the 1855 novel, *Ruth Hall*.[6]

The growth of cities helped create literary communities and publication centers in places such as New York, Philadelphia, and Boston that supported the work of all writers, male and female. In Boston, antebellum literary culture was dominated by Transcendentalism, a literary and intellectual reform movement of the mid-nineteenth century dedicated to the development of the individual self. At a time when women were defined by their social roles as daughters, wives, and mothers, Transcendentalism offered women a chance to think and write as individuals. Transcendentalist author Margaret Fuller focused on woman's need for self-improvement and intellectual independence in the first book of feminist theory published in the United States, *Woman in the Nineteenth Century* (1845). Bypassing explicitly political arguments for women's rights, Fuller argued, "What woman needs is not as a woman to act or rule, but as a nature to grow, as an intellect to discern,

Margaret Fuller (ca 1840s). Fuller was the first feminist theorist in the United States and had an active career as an author, literary critic, and newspaper editor. She was one of the key figures of the Transcendentalist movement, and her book *Woman in the Nine-teenth Century* provided philosophical and historical arguments for women's rights. (Schlesinger Library, Radcliffe Institute, Harvard University.)

as a soul to live freely and unimpeded, to unfold such powers as were given to her when we left our common home."[7] Fuller's career was devoted to promoting women's education and their individual talents, and to this end she played a significant literary role in the Transcendentalist movement. Between 1841 and 1844 she edited the main Transcendentalist literary journal, the *Dial*, before going on to become the first book reviewer and regular female columnist for the *New-York Tribune*. Paulina Wright Davis, the founder and editor of the first women's rights paper, the *Una* (1853–1855), acknowledged Margaret Fuller's influence on other women writers and intellectuals. As president of the first national women's rights convention held in Worcester, Massachusetts, in 1850, Davis reflected that Fuller, who unfortunately died in a shipwreck earlier that same year, "was, and still is, a leader of thought—a position far more desirable than of numbers."[8]

Transcendentalism influenced and was promoted by other women, as well. Lydia Maria Child's novel, *Philothea*, was published in 1836 just months before Ralph Waldo Emerson's *Nature*, and is often acknowledged as the first Transcendentalist novel. The networks between women were important in sustaining their work as writers, as Lydia Maria Child also published an essay in the *Dial* in 1843, entitled "What Is Beauty?" In an 1845 review of Margaret Fuller's *Woman in the Nineteenth Century*, Child declared her colleague "a woman of more powerful intellect, comprehensive thought, and thorough education, than any other American authoress, with whose productions I am acquainted."[9] Louisa May Alcott was also directly linked to Transcendentalism, but eventually became one of the most outspoken critics of the philosophy with her satirical short story, "Transcendental Wild Oats," published in 1873. Women writers of the early and mid-nineteenth century were not confined to a separate female literary culture, but had an active role in the intellectual and literary debates and communities of the time.

WOMEN POETS

Female poets also had a new role in the nineteenth century literary marketplace. American women had always written poetry, beginning with notable examples such as Anne Bradstreet in the colonial era and Phillis Wheatley in the Revolutionary era. There were several factors explaining the expanded presence of women poets in the nineteenth century. The same cultural and technological developments that gave rise to a magazine market for women journalists and fiction writers also provided a forum for poets. More important, however, a new focus on domesticity and on women's maternal and spiritual roles within the family led to increased public interest in women's particular voice on these topics and the most popular female poets emphasized such themes in their writing. Women's magazines regularly published poetry, as did more mainstream literary and news magazines such as the *Atlantic Monthly.* These publications and the popular taste for poetry provided new opportunities for women to generate an income from their poetry writing. At the height of her career, poet Lydia Sigourney was able to earn as much as $25 per poem.[10]

As with novelists, many female poets built careers and earned an income by publishing in a variety of genres. Elizabeth Oakes Smith was a poet as well as the editor of a literary magazine, a novelist, and a women's rights lecturer and author. As part of the emerging network of women's rights activists and writers in the 1850s, Smith had her novels and poetry volumes regularly advertised in the women's rights newspapers. The public careers of poets such as Lydia Sigourney or Elizabeth Oakes Smith are in contrast to the predominant image of the nineteenth-century woman poet exemplified by Emily Dickinson, who published only a handful of poems in her lifetime and was relatively unknown in the nineteenth century. Although it was true that most opportunities for publication were with magazines and presses located in New York and New England, not all women poets were privileged, well educated, or cloistered daughters of the Northeast. Western and Southern women published poems, as did working-class poets, such as Lucy Larcom.

As women poets had a greater role in the literary culture, they began to move away from strictly domestic or sentimental themes to larger political questions, including antislavery, the Civil War, and the women's rights critique of traditional gender roles. Not surprisingly, a great number of women reformers were also well-known writers. In these cases, poetry was not their primary vocation, but was merely a specific strategy for their cause, published interchangeably with their other writings in the form of essays, lectures, or novels. Maria Weston Chapman was active in the abolitionist cause as well as the early women's rights movement. At the first organized women's rights meeting, Chapman used poetry to articulate, somewhat humorously, women's early complaints about their limited public roles. Chapman read a poem at the 1848 meeting entitled "The Times That Try Men's Souls," in which she satirized men's anxiety about women's public roles, including their new roles as writers:

> Confusion has seized us, and all things go wrong, / The women have leaped from "their spheres," / . . . They've taken a notion to speak for themselves, / And are wielding the tongue and the pen; / They've mounted the rostrum, the termagant elves, / And, oh horrid, are talking to *men.*[11]

The Civil War also had a major impact on women's political writings, North and South, as many writers, including poets, felt compelled to contribute to the national discussion, offering either patriotism or critique, lamenting the human cost of war, or simply acknowledging the contribution of women to the war effort, such as nurse Clara Barton's 1892 poem, "The Women Who Went to the Field."

Like white female poets, many black women reformers published as essayists, novelists, and poets in service to the cause of gender and racial equality. Francis Ellen Watkins Harper's 1869 poem, "Moses: A Story of the Nile," recalled slave religion's emphasis on biblical metaphors to understand oppression and eventually freedom. In this case, however, Harper placed herself as a reformer-writer in the leadership role of Moses:

> I feel an earnest purpose binding all / My soul unto a strong resolve, which bid / Me put aside all other ends and aims, / Until the hour shall come when God—the God / Our fathers loved and worshipped—shall break our chains, / And lead our willing feet to freedom.[12]

SLAVE NARRATIVES AND ANTISLAVERY WRITING

Women had a prominent role as activists, lecturers, and as writers in the antislavery movement. Both black and white women authored anti-slavery novels, political treatises, and wrote articles for and edited antislav-ery newspapers. This literary work was part of the overall strategy in the antebellum decades to bring the issue of slavery into the white American consciousness. Harriet Beecher Stowe's *Uncle Tom's Cabin* critiqued the effect of slavery on both black and white family life, especially through the separation of families and the destruction of the mother-child bond. Whereas white women writers urged, in their newspapers and in the do-mestic literature, women to focus on their roles as wives and mothers as their primary occupation, black women writers, such as Harriet Wilson in *Our Nig*, emphasized how racism and slavery prevented black women from successfully pursuing or fulfilling those same roles. And although the majority of nineteenth-century slave narratives were by men, several im-portant female slave narratives provided a perspective on how slavery was different for women. As Harriet Jacobs declared in her 1861 *Incidents in the Life of a Slave Girl*, "Slavery is terrible for men; but it is far more terrible for women."[13] (See also Chapter 6, "Slavery and the Civil War.")

The abolitionist and free black communities of the antebellum North helped support the publication of personal narratives, fiction, and news-papers by black writers. By the 1830s African American communities sustained not only churches and businesses, but schools, newspapers, and reform organizations, all institutions that helped create an African American cultural community. The first black newspaper was *Freedom's Journal*, published in New York City beginning in 1827, and by 1865 there were more than 40 black periodicals produced in the North. The stability of black creative communities supported authorship and other intellectual pursuits, but black writers were still impeded by isolation and by the stress of segregation and Northern racism. Not all antebellum black writers and thinkers were former slaves, and not all were active as abolitionists, and those who did write about their experiences within slavery often moved into other genres.

Some of the first published black women were authors of spiritual narratives. Women such as Maria Stewart, Jarena Lee, and Zilpha Elaw were lecturers and preachers who eventually published autobiographical accounts of their spiritual journeys, explaining how they had overcome hardships, found the path to conversion, and been called to preach. Most of the authors of spiritual narratives were preachers in the African Methodist Episcopal (AME) Church, and their writings also served the political purpose of challenging the racial and gender discrimination facing women who felt called to be preachers. As black women, their published narratives called for social, political, and spiritual freedom for all African Americans, and became an important voice in the early abolitionist movement. (See also Chapter 3, "Religion.")

The slave narrative, however, was the most widely read literary genre for black writers and served an important role in the abolitionist movement, as well as in the post–Civil War continued struggle for civil rights. One of the most popular narratives was Harriet Jacobs's *Incidents in the Life of a Slave Girl,* published in 1861 at the outbreak of war, which was a unique and shocking view into the physical and sexual exploitation of enslaved women. Several other of the most important women's slave narratives were actually published after the Civil War, including Elizabeth Keckly's account of her years as a slave and then her life as a seamstress in the Lincoln White House, *Behind the Scenes* (published in 1868); *Narrative of Sojourner Truth* (1878); and Lucy A. Delaney's *From the Darkness Cometh the Light, or Struggles for Freedom* (1891). These narratives and many others were critical to the reform and civil rights movements of the nineteenth century and remain a crucial source for understanding the firsthand experience of slavery.

At times, the line between fiction and autobiography in regard to the slave experience was not clearly drawn. A recently discovered unpublished handwritten manuscript by a former slave named Hannah Crafts dates her fictionalized autobiography, *The Bondwoman's Narrative,* sometime in the 1850s, possibly as early as 1853. It is the story of the early life and escape of Crafts, a mulatto, born in Virginia, who lived there, in Washington, D.C., and in Wilmington, North Carolina.[14] However, Harriet E. Wilson's novel, the full title of which is, *Our Nig; or, Sketches from the Life of a Free Black, in a Two-Story White House, North. Showing That Slavery's Shadow Falls Even There* (1859), is generally considered the first published novel by an African

American woman. Wilson's controversial story is a different kind of reform novel because it focuses not on slavery but on racism in the nineteenth-century North, a North priding itself, in the 1850s, on its moral critique of slavery while ignoring its own complicity and its own racism. Wilson addresses these themes not by looking at the politics of antislavery, but through gender and race relations within the free states. At the center of the story is an interracial marriage, between a black man and a white woman, and it is white women who are the gravest perpetrators of racism, the villains, in the story.

WOMEN'S RIGHTS NEWSPAPERS, EDITORS, AND WRITERS

The women's rights movement propelled women into the public sphere, including into the literary culture. Beginning in the 1850s, radical reformers began to attack the idea of domesticity that kept women's interests confined to those of their families. Feminist lecturers, writers, and editors sought instead a wider sphere of activity and began by creating their own alternative public forum through the numerous women's rights newspapers of the day. The 1850s was the decade of the radical women's press, each with its own focus or specific approach to woman's issues. (See also Chapter 5, "Politics and Reform.")

The first paper devoted exclusively to the issue of women's rights was the *Una,* but others addressed multiple overlapping reform agendas, such as the *Lily* (which dealt primarily with temperance and dress reform), the *Woman's Advocate* (focused on labor), and the *Sybil* (dress and health reform). These were some of the most significant papers of the pre–Civil War era and the titles of articles published in the 1850s reveal the level of sophistication in the early stages of a feminist critique of American society and gender roles: "Sanctuary of Home Hides Male Tyranny" (*Woman's Advocate*), "Equitable Laws, Not Sentimentality" (the *Una*), "Men's Fear of Women's Competition" (*Woman's Advocate*), and "Chivalry as Class Maintenance" (the *Lily*).[15]

As a movement strategy, the press was intended, as *Una* editor Paulina Wright Davis explained, to serve as "a correct history, not only of this specific movement, but of the public lives engaged in it."[16] The mainstream urban newspapers might report on the women's rights conventions and lectures, but they could not be counted on to do so fairly or always in sympathy with the women's demands. In their own papers, reformers reprinted convention speeches and lectures; published original essays and articles, women's fiction and poetry, and news relating to discrimination against women; and celebrated women's accomplishments, in history as well as in contemporary times. In the post–Civil War era, the *Revolution* and *Woman's Journal* represented the different strands of the woman suffrage movement, and they were able to reach women readers geographically spread over the continent.

Women's rights newspapers not only provided a forum for reformers and other writers, but brought women into the business of newspaper production as editors and printers. Paulina Wright Davis explicitly recognized this aspect of their reform work when she wrote to coeditor Caroline Dall in October 1853:

> I have a fair prospect now of getting my paper printed by women. Our firm will take several apprentices and by the first of January I hope to be able to announce that the entire labor of Una passes through the hands of women. It will be more expensive but that is of no consequence in a work like this. The taking possession of every industrial avenue must be our great aim.[17]

Besides the specific issue of women's rights, reformers, writers, and newspaper editors also addressed themes related to women's roles as workers. In the antebellum era, female mill operatives started their own newspaper, *Lowell Offering,* and the *Woman's Advocate* was also committed to offering a voice for working women. Novelists as well examined women's work at mid-century, such as Louisa May Alcott in *Work: A Story of Experience* (1873). The novel's heroine, Christie Devon, explores the various vocational options available to American women in the nineteenth century. Christie works as a seamstress, a domestic servant, a Civil War nurse, and even an actress. Although Christie does not stay in any of these jobs long, Alcott reveals how women might learn about themselves through such employments. For example, rather than portray nursing simply as a natural extension of women's caretaking and domestic roles, Alcott has Christie learn how to nurture and have sympathy through such work, although ultimately finding it is not a suitable profession for her talents.

Whereas Alcott's middle-class heroine is free to sample these various professions (and free to give them up for marriage), Rebecca Harding Davis's novel, *Life in the Iron Mills,* published in 1861, dealt with the less glamorous plight of women factory workers and criticized the middle-class reformer out of touch with the reality of such women's lives. In the beginning of the novel, the narrator instructs the reader (most likely a white middle-class woman) "to hide your disgust, take no heed to your clean clothes, and come right down with me, . . . I want you to hear this story . . . I want to make it a real thing to you."[18]

WOMEN'S WRITING AND THE CIVIL WAR

Women, both North and South, were prolific writers during the Civil War. Louisa May Alcott addressed the issue of women's work and roles during wartime in another of her popular novels, *Hospital Sketches,* published in the middle of the war in 1863. Alcott herself had gone to Washington, D.C., during the war to work as a nurse and "let out my pent-up energy in some new way."[19] Although her "sketches" were presented somewhat humorously, her writing realistically addressed the issue of women taking on new roles outside of the family and outside conventional understandings of propriety or of female capabilities. In the end, war work empowered Alcott, and, through her writing, she sought to empower other women, as she explained, "I shall never regret going. . . . Let no one who sincerely desires to help the work on in this way, delay going through any fear; for the worth of life lies in the experiences that fill it, and this is one which cannot be forgotten."[20]

Southern women writers also created an impressive amount of Civil War fiction, reflecting on the war and on women's changing roles within the family and the larger society, both during and immediately following the war. One of the most popular Confederate women's wartime novels was Augusta Jane Evans's *Macaria; or, Altars of Sacrifice* (1864). Like Louisa May Alcott, Evans was interested in exploring women's roles through her writing, because they were "debarred from the dangers and earthless glory of the 'tented field,'" and so must find "Womanly Usefulness" in other ways. Evans herself found "Womanly Usefulness" through a literary contribution to the war effort, in this case, in support of the Confederacy. Through her stories she sought to rally both men and women to the Southern cause.[21]

Women writers, both North and South, documented and reflected upon the meaning and effect of the war, especially on women and families. Maria McIntosh's *Two Pictures; or, What We Think of Ourselves and What the World Thinks of Us* (1863) was a direct response to the image of Southern women as degraded and sometimes cruel victims of the slave system themselves, as portrayed in works such as Harriet Beecher Stowe's *Uncle Tom's Cabin* (1852). McIntosh's novel portrayed the marriage between an elite Southern woman and a Yankee man, not as a symbolic union of the nation, but to show the greater influence and superiority of the Southern woman, whose husband becomes a planter and slaveholder who eventually upholds the Southern way of life. Augusta Jane Evans also delivered the message through her novel that, upon "the women of our land, not less than upon the heroism of our armies, depends our national [Confederate] salvation."[22]

In justifying their public roles as authors and supporters of the Confederate cause, Southern women novelists made sure to distinguish their work from that of the Northern woman writer-reformer. They especially distanced themselves from any association with the women's rights movement. Florence O'Connor, for example, in her 1864 novel, *Heroine of the Confederacy; or, Truth and Justice,* explained that she was compelled to write so that the correct history of the South might be told, and did not want to be seen as "the female politician, the literary lady who affects the Madame de Stael."[23] In reality, these Southern women writers were making similar arguments about woman's duty to serve a public role, and even her individual right to do so, as were Northern women's rights activists. The difference was in their cause, for as Northern reformers fought to end hierarchy and inequalities, white Southern women of the Confederacy used their roles as writers to defend a society based upon the enslavement of other human beings.

Women not only wrote novels dealing with the themes of war, but also poetry, songs, and stories for newspapers and journals. The work of many women in telling stories about the war and about the South remained hidden away in private rather than public forums. Southern women's diaries, journals, and letters are filled with women's first-person accounts of the war, its impact on families, as well as perspectives on slavery, on the Southern cause, and on national politics. But novelists and essayists had an important role in putting those perspectives and those female insights in front of a larger public, national audience. Many wartime novelists, both North and South, had published other writings before the war and many continued their careers as writers after the war, but for a few brief years, the crisis of war provided new material and new justification for women's literary work.

WOMEN'S WRITING AFTER THE CIVIL WAR

In the latter decades of the century, the popular press and women's magazines emphasized the new, more consumer-oriented role that women played as housewives and as working women, and appealed to new audiences of immigrant and urban women. New products and household technologies were advertised in magazines such as the *Ladies' Home Journal,* founded in 1889. The home was still considered woman's primary sphere of activity, but the new woman consumer was acknowledged as educated and as concerned with a wider world beyond her children. The essays and advertisements in women's magazines of the late nineteenth and early twentieth century incorporated traditional information on motherhood, relationships, and domesticity, with new appeals to women's fashion and activities beyond the home.

Post–Civil War novelists were also more likely to take their heroines out of the home and show women involved in a variety of roles and activities. The domestic feminists of an earlier era, such as Catharine Beecher or Sarah Josepha Hale, were replaced by feminist writers such as Charlotte Perkins Gilman, who, in *The Yellow Wallpaper* (1892) and other works, showed the extreme damaging effects—socially, psychologically, and physically—of gender roles that kept women confined to the home. Other women writers also criticized restrictions on women's education and employment by venturing into new literary roles themselves. Writers such as Kate Chopin (*The Awakening*, 1899) and Sarah Orne Jewett (*A Country Doctor*, 1884, and *The Country of the Pointed Firs*, 1896) were at the forefront of the next generation of women as popular regional writers, focusing their stories on the Western frontiers or the New South.

After the Civil War, black women writers had a prominent role in remembering the history of slavery, but also in helping the race move forward in the continued struggle for freedom and civil rights. Octavia Victoria Rogers Albert was born a slave, but after the Civil War, she attended Atlanta University and studied to become a schoolteacher. She spent 13 years interviewing formerly enslaved men and women in an effort to record the history of American slavery and collected her interviews together as *The House of Bondage; or, Charlotte Brooks and Other Slaves* (1890). In their focus on community and on shared history, Albert's stories differed from the earlier slave narratives that focused on the experience of one individual, a necessary strategy in the racial uplift movement of the late nineteenth century that sought to counter the violence and discriminatory laws of the white supremacist South.

Barred from political power, many African American women used the written word as a political strategy. Katherine Chapman Tillman was a poet and essayist particularly interested in recording and recognizing the roles of black women writers. Among her published essays at the end of the century were "Afro-American Women and Their Work" (1895), "Afro-American Poets and Their Verse" (1898), and "The Negro among Angle-Saxon Poets" (1898). Tillman was a race reformer active in the club movement as a member of the National Colored Women's League, the National Federation of Afro-American Women, and the National Association of Colored Women's Clubs (NACW), for which she served as an officer. Other prominent black reformer-writers of the late nineteenth century included Anna Julia Cooper, author of *A Voice from the South by a Black Woman of the South* (1892); and Frances Ellen Watkins Harper, journalist, poet, and author of the novel, *Iola Leroy; or, Shadows Uplifted* (1892). (See also Chapter 5, "Politics and Reform.")

WOMEN AND THE ARTS

In addition to their participation in the literary world in the nineteenth century, women were active in the practical arts and fine arts. Historians in recent years have acknowledged the artistic contribution to American culture of women's traditional domestic arts such as home decorating, embroidery, sewing, quiltmaking, and other fiber arts. In the case of quiltmaking, such efforts were not entirely private, but did involve the entire community in their production as well as in their display. In her 1832 account, *Domestic Manners of the Americans*, English visitor Frances Trollope observed American quiltmakers and described the significance of the quilting bee: "[W]hen the external composition of one of these is completed, it is usual to call together their neighbors and friends to witness, and assist at the quilting, which is the completion of this elaborate work."[24] In this way many ordinary women nurtured their artistic tendencies, gathered with other women in the community, and displayed their domestic virtues, such as industry, frugality, and duty to their families. In the case of the slave community, African American women's artistic representations and symbols in quilts had the immediate political purpose of aiding fugitive slaves in the antebellum decades.[25] (See also Chapter 6, "Slavery and the Civil War.")

Ednah Dow Cheney sought to make practical or vocational art education available to more women through her New England School of Design for women in 1851. In addition to her other reform interests and writings, Cheney is regarded as the first American woman to publish on the aesthetics of art. Her definition of art as "thought in material form" revealed the early influence of Transcendentalism on her thought. After the Civil War, Cheney was invited by Bronson Alcott to be a founding member of his Concord School of Philosophy and Literature, where she was one of the few women to lecture every summer of the school's 10-year existence between 1879 and 1888. In addition to her autobiography, which included a chapter on art, she published several articles and memoirs of other artists, and collected together many of her later essays, including from her Concord School lectures, in a book entitled *Gleanings in the Fields of Art* (1881).[26]

Although few women received recognition for their domestic or "practical" arts, other women sought greater public recognition in careers as painters and sculptors. In these particular fields, a few women of the nineteenth century did manage to obtain entrance into professional schools, associations, and circles. Anne Whitney briefly attended the Philadelphia Academy of Fine Arts with plans to become a sculptor, and, unlike many women artists who did not have the freedom or the finances, she was able to spend time in Europe before returning to the United States to open her own studio where she specialized in bronze and marble statues. Mary Edmonia Lewis was born in Ohio in 1845 to a free black father and a Chippewa Indian mother, and specialized in sculptures depicting strong female figures. Lewis attended Oberlin College and completed busts of important nineteenth-century American figures, such as poet Henry Wadsworth Longfellow and President Abraham Lincoln. She was the only black artist to have works displayed at the Philadelphia Centennial Exposition in 1876, where six of her sculptures were exhibited.

Perhaps the best-known American woman artist of the late nineteenth and early twentieth centuries was Impressionist painter Mary Cassatt, born in Pennsylvania in 1844. The theme of many of Cassatt's paintings was the special bond between mothers and children. She knew Claude Monet and was one of the few women to exhibit her work along with other Impressionists. By the end of the century, however, just as in other professions, women artists were beginning to organize and find ways to support each other in their roles as artists. The Woman's Art Club, for example, was founded in 1889 and held its own exhibitions, and allowed women the opportunity to "show their own work by itself, unaffected by the opinion or the prejudice of masculine juries of acceptance and masculine hanging committees."[27] Even already established artists, such as Mary Cassatt, exhibited with the club in the 1890s. Cassatt, however, feared (perhaps rightly) that such separate organizations could be used to justify women's continued exclusion from professional exhibits and associations. Still, the Woman's Art Club became an important stepping-stone for many women artists who went on to have professional careers in the early twentieth century.

In some ways, all women writers and artists challenged women's traditional roles and societal expectations for women simply through the act of producing their work. They did so whether privately or in public, and, often, in an effort to specifically work toward an expansion or reconsideration of women's roles. It was up to the next generations of women in the twentieth century and beyond to imagine and continue to work toward a

"Section of Tympanum in the Woman's Building by Miss Mary Cassatt, Painter," *Harper's New Monthly Magazine* 86, no. 516 (May 1893): p. 837. American Impressionist painter Cassatt completed this mural for the Woman's Building at the 1893 World's Columbian Exposition in Chicago. The mural was meant to represent women's achievements and includes scenes of women participating in the arts and sciences and, in this panel, harvesting the fruits of knowledge. (Division of Rare and Manuscript Collections, Cornell University Library.)

future where women were free to pursue their talents and interests and have their contributions recognized, regardless of society's definition of their proper roles.

NOTES

1. Margaret Fuller, *Woman in the Nineteenth Century* (1845), excerpted in Eve Kornfeld, *Margaret Fuller: A Brief Biography with Documents* (Boston: Bedford/ St. Martins, 1997), p. 175.

2. On Child's prolific and varied writing career in the context of nineteenth-century literary culture, see Carolyn Karcher, *The First Woman in the Republic: A Cultural Biography of Lydia Maria Child* (Durham, N.C.: Duke University Press, 1994).

3. For the role of such magazines in middle-class women's religious life, see Mary Ryan, *Cradle of the Middle Class: The Family in Oneida County, New York, 1790–1865* (New York: Cambridge University Press, 1981).

4. Hale quoted in Barbara Solomon, *In the Company of Educated Women: A History of Women and Higher Education in America* (New Haven, Conn.: Yale University Press, 1985), p. 36.

5. Nina Baym, "Again and Again, the Scribbling Women," in *Hawthorne and Women: Engendering and Expanding the Hawthorne Tradition*, ed. John L. Idol and Melinda Ponder (Amherst: University of Massachusetts Press, 1999), quote on pp. 21–22.

6. See Joyce W. Warren, "Uncommon Discourse: Fanny Fern and the *New York Ledger*," in *Periodical Literature in Nineteenth-Century America*, ed. Kenneth M. Price and Susan Belasco Smith (Charlottesville: University Press of Virginia, 1995), pp. 51–68.

7. Kornfeld, *Margaret Fuller*, p. 165.

8. Davis quoted in Tiffany K. Wayne, *Woman Thinking: Feminism and Transcendentalism in Nineteenth-Century America* (Lanham, Md.: Lexington Books, 2005), p. 47.

9. Lydia Maria Child, *Broadway Journal* (Feb. 15, 1845), qtd. in Kornfeld, *Margaret Fuller*, p. 231.

10. Cheryl Walker, ed., *American Women Poets of the Nineteenth Century: An Anthology* (New Brunswick, N.J.: Rutgers University Press, 1992), p. xxi.

11. Paula Bernat Bennett, *Poets in the Public Sphere: The Emancipatory Project of American Women's Poetry, 1800–1900* (Princeton, N.J.: Princeton University Press, 2003), p. 46.

12. Bennett, *Poets in the Public Sphere*, pp. 88–89.

13. Harriet Jacobs, *Incidents in the Life of a Slave Girl, Written by Herself*, ed. Jean Fagan Yellin (Cambridge, Mass.: Harvard University Press, 2000), p. 77.

14. See Henry Louis Gates, Jr., ed., *The Bondwoman's Narrative, a Novel by Hannah Crafts* (New York: Warner Books, 2002).

15. See Ann Russo and Cheris Kramarae, eds., *The Radical Women's Press of the 1850s* (New York: Routledge, 1991).

16. Wayne, *Woman Thinking*, p. 56.

17. Wayne, *Woman Thinking*, pp. 83–84.

18. Alcott and Davis both discussed in Lyde Cullen Sizer, *The Political Work of Northern Women Writers and the Civil War, 1850–1872* (Chapel Hill: University of North Carolina Press, 2000), quote on p. 41.

19. Sizer, *Political Work of Northern Women Writers*, p. 46.

20. Sizer, *Political Work of Northern Women Writers*, p. 98.

21. See Drew Gilpin Faust, *Mothers of Invention: Women of the Slaveholding South in the American Civil War* (Chapel Hill: University of North Carolina Press, 1996), pp. 168–69.

22. Sarah E. Gardner, *Blood and Irony: Southern White Women's Narratives of the Civil War, 1861–1937* (Chapel Hill: University of North Carolina Press, 2004), p. 30.

23. Gardner, *Blood and Irony*, p. 31.

24.Trollope quoted in S. J. Kleinberg, *Women in the United States, 1830–1945* (New Brunswick, N.J.: Rutgers University Press, 1999), p. 70.

25. See Jacqueline L. Tobin and Raymond G. Dobard, *Hidden in Plain View: A Secret Story of Quilts and the Underground Railroad* (New York: Doubleday, 1999).

26. Therese B. Dykeman, "Ednah Dow Cheney's American Aesthetics," in *Presenting Women Philosophers,* ed. Sara Ebenreck and Cecile T. Tougas (Philadelphia: Temple University Press, 2000), pp. 41–50.

27. Kirsten Swinth, *Painting Professionals: Women Artists and the Development of Modern American Art, 1870–1930* (Chapel Hill: University of North Carolina Press, 2001), p. 119.

SUGGESTED READING

Baym, Nina. *American Women Writers and the Work of History, 1790–1860.* New Brunswick, N.J.: Rutgers University Press, 1995.

Bennett, Paula Bernat. *Poets in the Public Sphere: The Emancipatory Project of American Women's Poetry, 1800–1900* Princeton, N.J.: Princeton University Press, 2003.

Carby, Hazel V. *Reconstructing Womanhood: The Emergence of the Afro-American Woman Novelist* (New York: Oxford University Press, 1987).

Fahs, Alice. *The Imagined Civil War: Popular Literature of the North and South, 1861–1865.* Chapel Hill: University of North Carolina Press, 2001.

Foster, Francis Smith. *Written by Herself: Literary Production by African American Women, 1746–1892.* Bloomington: Indiana University Press, 1993.

Gardner, Sarah E. *Blood and Irony: Southern White Women's Narratives of the Civil War, 1861–1937.* Chapel Hill: University of North Carolina Press, 2004.

Harris, Sharon M., and Ellen Gruber Garvey, eds. *Blue Pencils and Hidden Hands: Women Editing Periodicals, 1830–1910.* Boston: Northeastern University Press, 2004.

Okker, Patricia. *Our Sister Editors: Sarah J. Hale and the Tradition of Nineteenth-Century American Women Editors.* Athens: University of Georgia Press, 1995.

Price, Kenneth M., and Susan Belasco Smith, eds. *Periodical Literature in Nineteenth-Century America.* Charlottesville: University Press of Virginia, 1995.

Rhodes, Jean. *Mary Ann Shadd Cary: The Black Press and Protest in the Nineteenth Century.* Bloomington: Indiana University Press, 1998.

Sizer, Lyde Cullen. *The Political Work of Northern Women Writers and the Civil War, 1850–1872.* Chapel Hill: University of North Carolina Press, 2000.

Solomon, Martha M., ed. *A Voice of Their Own: The Woman Suffrage Press, 1840–1910.* Tuscaloosa: University of Alabama, 1991.

Swinth, Kirsten. *Painting Professionals: Women Artists and the Development of Modern American Art, 1870–1930.* Chapel Hill: University of North Carolina Press, 2001.

Tonkovich, Nicole. *Domesticity with a Difference: The Nonfiction of Catharine Beecher, Sarah J. Hale, Fanny Fern, and Margaret Fuller.* Jackson: University Press of Mississippi, 1997.

Wayne, Tiffany K. *Woman Thinking: Feminism and Transcendentalism in Nineteenth-Century America.* Lanham, Md.: Lexington Books, 2005.

Young, Elizabeth. *Disarming the Nation: Women's Writing and the American Civil War.* Chicago: University of Chicago Press, 1999.

Selected Bibliography

Abram, Ruth J., ed. *"Send Us a Lady Physician": Women Doctors in America, 1835–1920.* New York: Norton, 1985.

Anderson, Bonnie. *Joyous Greetings: The First International Women's Movement, 1830–1860.* New York: Oxford University Press, 2000.

Andrews, William L., ed. *Sisters of the Spirit: Three Black Women's Autobiographies of the Nineteenth Century.* Bloomington: Indiana University Press, 1986.

Armitage, Susan, and Elizabeth Jameson, eds., *The Women's West.* Norman: University of Oklahoma Press, 1987.

Attie, Jeanie. *Patriotic Toil: Northern Women and the American Civil War.* Ithaca, N.Y.: Cornell University Press, 1998.

Bacon, Margaret Hope. *Mothers of Feminism: The Story of Quaker Women in America.* New York: Harper, 1986.

Bakken, Gordon, and Brenda Farrington, eds. *Encyclopedia of Women in the American West.* Thousand Oaks, Calif.: Sage, 2003.

Baron, Ava, ed. *Work Engendered: Toward a New History of American Labor.* Ithaca, N.Y.: Cornell University Press, 1991.

Bartlett, Elizabeth Ann. *Liberty, Equality, Sorority: The Origins and Interpretations of American Feminist Thought: Frances Wright, Sarah Grimke, and Margaret Fuller.* Brooklyn, N.Y.: Carlson, 1994.

Baym, Nina. *American Women Writers and the Work of History, 1790–1860.* New Brunswick, N.J.: Rutgers University Press, 1995.

Bederman, Gail. *Manliness and Civilization: A Cultural History of Gender and Race in the United States.* Chicago: University of Chicago Press, 1995.

Bennett, Paula Bernat. *Poets in the Public Sphere: The Emancipatory Project of American Women's Poetry, 1800–1900.* Princeton, N.J.: Princeton University Press, 2003.

Bennion, Sherilyn Cox. *Equal to the Occasion: Women Editors of the Nineteenth-Century Frontier.* Reno: University of Nevada Press, 1990.

Blair, Karen. The *Clubwoman as Feminist: True Womanhood Redefined, 1868–1914.* New York: Holmes and Meier, 1980.

Bleser, Carol, ed. *In Joy and in Sorrow: Women, Family, and Marriage in the Victorian South, 1830–1900.* New York: Oxford University Press, 1992.

Blewett, Mary. *Men, Women, and Work: Class, Gender, and Protest in the New England Shoe Industry, 1780–1910.* Urbana: University of Illinois Press, 1988.

———. *We Will Rise in Our Might: Workingwomen's Voices from Nineteenth-Century New England.* Ithaca, N.Y.: Cornell University Press, 1991.

Bordin, Ruth. *Alice Freeman Palmer: The Evolution of a New Woman.* Ann Arbor: University of Michigan Press, 1993.

———. *Woman and Temperance: The Quest for Power and Liberty, 1873–1900.* New Brunswick, N.J.: Rutgers University Press, 1990.

Boydston, Jeanne. *Home and Work: Housework, Wages, and the Ideology of Labor in the Early Republic.* New York: Oxford University Press, 1990.

———. *The Limits of Sisterhood: The Beecher Sisters on Women's Rights and Woman's Sphere.* Chapel Hill: University of North Carolina Press, 1988.

Boylan, Anne M. *The Origins of Women's Activism: New York and Boston, 1797–1840.* Chapel Hill: University of North Carolina Press, 2002.

———. *Sunday School: The Formation of an American Institution, 1790–1880.* New Haven, Conn.: Yale University Press, 1990.

Braude, Ann. *Radical Spirits: Spiritualism and Women's Rights in Nineteenth-Century America.* Bloomington: Indiana University Press, 2001.

Brekus, Catherine Anne. *Strangers and Pilgrims: Female Preaching in America, 1740–1845.* Chapel Hill: University of North Carolina Press, 1998.

Brewer, Priscilla. *Shaker Communities, Shaker Lives.* Hanover, N.H.: University Press of New England, 1986.

Brodie, Janet Farrell. *Contraception and Abortion in 19th-Century America.* Ithaca, N.Y.: Cornell University Press, 1994.

Brown, Victoria Bissell. *The Education of Jane Addams.* Philadelphia: University of Pennsylvania Press, 2004.

Butler, Anne M. *Daughters of Joy, Sisters of Mercy: Prostitutes in the American West, 1865–1890.* Urbana: University of Illinois Press, 1985.

Campbell, Edward, and Kym Rice, eds. *A Woman's War: Southern Women, Civil War, and the Confederate Legacy.* Charlottesville: University Press of Virginia, 1996.

Capper, Charles. *Margaret Fuller: An American Romantic Life.* Vol. 1. New York: Oxford University Press, 1992.

Carby, Hazel V. *Reconstructing Womanhood: The Emergence of the Afro-American Woman Novelist.* New York: Oxford University Press, 1987.

Carter, Christine Jacobson. *Southern Single Blessedness: Unmarried Women in the Urban South, 1800–1865.* Urbana: University of Illinois Press, 2006.

Cashin, Joan E. *A Family Venture: Men and Women on the Southern Frontier.* Baltimore: Johns Hopkins University Press, 1991.

Cayleff, Susan. *Wash and Be Healed: The Water Cure Movement and Women's Health.* Philadelphia: Temple University Press, 1987.

Censer, Jane Turner. *The Reconstruction of White Southern Womanhood, 1865–1895.* Baton Rouge: Louisiana State University Press, 2003.

Chambers-Schiller, Lee. *Liberty, a Better Husband: Single Women in America, the Generations of 1780–1840.* New Haven, Conn.: Yale University Press, 1984.

Clinton, Catherine. *Harriet Tubman: The Road to Freedom.* New York: Little, Brown, 2004.

———. *The Plantation Mistress: Woman's World in the Old South.* New York: Pantheon Books, 1982.

———, ed. *Southern Families at War: Loyalty and Conflict in the Civil War South.* New York: Oxford University Press, 2000.

———, and Nina Silber, eds., *Divided Houses: Gender and the Civil War.* New York: Oxford University Press, 1992.

Cohen, Ruth Schwartz. *More Work for Mother: The Ironies of Household Technology from the Open Hearth to the Microwave.* New York: Basic Books, 1985.

Collins, Gail. *America's Women: 400 Years of Dolls, Drudges, Helpmates, and Heroines.* New York: HarperCollins, 2003.

Cott, Nancy F. *The Bonds of Womanhood: "Woman's Sphere" in New England, 1780–1835,* 2nd ed. New Haven, Conn.: Yale University Press, 1997.

———. *Public Vows: A History of Marriage and the Nation.* Cambridge, Mass.: Harvard University Press, 2000.

———, ed. *No Small Courage: A History of Women in the United States.* New York: Oxford University Press, 2000.

Culpepper, Marilyn Mayer, *All Things Altered: Women in the Wake of Civil War and Reconstruction.* Jefferson, N.C.: McFarland, 2002.

Cutter, Barbara. *Domestic Devils, Battlefield Angels: The Radicalism of American Womanhood, 1830–1865.* DeKalb: Northern Illinois University, 2003.

Davis, Marjorie. *Woman's Place Is at the Typewriter: Office Work and Office Workers, 1870–1930.* Philadelphia: Temple University Press, 1982.

Daynes, Kathryn M. *More Wives Than One: Transformation of the Mormon Marriage System, 1840–1910.* Urbana: University of Illinois Press, 2001.

Deutsch, Sarah. *No Separate Refuge: Culture, Class, and Gender on the Anglo-Hispanic Frontier in the American Southwest, 1880–1940.* New York: Oxford University Press, 1987.

———. *Women and the City: Gender, Space, and Power in Boston, 1870–1940.* New York: Oxford University Press, 2000.

Diner, Hasia. *Erin's Daughters in America: Irish Immigrant Women in the Nineteenth Century.* Baltimore: Johns Hopkins University Press, 1983.

Dixon, Chris. *Perfecting the Family: Antislavery Marriages in Nineteenth-Century America.* Amherst: University of Massachusetts Press, 1997.

Dorsey, Bruce. *Reforming Men and Women: Gender in the Antebellum City.* Ithaca, N.Y.: Cornell University Press, 2002.

Douglas, Ann. *The Feminization of American Culture.* New York: Knopf, 1977.

Dublin, Thomas. *Transforming Women's Work: New England Lives in the Industrial Revolution.* Ithaca, N.Y.: Cornell University Press, 1994.

———, ed. *Farm to Factory: Women's Letters, 1830–1860.* New York: Columbia University Press, 1993.

DuBois, Ellen Carol. *Feminism and Suffrage: The Emergence of an Independent Women's Movement in America, 1848–1869.* Ithaca, N.Y.: Cornell University Press, 1999.

———. *Harriot Stanton Blatch and the Winning of Woman Suffrage.* New Haven, Conn.: Yale University Press, 1999.

———, and Lynn Dumenil, eds. *Through Women's Eyes: An American History with Documents.* 3rd ed. Boston: Bedford/St. Martin's, 2005.

——, and Vicki L. Ruiz, eds. *Unequal Sisters: A Multicultural Reader in U.S. Women's History.* 3rd ed. New York: Routledge, 2000.

Edwards, Laura. *Gendered Strife and Confusion: The Political Culture of Reconstruction.* Urbana: University of Illinois Press, 1997.

——. *Scarlett Doesn't Live Here Anymore: Southern Women in the Civil War Era.* Urbana: University of Illinois Press, 2000.

Edwards, Rebecca. *Angels in the Machinery: Gender in American Party Politics from the Civil War to the Progressive Era.* New York: Oxford University Press, 1997.

Eisler, Benita, ed. *The* Lowell Offering: *Writings by New England Mill Women (1840–1845).* New York: Norton, 1997.

Epstein, Barbara L. *The Politics of Domesticity: Women, Evangelism, and Temperance in Nineteenth-Century America.* Middletown, Conn.: Wesleyan University Press, 1981.

Fahs, Alice. *The Imagined Civil War: Popular Literature of the North and South, 1861–1865.* Chapel Hill: University of North Carolina Press, 2001.

Farnham, Christie Anne. *The Education of the Southern Belle: Higher Education and Student Socialization in the Antebellum South.* New York: New York University Press, 1994.

Faulkner, Carol. *Women's Radical Reconstruction: The Freedmen's Aid Movement.* Philadelphia: University of Pennsylvania Press, 2003.

Faust, Drew Gilpin. *Mothers of Invention: Women of the Slaveholding South in the American Civil War.* Chapel Hill: University of North Carolina Press, 1996.

Ferris, Jeri. *Native American Doctor: The Story of Susan La Flesche Picotte.* Minneapolis, Minn.: Carolrhoda Books, 1991.

Fischer, Gayle V. *Pantaloons and Power: Nineteenth-Century Dress Reform in the United States.* Kent, Ohio: Kent State University Press, 2001.

Fleischner, Jennifer. *Mrs. Lincoln and Mrs. Keckly: The Remarkable Story of the Friendship between a First Lady and a Former Slave.* New York: Broadway Books, 2003.

Foote, Cheryl J. *Women of the New Mexico Frontier, 1846–1912.* Albuquerque: University of New Mexico Press, 2005.

Foster, Francis Smith. *Written by Herself: Literary Production by African American Women, 1746–1892.* Bloomington: Indiana University Press, 1993.

Foster, Lawrence. *Religion and Sexuality: The Shakers, the Mormons, and the Oneida Community.* Urbana: University of Illinois Press, 1984.

Fox-Genovese, Elizabeth. *Within the Plantation Household: Black and White Women in the Old South.* Chapel Hill: University of North Carolina Press, 1988.

Frankel, Noralee. *Freedom's Women: Black Women and Families in Civil War Era Mississippi.* Bloomington: Indiana University Press, 1999.

Freeberg, Ernest. *The Education of Laura Bridgman: First Deaf and Blind Person to Learn Language.* Cambridge, Mass.: Harvard University Press, 2001.

Frey, Sylvia R., and Betty Wood. *Come Shouting to Zion: African-American Protestantism in the American South and British Caribbean to 1830.* Chapel Hill: University of North Carolina Press, 1998.

Friedman, Jane. *America's First Woman Lawyer: The Biography of Myra Bradwell.* Buffalo, N.Y.: Prometheus Books, 1993.

Gabaccia, Donna. *From the Other Side: Women, Gender, and Immigrant Life in the U.S., 1820–1990.* Bloomington: Indiana University Press, 1994.

Gamber, Wendy. *The Female Economy: The Millinery and Dressmaking Trades, 1860–1930.* Urbana: University of Illinois Press, 1997.

Gardner, Sarah E. *Blood and Irony: Southern White Women's Narratives of the Civil War, 1861–1937.* Chapel Hill: University of North Carolina Press, 2004.

Gaspar, David Barry, and Darlene Clark Hine, eds. *More Than Chattel: Black Women and Slavery in the Americas.* Bloomington: Indiana University Pres, 1996.

Gedge, Karin E. *Without Benefit of Clergy: Women and the Pastoral Relationship in Nineteenth-Century American Culture.* New York: Oxford University Press, 2003.

Giddings, Paula. *When and Where I Enter: The Impact of Black Women on Race and Sex in America.* New York: Morrow, 1984.

Giesberg, Judith Ann. *Civil War Sisterhood: The U.S. Sanitary Commission and Women's Politics in Transition.* Boston: Northeastern University Press, 2000.

Gilmore, Glenda. *Gender and Jim Crow: Women and the Politics of White Supremacy in North Carolina, 1896–1920.* Chapel Hill: University of North Carolina Press, 1996.

Ginzberg, Lori. *Women and the Work of Benevolence: Morality, Politics, and Class in the Nineteenth Century.* New Haven, Conn.: Yale University Press, 1992.

Goldsmith, Barbara. *Other Powers: The Age of Suffrage, Spiritualism, and the Scandalous Victoria Woodhull.* New York: Knopf, 1998.

Gonzalez, Deena J. *Refusing the Favor: The Spanish-Mexican Women of Santa Fe, 1820–1880.* New York: Oxford University Press, 1999.

Gordon, Ann D., Joyce A. Berkman, and John H. Bracey, eds. *African American Women and the Vote, 1837–1965.* Bloomington: Indiana University Press, 1998.

Gordon, Linda. *Heroes of Their Own Lives: The Politics and History of Family Violence, Boston, 1880–1960.* Urbana: University of Illinois Press, 2002.

Grimshaw, Patricia. *Paths of Duty: American Missionary Wives in Nineteenth-Century Hawaii.* Honolulu: University of Hawaii Press, 1989.

Groneman, Carol, and Mary Beth Norton, eds. *To Toil the Livelong Day: America's Women at Work, 1780–1980.* Ithaca, N.Y.: Cornell University Press, 1987.

Gustafson, Melanie. *Women and the Republican Party, 1854–1924.* Urbana: University of Illinois Press, 2001.

Hansen, Debra Gold. *Strained Sisterhood: Gender and Class in the Boston Female Anti-Slavery Society.* Amherst: University of Massachusetts Press, 1993.

Harris, Barbara. *Beyond Her Sphere: Women and the Professions in American History.* Westport, Conn.: Greenwood, 1978.

Harris, Sharon M., and Ellen Gruber Garvey, eds. *Blue Pencils and Hidden Hands: Women Editing Periodicals, 1830–1910.* Boston: Northeastern University Press, 2004.

Hedrick, Joan. *Harriet Beecher Stowe: A Life.* New York: Oxford University Press, 1994.

Herbert, T. Walter. *Dearest Beloved: The Hawthornes and the Making of the Middle-Class Family.* Berkeley: University of California Press, 1993.

Hewitt, Nancy. *Women's Activism and Social Change, Rochester, New York, 1822–1872.* Lanham, Md.: Lexington Books, 2001.

———, ed. *A Companion to American Women's History.* Malden, Mass.: Blackwell, 2002.

Higginbotham, Evelyn Brooks. *Righteous Discontent: The Women's Movement in the Black Baptist Church, 1880–1920.* Cambridge, Mass.: Harvard University Press, 1993.

Hill, Patricia. *The World Their Household: The American Woman's Foreign Missionary Movement and Cultural Transformation, 1870–1920.* Ann Arbor: University of Michigan Press, 1985.

Hine, Darlene Clark, and Kathleen Thompson. *A Shining Thread of Hope: The History of Black Women in America.* New York: Broadway Books, 1998.

Hodes, Martha. *White Women, Black Men: Illicit Sex in the 19th-Century South.* New Haven, Conn.: Yale University Press, 1997.

Hoffert, Sylvia. *When Hens Crow: The Woman's Rights Movement in Antebellum America.* Bloomington: Indiana University Press, 1995.

——, ed. *A History of Gender in America.* Upper Saddle River, N.J.: Prentice Hall/Pearson, 2003.

Horowitz, Helen. *Alma Mater: Design and Experience in the Women's Colleges from Their 19th-Century Beginnings to the 1930s.* Amherst: University of Massachusetts Press, 1993.

——. *Rereading Sex: Battles over Sexual Knowledge and Suppression in Nineteenth-Century America.* New York: Knopf, 2002.

Hunter, Tera. *To 'joy My Freedom: Southern Black Women's Lives and Labors after the Civil War.* Cambridge, Mass.: Harvard University Press, 1997.

Isenberg, Nancy. *Sex and Citizenship in Antebellum America.* Chapel Hill: University of North Carolina Press, 1998.

Jeffrey, Julie Roy. *Converting the West: A Biography of Narcissa Whitman.* Norman: University of Oklahoma Press, 1991.

——. *Frontier Women: The Trans-Mississippi West, 1840–1880.* New York: Hill and Wang, 1979.

——. *The Great Silent Army of Abolitionism: Ordinary Women in the Antislavery Movement.* Chapel Hill: University of North Carolina Press, 1998.

Johnson, Paul E. *A Shopkeeper's Millennium: Society and Revivals in Rochester, New York, 1815–1837.* New York: Hill and Wang, 1978.

Jones, Beverly Washington. *Quest for Equality: The Life and Writings of Mary Eliza Church Terrell, 1863–1954.* Brooklyn, N.Y.: Carlson, 1990.

Jones, Jacqueline. *Labor of Love, Labor of Sorrow: Black Women, Work, and the Family from Slavery to the Present.* New York: Basic Books, 1985.

Juster, Susan. *Disorderly Women: Sexual Politics and Evangelicalism in Revolutionary New England.* Ithaca, N.Y.: Cornell University Press, 1994.

Karcher, Carolyn. *The First Woman in the Republic: A Cultural Biography of Lydia Maria Child.* Durham, N.C.: Duke University Press, 1994.

Kaufman, Polly Welts. *Women Teachers on the Frontier.* New Haven, Conn.: Yale University Press, 1984.

Kelley, Mary. *Private Woman, Public Stage: Literary Domesticity in Nineteenth-Century America.* Chapel Hill: University of North Carolina Press, 1984; rev. ed. 2002.

Kerber, Linda. *Toward an Intellectual History of Women.* Chapel Hill: University of North Carolina Press, 1997.

——, and Jane Sherron de Hart, eds., *Women's America: Refocusing the Past.* 6th ed. New York: Oxford University Press, 2003.

——, Alice Kessler-Harris, and Kathryn Kish Sklar, eds., *U.S. History as Women's History: New Feminist Essays.* Chapel Hill: University of North Carolina Press, 1995.

Kern, Kathi. *Mrs. Stanton's Bible.* Ithaca, N.Y.: Cornell University Press, 2001.

Kessler-Harris, Alice. *Out to Work: A History of Wage-Earning Women in the United States*. Rev. ed. New York: Oxford University Press, 2003.

Klein, Laura, ed. *Women and Power in Native North America*. Norman: University of Oklahoma, 1995.

Kornfeld, Eve. *Margaret Fuller: A Brief Biography with Documents*. Boston: Bedford/St. Martin's, 1997.

Lasch-Quinn, Elizabeth. *Black Neighbors: Race and the Limits of Reform in the American Settlement House Movement, 1890–1945*. Chapel Hill: University of North Carolina Press, 1993.

Leach, Kristine. *In Search of a Common Ground: Nineteenth and Twentieth Century Immigrant Women in America*. San Francisco: Austin & Winfield, 1995.

Leach, William. *True Love and Perfect Union: The Feminist Reform of Sex and Society*. New York: Basic Books, 1980.

Lebsock, Suzanne. *The Free Women of Petersburg: Status and Culture in a Southern Town, 1784–1860*. New York: Norton, 1984.

Leonard, Elizabeth D. *All the Daring of the Soldier: Women of the Civil War Armies*. New York: Norton, 1999.

———. *Yankee Women: Gender Battles in the Civil War*. New York: Norton, 1994.

Lerner, Gerda. *The Grimké Sisters from North Carolina: Pioneers for Women's Rights and Abolition*. Chapel Hill: University of North Carolina Press, 2004.

Levy, Joanne. *They Saw the Elephant: Women in the California Gold Rush*. Hamden, Conn.: Archon Books, 1990.

Lewenson, Sandra. *Taking Charge: Nursing, Suffrage, and Feminism in America, 1873–1920*. New York: National League for Nursing Press, 1996.

Lindley, Susan Hall. *"You Have Stept Out of Your Place": A History of Women and Religion in America*. Louisville, Ky.: Westminster John Knox Press, 1996.

Luchetti, Cathy. *"I Do!": Courtship, Love and Marriage on the American Frontier*. New York: Crown, 1996.

———, and Carol Olwell. *Women of the West*. New York: Orion Books, 1982.

Maher, Mary Denis. *To Bind up the Wounds: Catholic Sister Nurses in the U.S. Civil War*. New York: Greenwood, 1989.

Mankiller, Wilma, Gloria Steinem, Gwendolyn Mink, Barbara Smith, and Marysa Navarro, eds. *The Reader's Companion to U.S. Women's History*. Boston: Houghton Mifflin, 1999.

Marshall, Megan. *The Peabody Sisters: Three Women Who Ignited American Romanticism*. Boston: Houghton Mifflin, 2005.

Mathes, Valerie Sherer. *Helen Hunt Jackson and Her Indian Reform Legacy*. Norman: University of Oklahoma Press, 1997.

Matthews, Jean V. *Women's Struggle for Equality: The First Phase, 1828–1876*. Chicago: Ivan R. Dee, 1997.

Mattingly, Carol, *Appropriate[ing] Dress: Women's Rhetorical Style in Nineteenth-Century America*. Carbondale: Southern Illinois University Press, 2002.

May, Elaine Tyler. *Great Expectations: Marriage and Divorce in Post-Victorian America*. Chicago: University of Chicago Press, 1983.

McClymer, John F. *This High and Holy Moment: The First National Woman's Rights Convention, Worcester, 1850*. Orlando, Fla.: Harcourt Brace, 1999.

McCurry, Stephanie. *Masters of Small Worlds: Yeoman Households, Gender Relations, and the Political Culture of the Antebellum South Carolina Low Country*. New York: Oxford University Press, 1995.

McLaurin, Melton A. *Celia, a Slave: A True Story of Violence and Retribution in Antebellum Missouri.* Athens: University of Georgia Press, 1991.

McMillen, Sally. *Motherhood in the Old South: Pregnancy, Childbirth, and Infant-Rearing.* Baton Rouge: Louisiana State University Press, 1990.

———. *Southern Women: Black and White in the Old South.* Arlington Heights, Ill.: Harlan Davidson, 1992.

———. *To Raise Up the South: Sunday Schools in Black and White Churches, 1865–1915.* Baton Rouge: Louisiana State University Press, 2001.

McMurry, Linda O. *To Keep the Waters Troubled: The Life of Ida B. Wells.* New York: Oxford University Press, 1998.

Mead, Rebecca. *How the Vote Was Won: Woman Suffrage in the Western United States, 1868–1914.* New York: New York University Press, 2004.

Meyerowitz, Joanne. *Women Adrift: Independent Wage Earners in Chicago, 1880–1930.* Chicago: University of Chicago Press, 1988.

Mihesuah, Devon. *Cultivating the Rosebuds: The Education of Women at the Cherokee Female Seminary, 1851–1909.* Urbana: University of Illinois Press, 1993.

Million, Joelle. *Woman's Voice, Woman's Place: Lucy Stone and the Birth of the Woman's Rights Movement.* Westport, Conn.: Praeger, 2003.

Moran, William. *The Belles of New England: The Women of the Textile Mills and the Families Whose Wealth They Wove.* New York: St. Martin's, 2002.

Muncy, Robin. *Creating a Female Dominion in American Reform, 1890–1935.* New York: Oxford University Press, 1991.

Murphy, Teresa Anne. *Ten Hours' Labor: Religion, Reform, and Gender in Early New England.* Ithaca, N.Y.: Cornell University Press, 1992.

Norton, Mary Beth, and Ruth M. Alexander, eds. *Major Problems in American Women's History.* 3rd ed. Boston: Houghton Mifflin, 2003.

Okker, Patricia. *Our Sister Editors: Sarah J. Hale and the Tradition of Nineteenth-Century American Women Editors.* Athens: University of Georgia Press, 1995.

Painter, Nell Irvin. *Sojourner Truth: A Life, a Symbol.* New York: Norton, 1996.

Pascoe, Peggy. *Relations of Rescue: The Search for Female Moral Authority in the American West, 1874–1939.* New York: Oxford University Press, 1990.

Passet, Joanne Ellen. *Sex Radicals and the Quest for Women's Equality.* Urbana: University of Illinois Press, 2003.

Peiss, Kathy. *Cheap Amusements: Working Women and Leisure in Turn-of-the-Century New York.* Philadelphia: Temple University Press, 1986.

Perdue, Theda. *Cherokee Women: Gender and Culture Change, 1700–1835.* Lincoln: University of Nebraska Press, 1998.

———, ed. *Sifters: Native American Women's Lives.* New York: Oxford University Press, 2001.

Porter, Susan L., ed. *Women of the Commonwealth: Work, Family, and Social Change in Nineteenth-Century Massachusetts.* Amherst: University of Massachusetts Press, 1996.

Price, Kenneth M., and Susan Belasco Smith, eds. *Periodical Literature in Nineteenth-Century America.* Charlottesville: University Press of Virginia, 1995.

Pryor, Elizabeth Brown. *Clara Barton: Professional Angel.* Philadelphia: University of Pennsylvania Press, 1987.

Rable, George. *Civil Wars: Women and the Crisis of Southern Nationalism.* Urbana: University of Illinois Press, 1989.

Rhodes, Jean. *Mary Ann Shadd Cary: The Black Press and Protest in the Nineteenth Century.* Bloomington: Indiana University Press, 1998.

Riley, Glenda. *Women and Indians on the Frontier, 1825–1915.* Albuquerque: University of New Mexico Press, 1984.

Ronda, Bruce. *Elizabeth Palmer Peabody: A Reformer on Her Own Terms.* Cambridge, Mass.: Harvard University Press, 1999.

Rosenzweig, Linda W. *The Anchor of My Life: Middle-Class American Mothers and Daughters, 1880–1920.* New York: New York University Press, 1993.

Rothman, Joshua. *Notorious in the Neighborhood: Sex and Families across the Color Line in Virginia, 1787–1861.* Chapel Hill: University of North Carolina Press, 2003.

Royster, Jacqueline Jones, ed. *Southern Horrors and Other Writings: The Anti-Lynching Campaign of Ida B. Wells, 1892–1900.* Boston: Bedford/St. Martin's, 1997.

Ruether, Rosemary R., and Rosemary S. Keller, eds. *Women and Religion in America.* Vol. I, *The Nineteenth Century.* San Francisco: Harper and Row, 1981.

Russo, Ann, and Cheris Kramarae, eds., *The Radical Women's Press of the 1850s.* New York: Routledge, 1991.

Ryan, Mary. *Cradle of the Middle Class: The Family in Oneida County, New York, 1790–1865.* New York: Cambridge University Press, 1981.

———. *Women in Public: Between Banners and Ballots, 1825–1880.* Baltimore: Johns Hopkins University Press, 1990.

Schlissel, Lillian. *Women's Diaries of the Westward Journey.* New York: Schocken Books, 1992.

Schultz, Jane E. *Women at the Front: Hospital Workers in Civil War America.* Chapel Hill: University of North Carolina Press, 2004.

Scott, Anne Firor. *Making the Invisible Woman Visible.* Urbana: University of Illinois Press, 1984.

———. *Natural Allies: Women's Associations in American History.* Urbana: University of Illinois Press, 1992.

Sherr, Lynn, and Jurate Kazickas. *Susan B. Anthony Slept Here: A Guide to American Women's Landmarks.* New York: Random House, 1994.

Shoemaker, Nancy, ed. *Negotiators of Change: Historical Perspectives on Native American Women.* New York: Routledge, 1995.

Sizer, Lyde Cullen. *The Political Work of Northern Women Writers and the Civil War, 1850–1872.* Chapel Hill: University of North Carolina Press, 2000.

Sklar, Kathryn Kish. *Catharine Beecher: A Study in American Domesticity.* New York: Norton, 1976.

———. *Florence Kelley and the Nation's Work: The Rise of Women's Political Culture, 1830–1900.* New Haven, Conn.: Yale University Press, 1997.

———. *Women's Rights Emerges within the Antislavery Movement, 1830–1870: A Brief History with Documents.* Boston: Bedford/St. Martin's, 2000.

Smith-Rosenberg, Carroll. *Disorderly Conduct: Visions of Gender in Victorian America.* New York: Knopf, 1985.

Solomon, Barbara. *In the Company of Educated Women: A History of Women and Higher Education in America.* New Haven, Conn.: Yale University Press, 1985.

Solomon, Martha M., ed. *A Voice of Their Own: The Woman Suffrage Press, 1840–1910.* Tuscaloosa: University of Alabama Press, 1991.

Sonneborn, Liz. *A to Z of Native American Women.* New York: Facts on File, 1998.

Stanley, Amy Dru. *From Bondage to Contract: Wage Labor, Marriage, and the Market in the Age of Slave Emancipation.* New York: Cambridge University Press, 1998.

Stansell, Christine. *City of Women: Sex and Class in New York, 1789–1860.* Urbana: University of Illinois Press, 1987.

Sterling, Dorothy, ed. *We Are Your Sisters: Black Women in the Nineteenth Century.* New York: Norton, 1997.

Stevenson, Brenda. *Life in Black and White: Family and Community in the Slave South.* New York: Oxford University Press, 1996.

Strane, Susan. *A Whole-Souled Woman: Prudence Crandall and the Education of Black Women.* New York: Norton, 1990.

Sutherland, Daniel E. *Americans and Their Servants: Domestic Service in the United States from 1800 to 1920.* Baton Rouge: Louisiana State University Press, 1981.

Swinth, Kirsten. *Painting Professionals: Women Artists and the Development of Modern American Art, 1870–1930.* Chapel Hill: University of North Carolina Press, 2001.

Terborg-Penn, Rosalyn. *African American Women in the Struggle for the Vote, 1850–1920.* Bloomington: Indiana University Press, 1998.

Tobin, Jacqueline L., and Raymond G. Dobard. *Hidden in Plain View: A Secret Story of Quilts and the Underground Railroad.* New York: Doubleday, 1999.

Tonkovich, Nicole. *Domesticity with a Difference: The Nonfiction of Catharine Beecher, Sarah J. Hale, Fanny Fern, and Margaret Fuller.* Jackson: University Press of Mississippi, 1997.

Tyrrell, Ian. *Woman's World/Woman's Empire: The Woman's Christian Temperance Union in International Perspective, 1880–1930.* Chapel Hill: University of North Carolina Press, 1991.

Ulrich, Laurel Thatcher. *A Midwife's Tale: The Life of Martha Ballard, Based on Her Diary, 1785–1812.* New York: Vintage Books, 1991.

Varon, Elizabeth. *We Mean to Be Counted: White Women and Politics in Antebellum Virginia.* Chapel Hill: University of North Carolina Press, 1998.

Venet, Wendy Hamand. *Neither Ballots nor Bullets: Women Abolitionists and the Civil War.* Charlottesville: University Press of Virginia, 1991.

Vertinsky, Patricia A. *The Eternally Wounded Woman: Women, Doctors, and Exercise in the Late Nineteenth Century.* Urbana: University of Illinois Press, 1994.

Walker, Cheryl, ed. *American Women Poets of the Nineteenth Century: An Anthology.* New Brunswick, N.J.: Rutgers University Press, 1992.

Wayne, Tiffany K. *Woman Thinking: Feminism and Transcendentalism in Nineteenth-Century America.* Lanham, Md.: Lexington Books, 2005.

Weatherford, Doris. *Foreign and Female: Immigrant Women in America, 1840–1930.* New York: Schocken Books, 1986.

Weiner, Marli. *Mistresses and Slaves: Plantation Women in South Carolina, 1830–1880.* Urbana: University of Illinois Press, 1998.

Wertz, Richard W., and Dorothy C. Wertz. *Lying-In: A History of Childbirth in America.* New York: Free Press, 1977.

West, Emily. *Chains of Love: Slave Couples in Antebellum South Carolina.* Urbana: University of Illinois Press, 2004.

Westerkamp, Marilyn. *Women and Religion in Early America, 1600–1850: The Puritan and Evangelical Traditions.* New York: Routledge, 1999.

White, Barbara A. *The Beecher Sisters.* New Haven, Conn.: Yale University Press, 2003.

White, Deborah Gray. *Ar'n't I a Woman?: Female Slaves in the Plantation South*. New York: Norton, 1985.

Yee, Shirley. *Black Women Abolitionists: A Study in Activism, 1828–1860*. Knoxville: University of Tennessee Press, 1992.

Yellin, Jean Fagan. *Harriet Jacobs: A Life*. New York: Basic Civitas Books, 2004.

———. *Women and Sisters: The Antislavery Feminists in American Culture*. New Haven, Conn.: Yale University Press, 1989.

———, and John Van Horne, eds. *The Abolitionist Sisterhood: Women's Political Culture in Antebellum America*. Ithaca, N.Y.: Cornell University Press, 1994.

Young, Elizabeth. *Disarming the Nation: Women's Writing and the American Civil War*. Chicago: University of Chicago Press, 1999.

Yung, Judy. *Unbound Feet: A Social History of Chinese Women in San Francisco*. Berkeley: University of California Press, 1995.

Zaeske, Susan. *Signatures of Citizenship: Petitioning, Antislavery, and Women's Political Identity*. Chapel Hill: University of North Carolina Press, 2003.

Zanjani, Sally. *A Mine of Her Own: Women Prospectors in the American West, 1850–1950*. Lincoln: University of Nebraska Press, 2000.

Zophy, Angela Howard, and Frances M. Kavenik, eds. *Handbook of American Women's History*. New York: Garland, 1990.

Index

About the Author

TIFFANY K. WAYNE, a former Affiliated Scholar of the Institute for Research on Women and Gender at Stanford University, teaches U.S. history and American women's history at Cabrillo College in Aptos, California. She is the author of *Women Thinking: Feminism and Transcendentalism in 19th-Century America* (2005) and *Encyclopedia of Transcendentalism* (2006).